The Ethiopian War
1935-1941

THE

ETHIOPIAN

WAR

1935-1941

by Angelo Del Boca

TRANSLATED FROM THE ITALIAN BY
P. D. CUMMINS

The University of Chicago Press

CHICAGO AND LONDON

Translated from the Italian La guerra d'Abissinia, 1935–1941
© *1965 by Giangiacomo Feltrinelli Editore, Milan*

Standard Book Number: 226–14217–5
Library of Congress Catalog Card Number: 71–79562

The University of Chicago Press, Chicago 60637
The University of Chicago Press, Ltd., London W.C. 1

Contents

	Acknowledgments	ix
Chapter one:	The "Adowa Complex"	3
Chapter two:	Italy's Preparations for War	17
Chapter three:	In the "Enemy's" Camp	30
Chapter four:	The De Bono Phase of the War	43
Chapter five:	Conscripts, Volunteers, and War Correspondents	56
Chapter six:	The Ethiopian Counter-offensive	70
Chapter seven:	Under the Banner of the Lion of Judah	85
Chapter eight:	The First Battle of Tembien	98
Chapter nine:	The Occupation of Negelli	112
Chapter ten:	The Battle of Enderta	124
Chapter eleven:	The Second Battle of Tembien	137
Chapter twelve:	The Battle of Shire	149
Chapter thirteen:	The Battle of Mai Chew	161
Chapter fourteen:	The Massacre of Lake Ashangi	174
Chapter fifteen:	The Battle of the Ogaden	186
Chapter sixteen:	The Train to Jibouti	199
Chapter seventeen:	Italy's Colonial Policy	212
Chapter eighteen:	An Empire on the Map	227
Chapter nineteen:	The Guerrilla War of the Arbaññoch	239
Chapter twenty:	The Return of the Exile	253
Chapter twenty-one:	The Reconciliation	265
	Glossary	279
	Index	281

Maps

Map one: **Ethiopia, 1935** following page 9
Map two: **Operations of De Bono, Autumn 1935** 46
Map three: **"Christmas offensive"** 73
Map four: **The first battle of Tembien** 101
Map five: **The southern front** 115
Map six: **The trap around Amba Aradam** 127
Map seven: **The second battle of Tembien** 139
Map eight: **The battle of Shire** 152
Map nine: **Movements after the battle of Lake Ashangi** 178
Map ten: **Graziani's plan in the Ogaden** 189

Acknowledgments

For the help I received while writing this book (part of a more ambitious project, a history of Italo-Ethiopian relations from the reign of Menelik to that of the present emperor), let me express first my profound gratitude to His Imperial Majesty Haile Selassie, and His Royal Highness Imru Mangasha, who so generously answered the many questions I put to them. I am also deeply indebted to His Excellency Daniel Abebe, governor of Arussi, and Colonel Kosrof Boghossian for the information they provided me. My particular thanks are due Dr. Hans W. Lockot, who assisted me with my research work for more than a month, and allowed me free access to the books and documents of the National Library in Addis Ababa. I also take this opportunity to thank once more: General Quirino Armellini, General Emilio Faldella, Paola Cesarini, Luigi Lino, Tullio Pastori, my friend Enrico Emanuelli who put precious documents at my disposal, the Bassi family, who permitted me to consult the notebooks and maps of the late journalist Mario Bassi, and all those too numerous to name who supplied me with valuable evidence. I owe more than I can say to Giorgio Vecchiato, editor of the Turin *Gazzetta del Popolo*, who commissioned me to write a series of articles from the Ethiopian viewpoint of the events that led to the Italo-Ethiopian war, the war itself, and the subsequent occupation. That he published these articles in his newspaper is proof he possesses a degree of broadmindedness that is rarely found, and it was largely due to his encouragement that I wrote this book. Lastly, my affectionate thanks go to my wife, Maria Teresa, for the most helpful comments she made when she read my manuscript.

The Ethiopian War
1935-1941

Chapter one

The "Adowa Complex"

To those who remember it in the mid-thirties, Massawa is dead. The port described by Ferdinando Martini as "affording first-class anchorage" and "unquestionably the finest on the Red Sea," is empty. Gerar Bay, where the ships of the Royal Italian Navy once rode proudly, is a vast, deserted basin above whose waters dense clouds of seagulls storm. Taulud Bay, filled to capacity in those days with tankers and coal freighters, is equally deserted and reflects a bleak and gloomy sky. Only this sky drained of color, the blinding glare, the sweltering heat, and the mists that blur every outline remain unchanged.

The view from the veranda of the Italian consulate is dominated by the port with its abandoned quays, its motionless cranes. The silence is complete, that same unbroken silence which made such an impression on me as I crossed the burning regions between Dogali and Otumlo. "Massawa seems to come to life when the mail boat from the Arabian ports arrives or when some ship from Europe puts in," Signor Brancato, the vice-consul, told me, "but it's an event that only happens once a day." Brancato, who was born in Massawa, has experienced all its changes of fortune, and as his memories came surging back, it was only natural that he preferred to speak of the golden age in the mid-thirties when the port was so crowded that there were as many as forty ships anchored in the bay waiting to berth. Massawa was the gateway of the "empire," and there were so many cargoes of arms, ammunition, and goods of all kinds to handle that there was a crying need for more quays. In Massawa there was abundance, whereas in Italy men were holding forth on autarchy and swallowing their "sanction soup," and there were still people like the inhabitants of Matera reduced to living in caves. This blisteringly hot port was the point of departure for Italy's "Far West," the first stage on the trail rising precipitously upward to the vast tablelands whose rich black soil yielded two crop a year. It was from Massawa that Italy had embarked on her first African adventure in 1885.

In 1934, the sixty-eight-year-old General Emilio de Bono was entrusted with the task of securing a place in the sun for the most disinherited nation in Europe. "Money will be needed, Leader, lots of money," he warned the Duce. "There will be no lack of money," Mussolini assured him.[1] Nor was there, in fact. Italy's entire gold reserves ended up in East Africa, transformed into guns, tanks, roads, mineral water and Maria Theresa thalers with which to trade with the Ethiopians. In Sicily drastic economic measures were imposed, and the authorities cherished the illusion that the activities of the police and the astuteness of super-Prefect Mori would put an end to the Mafia and the misery of the Sicilian people. In Sicily lawlessness and despair; in Massawa the horn of plenty, and more than once the riches it poured out deliberately thrown away. "On the day that Teruzzi, our new Colonial Minister, arrived," said Brancato, "all the goods piled up on the quay

[1] Emilio de Bono, *Anno XIII: The Conquest of an Empire* (London: Cresset Press, 1937), p. 15.

were dumped into the sea to make room for the *Victoria*.[2] In addition to Teruzzi and his staff, the *Victoria* brought the comedian Totò and his troupe of lovelies to Massawa. In the wake of the guns came wisecracks and cheesecake. Only the stagecoaches were missing from Italy's "Far West."

After considerable water had flowed over the dam, history condemned Italy harshly for her Ethiopian venture and branded the instigators as criminals. But the minor protagonists, the hundreds and thousands of soldiers and laborers who took part in "the conquest of the Empire" and who were absolved of guilt en bloc, have never been able to bring themselves to endorse the verdict passed on their country. On the contrary they look back on those years as their most exalting experience. Suddenly removed from the deadly monotony of Italian provincial life, from dull drudgery, starvation wages, and unemployment, they found in Africa a breathtaking spaciousness and the individual right to at least a small measure of power. Only a few of them hypocritically cultivated the presumptuous notion that they represented "the hand of God," that they were crusaders of civilization. The majority were fully aware they were engaged in a war of conquest, a war initiated by a poor but industrious nation against one that was still poorer and utterly inept. With almost complete conviction they sang:

> Hardworking, warrior people who
> Follow your leader, Mussolini,
> We'll open up the way for you,
> You shall have bread for your bambini.

For the first time they felt they were fighting for something concrete. Other Italians had fallen to no end amidst the sand dunes of Tripoli, the lunar volcanoes of the Mijjertein and the

[2] My conversation with Signor Brancato took place April 5, 1965. Terruzi arrived in Massawa May 26, 1938.

oases of Kufra. Now they were ready to die—and not many were destined to die—for the fertile plains of Kaffa and Gojjam, the forests of Jimma, the gold and platinum of Yubdo and Birbir. But over and above these mirages that were never to materialize, the hundreds and thousands of Italians who flocked to Ethiopia between 1935 and 1940 responded to a call that had nothing whatsoever to do with the directives of the Fascist regime or geopolitical laws. It was the stimulating, enthralling call of their Far West, with its unexplored riches, its unknown hazards and dangers. Some of these pioneers drove 634 trucks along the terrifyingly steep and dangerous roads of Wolkefit and Termaber; thousands worked on the construction of the Danakil road, breaking up the burning lava in the sweltering heat; others became big game hunters whose quarries were the hippo of the River Takkaze; and still others (although this was against the law), settled down happily with gentle, affectionate Ethiopian women, women so different from those of their own country. It was because the Italians saw East Africa as the springboard of escape to a thrilling new life that they lined themselves up with the expansionist schemes of the Fascist regime. True, Italy was still suffering from the "Adowa complex," but it was the longing for adventure, not obsessive rancor, that weighed down the scales decisively. "Everything was easy here in those days," Roscigno, a Neapolitan who has made his home in Addis Ababa, told me. "It was like living in a dream. For any kind of work you did, the pay was ten times better than in Italy. I changed jobs a dozen times and at the end of each of them, I wound up with a bundle. When I went back to Naples to visit my old folks in 1938, I spent 70,000 lire—more than ten laborers working full time for a year could earn between them. If I wanted change for a 1,000-lire note, I had to comb the neighborhood to find someone who had enough cash." [3]

Exactly thirty years after the outbreak of the Italo-Ethio-

[3] In a conversation with me on March 26, 1965.

pian war, I returned to Massawa, and from the Regina Elena
quay where most ships dock, set out on a 5,000 kilometer
journey on the trail of the Italian troops, laborers, traders, and
adventurers who had deluded themselves into believing that
they were founding a colonial empire in an era when other
empires, centuries old, were beginning to disintegrate. Notwithstanding the fact that there are at least a thousand books
on this "epic" written by military experts and men who were
prominent during the Fascist regime, and that an exceptional
amount of material has been made available, the war and the
four years of "grand colonial policy" that followed it, still
present the most informed reader and even the men who took
part in the enterprise with a long series of lacunae and question marks. Hence we may well say that "the greatest colonial
war in history," as King Victor Emmanuel III called it, is also
the most obscure, encrusted as it is by a mass of one-sided
rhetoric.

In the hope of filling in the most glaring gaps and amending
certain conclusions, I followed the routes of the invading
armies step by step, reconnoitered and evaluated the various
battlefields, and obtained as many eyewitness accounts as
possible from both Italians and Ethiopians. I had, of course,
extracted all the essential information from our own sources,
but I also went carefully through the Ethiopian archives that
Italian historians have ignored. Furthermore, I was privileged
to hear the Ethiopian version of the facts from the lips of the
Emperor Haile Selassie I, Commander-in-Chief of the Armed
Forces, Ras Imru, commander of the Shire army, and several
of the most notable leaders of the resistance. The new evidence
I succeeded in collecting casts an ugly shadow on many of the
glowing images of fascist iconography while, by way of avenging the Ethiopians, it sheds light on their unrecognized virtues
and their spirit of self-sacrifice. It is truly comforting, however, to recall that in the country that was the scene of such
savage reprisals, the people responded wholeheartedly to their
emperor's appeal to "forgive the enemies of yesterday," and

that twenty years of peaceful collaboration have proved far more fruitful for Italy and Ethiopia than five years of inglorious victories, rapine, and brutal repression.

The first question that springs spontaneously to the mind of the historian who has set himself the task of examining the facts that led to the Italo-Ethiopian war is fated to remain without a definite answer. That question is, of course, when did Mussolini first consider the conquest of Ethiopia? I know of no documents that would help to establish the date, and even those men who were closest to the Duce have been unable to pinpoint it, though all of them agree that it could not have been earlier than 1932. I myself, however, as I hope to prove, am convinced that this is putting it much too late and that as far back as 1925, Mussolini was making the initial plans for the conquest of Ethiopia. In the first place I have the most valuable testimony of the emperor himself: "It must be borne in mind that the war was premeditated and that preparations were made years in advance. When we visited Europe in 1924, certain persons informed us of the project to invade our country, and we were also told that the invasion might be launched from both Eritrea and Italian Somaliland." [4] In answer to a similar question put by a foreign journalist, the negus replied, "Four years after my meeting with Mussolini [1924], a Treaty of Friendship and Arbitration was signed between Italy and Ethiopia; at the same time, however, Fascist Italy embarked on her lengthy program of preparations for the invasion of our country. Italy, in fact, had never relinquished her dream of reconquest. Her overtures to us in 1923, 1924, and 1928, supposedly friendly, were deliberately made to mask her real intentions and her military buildup. This policy, the bitter fruit of Menelik's victory, conditioned every move." [5]

In his socialist days Mussolini had opposed the Libyan War

[4] The emperor granted me this interview May 14, 1965.

[5] From an interview with Serge Groussard published in *Figaro* (Paris), March 25, 1959.

of 1911, and had defined Crispi's efforts to increase the Italian foothold in Ethiopia as "the dream of a jingoist minister," [6] but underwent a radical change of heart the moment he found himself installed in the Palazzo Venezia. Indeed, only a year later he ordered the reoccupation of Tripolitania and Cyrenaica, and gave Cesare Maria De Vecchi di Val Cismon a free hand to carry out the war against the sultans of Obbia and Mijjarten. But Libya and Italian Somaliland were wretchedly poor colonies and could never have solved the peninsula's critical demographic problems, as Mussolini realized when he visited Tripoli in 1926. According to Beatrice Baskerville, it was precisely on this occasion, after pondering on the pitifully limited opportunities this "sandbox" had to offer, that the Duce made up his mind to invade Ethiopia. [7]

Once he had settled on the new objective for the Fascist regime's expansionist policy, the Duce found that the ground had been abundantly prepared by such flaming nationalists as Oriani, Corradini, Forges Davanzati, Coppola, Pedrazzi and Scarfoglio, and by the ever-active propagandists of the Africa Society. After Adowa, Alfredo Oriani had written: "We have signed a peace but there will be no peace. We will never give up Africa—the war will be resumed." The defeat seared their minds and the words of the boastful patriotic ditties the soldiers had sung, words such as these stung them like whips:

> Baldissare, hey, beware
> Of these black folk with woolly hair!
> Menelik, you're dead—here comes
> A shower of lead, not sugar-plums!

By and large Italy could not bring herself to accept the fact that the "barbarous Shoan hordes" had succeeded in annihi-

[6] Herbert L. Matthews, *The Fruits of Fascism* (New York: Harcourt, Brace Co.), p. 223.

[7] Beatrice Baskerville, *What next, O Duce?* (London: Longmans, 1937), p. 8.

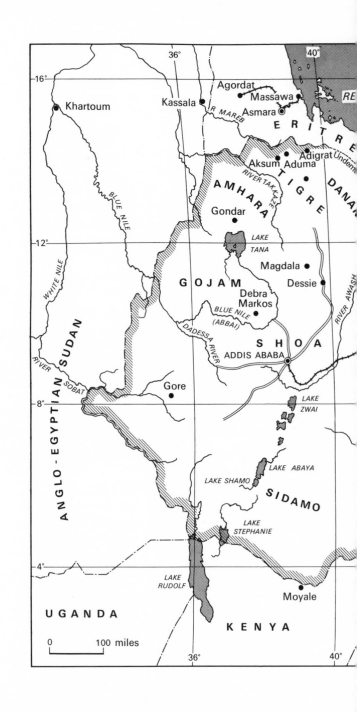

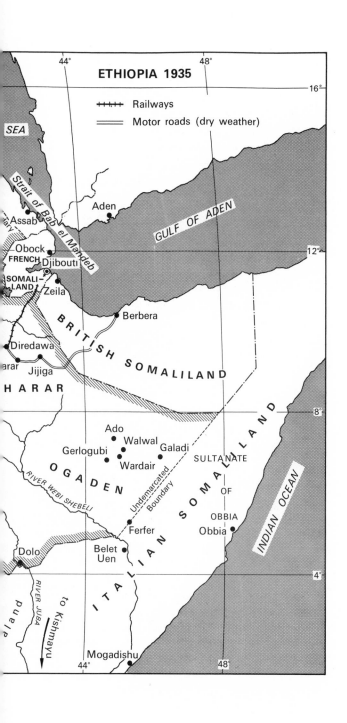

ETHIOPIA 1935

+++++ Railways
===== Motor roads (dry weather)

16°

SEA

Strait of Bab el Mandeb

Aden

GULF OF ADEN

Assab
Obock
FRENCH Djibouti
SOMALI-
LAND Zeila

12°

Berbera

B R I T I S H   S O M A L I L A N D

Diredawa
arar Jijiga

H A R A R

8°

Ado
Walwal
Gerlogubi   Galadi
Wardair

SULTANATE

O G A D E N

RIVER WEBI SHEBELI

OF

Undemarcated Boundary

INDIAN OCEAN

I T A L I A N   S O M A L I L A N D

OBBIA

Ferfer   Obbia

Dolo   Belet
Uen

4°

aland

RIVER JUBA

to Kishmayu

Mogadishu

44°   48°

CHAPTER ONE

lating a European army. The Nationalists, mentally unbalanced by the "Adowa complex," flocked to the Fascist Party and, as Chabod noted, brought their "doctrinaire influence" to bear on Mussolini.[8] As a result, the man of Predappio gradually consolidated his power, becoming more and more dominated by the desire to increase the prestige and might of his country. He must have been enthralled by the idea of "settling, once and for all, the great account that had been left over since 1896."[9]

Enthralled, yes, but also tormented, for Mussolini knew only too well that Italy, already engaged in the reconquest of Libya and Somaliland, was in no position to undertake a long and insidious colonial campaign thousands of miles from her shores. This probably explains why he temporized and made such a show of friendship to the regent of Ethiopia, Ras Tafari Makonnen, the emperor-to-be.* Indeed it was largely owing to the Duce's support that Ethiopia was admitted as a charter member of the League of Nations in 1923.[10] The following year he invited the regent to visit Italy. While he was displaying so much cordiality, however, Mussolini entered into an agreement with Great Britain under which both countries agreed to "stabilize their spheres of influence" in Ethiopia, which meant nothing more or less than that Great Britain

[8] Federico Chabod, *L'Italia contemporanea* (*1918–1948*) (Turin: Einaudi, 1961), p. 92.

[9] From Mussolini's introduction to the above-mentioned book by De Bono, p. viii.

* Menelik was succeeded by his grandson, the vicious and corrupt *Lij* (Prince) Yasu. He was deposed in 1916, and Menelik's daughter, Zauditu, became empress. At the same time, Ras Tafari Makonnen, the son of Menelik's right-hand Ras, was appointed regent and heir presumptive. He took the name of Haile Selassie (Might of the Trinity) at his coronation in 1930 (TRANS.).

[10] Note that Mussolini, who had intervened in Corfu, supported Ethiopia not so much because he wished to show favor to the regent but because he was anxious to conciliate France, which had sponsored Ethiopia's application for membership in the League of Nations.

12

would support Italy's claims to certain concessions and vice versa.[11]

While Mussolini was discreetly testing the diplomatic climate of Europe and waiting for the time when he would be strong enough to strike, he was playing the card of corruption in Ethiopia, hoping that it would lead to the collapse of the already shaken empire. "It is strange to recall that those who did their utmost many years later to persuade the League of Nations to expel Ethiopia on the ground that she completely lacked unity, were the very men who had done everything in their power—but without success—to disintegrate our empire . . . Let me remind you that the revolt of Ras Gugsa, Governor of Begemdor and the morganatic husband of the Empress Zauditu, was fomented by the Italians . . . In 1932, with Italian aid, Ras Hailu organized the flight of his son-in-law, *Lij* Yasu, to Gojjam and attempted to join him there in order to raise the country against us. . . ."[12] Haile Selassie's accusations of subversive Italian activities were, in fact, confirmed point by point by the ingenuous General De Bono who, after giving the names of the Italian agents and those of the rases who were bought over, wound up: "The important thing to understand is this: that from the very outset of the campaign there were signs of the results of this disintegrating political action, and that it deprived our enemy of at least 200,000 men who either did not take up arms or who, although enrolled and armed, remained inert."[13] The general also gave it as his

---

[11] This agreement was defined in a letter dated December 14, 1925, from Sir Ronald Graham, British ambassador in Rome, to Mussolini, and in a letter from the Duce to Sir Ronald dated December 20. These texts, which only became known six months later to the Ethiopian government, will be found in the *Official Journal* of the League of Nations (November 1926), pp. 1518 ff.

[12] *Une victoire de la civilisation* (an account of the war given by the emperor to Marcel Griaule, published as a special supplement in *Vu*, Paris, 1936).

[13] De Bono, *Anno XIII*, p. 36.

opinion that, taking advantage of Ras Gugsa's rebellion, Italy might have attacked and overrun Ethiopia in 1930: "I believe that the thing could have been done with fascist audacity. I must add, however, that we were not ready." [14]

Mussolini's observance of the Treaty of Friendship was, to put it mildly, strange to a degree, but for Italian propagandists the villain of the piece was the negus who was doing his utmost to hold up the construction of the Assab-Dessie road, for which one clause of the treaty provided. The emperor's reluctance to furnish the country which had a common frontier with his own the most rapid route for an invasion was fully justified, of course, and Mussolini knew it. But from this time on we were the archangelic messengers of light and civilization, the Ethiopians the lowest, most deeply damned race on earth, the personification of all that was evil and abominable. Utterly puerile as this counterblast was, the majority of Italians honestly believed this rubbish was true; consequently, when the hour struck, they gladly acclaimed the act of aggression.

Meanwhile, Mussolini was making plans for the invasion even though, on the eve of the hostilities, he sought to convince the world that the war was completely unpremeditated. Badoglio tells us in his book that studies for the defense of Eritrea in the event of an armed conflict were begun in 1925.[15] In the same year, as we learn from De Bono, the Duce asked Prince Scalea, then colonial secretary, to draft a scheme for

[14] *Ibid.* Regarding this "opportunity," Corrado Zoli, a former governor of Eritrea, wrote, "The governor of Eritrea did his utmost to spread this revolt, and provoke even more serious trouble in Ethiopia. Most probably, he had had on several occasions reason to believe—and he was to be provided with fresh grounds for his belief in the following months—that the intervention by Italy on however modest a scale would trigger off an uprising in Tigre and Amhara, and possibly in Shoa, and so precipitate the fall of the negus and his empire." See *Etiopia d'Oggi* (Rome: Società Anonima Italiana Arti Grafiche, 1935), pp. 151–52.

[15] Pietro Badoglio, *The War in Abyssinia* (London: Methuen, 1937), pp. 4–5.

the formation and mobilization of a massive Eritrean corps. In 1932 he sent the quadrumvir De Bono to Eritrea "to see how matters stand and report to me," [16] and this was certainly the year when the "irrevocable" decision was made. In September King Victor Emmanuel III paid a state visit to the "first-born colony," toured the battlefields, and pronounced himself "deeply moved" by the homage of the disabled Eritrean soldiers who had fought under our colors at Adowa. Again in 1932 the Italian High Command elaborated Project OME,* the defensive-offensive plan for Eritrea in the event of war. By this time, in addition to those in the military sphere, several members of the Fascist hierarchy knew of Mussolini's "Grand Design." Dino Grandi, the Italian ambassador at the Court of St. James, confided the secret to Sir John Simon, possibly in order to find out which way the wind was blowing in Great Britain. [17] A year later, irked by all the delays, De Bono decided to confront Mussolini squarely: "One day I said to the Duce, 'Listen, if there is a war down there—and if you think me worthy and capable of it—you ought to grant me the honor of conducting the campaign.' The Duce looked at me hard and at once replied, 'Surely.' 'You don't think I'm too old?' I asked. 'No,' he said, 'because we mustn't lose time.' " [18] There were still two years to go till the Wal Wal incident, but Mussolini already had a plan of campaign and a commander-in-chief to carry it out.

In the neoclassical "Yellow Room" of the Hotel Minghetti-

---

[16] De Bono, *Anno XIII*, pp. 1–2. In *Fronte Sud* (Milan: Mondadori, 1938), p. 31, General Rodolfo Graziani tells of the conversation he had with Mussolini before leaving for Mogadishu: " 'Everything has been worked out,' said the Duce. 'My plans for the war, my calculations as to the necessary number of divisions and the time it will take to prepare for the invasion were not made yesterday.' "

* *Ordini Militari Eritrea:* Military Order for Eritrea (TRANS.).

[17] A. de la Pradelle, *Le conflit italo-éthiopien* (Paris: Editions Internationales, 1936).

[18] De Bono, *Anno XIII*, p. 18.

Italia in Asmara, I was given a most valuable piece of evidence on this prewar period. It came from my guest Tullio Pastori, the geologist and explorer. Pastori, who was a friend of the Emperor Menelik and who has traveled throughout Ethiopia for the past 64 years, has an unrivaled knowledge of the country's complex geography. "I can vouch for the fact that shortly after the Fascist regime had established itself, the Italians in Eritrea began to think of the reconquest of Ethiopia," he told me. "In 1924 I was approached by Captain Malladra, now a general, who asked me if I would undertake a delicate mission. During the course of my annual explorations for minerals, he wished me to make an exhaustive study of the rivers that form the defensive system of the Ethiopian highlands. I was to measure the water level in the dry and rainy seasons, indicate where these rivers could be forded, and so on. I agreed to do so and for years sent notebooks crammed with figures to Malladra. In 1928 when I was about to set out with the English geologist L. M. Nesbitt on an expedition from Addis Ababa to Dallol, I was entrusted with an even more delicate mission which made me suspect that an invasion had already been planned and that war would not be long delayed. I was to make a careful examination of the bridge over the Awash on the Addis Ababa-Jibouti line, and establish its weakest points in case a day came when it would have to be blown up. Later on the policy of making direct contact with those rases and notables who bore some grudge against the emperor was intensified. *Dejatch* Haile Selassie Gugsa, for instance, was subtly undermined, not by Baron Franchetti as is generally believed, but by two unpublicized agents, Sergeant Erre and Signor De Meo. When the war broke out, a good third of the Ethiopian army was paralyzed. Men like *Dejatch* Ayelu Birru, for example, bent over backward in their anxiety to cause us no trouble. Our political officers had done their work well." [19]

[19] This conversation took place April 5, 1965.

Chapter two

Italy's Preparations for War

Small and provincial Asmara may be, but not so long ago, up to the time, that is, of the building boom in Nairobi, Dakar, Abidjan and Accra, it was the most "Europeanized" and enchanting town in Africa. This is the opinion held by all the writers who have traveled extensively in Africa in search of material for their books. "The Italians built Asmara from scratch and built it well," noted Smith Hempstone. "By comparison, Addis Ababa makes a poor show." [1] "Addis Ababa is a large village, but Asmara is a small *city*," observed John Gunther shrewdly,[2] and the Swiss author Charles-Henri Favrod captured its very spirit: "Asmara, with its cathedral,

---

[1] Smith Hempstone, *The New Africa* (London: Faber and Faber, 1961), p. 82.
[2] John Gunther, *Inside Africa* (New York: Harper and Brothers, 1963), p. 278.

town hall, terraces and porticoes, its streets crowded with strollers, its civic pride, simple piety and love of pageantry, is a real Italian town. It gives one the impression that it was built and perfected down to the last detail in Apulia and wafted over the sea to Africa where it came down like a meteorite and landed intact on this particular spot." [3] But it is not only Apulia that Asmara recalls—the cathedral with its red-brick towers brings to mind the churches of Lombardy, the palm-lined Corso Italia might well be in the heart of San Remo, and when dusk falls and the inhabitants turn out for the customary evening promenade, Asmara is twin to Trapani.

It is hard to believe that this almost perfectly laid-out town took only three years to build (1935, 1936, 1937). "At the beginning of 1935, Asmara contained exactly 3,873 Italians, including officials and white soldiers," De Bono tells us,[4] but by May of the same year the number had risen to 15,000, and at the end of the war, 50,000 Italians were living in Asmara. During the first months of the "rush," gangs of laborers worked night and day to build barracks, offices, warehouses, and arsenals for the greatest expeditionary force that Africa had ever seen. Round the old center of the town, car parks, repair shops, and laboratories were hastily erected. It was not long, however, before the wooden barracks and corrugated iron hangars were pulled down to make way for solidly built houses. Although Mussolini had not, as Hitler, promised his people that his regime would last for a millennium, the Italians, with a faith that was unprecedented, never doubted the empire would endure, that it could easily be developed and that it held a store of fabulous riches. Consequently, because they were looking toward the future, Asmara is a harmonious whole, although built in such an incredibly short time, utterly unlike Mogadishu, with its makeshift, impermanent air.

---

[3] Charles-Henri Favrod, *Le poids de l'Afrique* (Paris: Editions du Seuil, 1958), pp. 353–55.

[4] De Bono, *Anno XIII*, p. 21.

Italy's Preparations for War

It all began in December 1934, the day after the Wal Wal incident. The sound of firing round the wells had scarcely died away than Mussolini personally compiled the top-secret document (of which only five copies were made), known as "Directives and Plan of Action for the Solution of the Italo-Ethiopian Question." Barely a week later the Duce sent De Bono to Eritrea as High Commissioner, a title he exchanged in March for one far more significant and provocative, Commander-in-Chief of the Italian Armed Forces in Africa.

Mussolini had been seeking for months for a pretext to mobilize; the Wal Wal affair provided him with one. Yet border skirmishes of this kind, even if not quite so serious, had been common occurrences from the day that Italy first set foot in East Africa. These acts of aggression or attempts to invade our colonies were, as A. H. M. Jones and Elizabeth Monroe rightly point out, "of a type with which the British and French frontier authorities were familiar and handled purely as tribal feuds, with a subaltern and a few native troops." [5] But Mussolini had made up his mind that Wal Wal should be the *casus belli*, and accordingly he ordered the press to blow it up into a front-line story, featuring the incident as a deliberate act of aggression on the part of Ethiopia, an act of so grave a nature that it could not be condoned. But the Wal Wal dispute could and should have been settled in the same way as the hundreds of previous forays, particularly because the whole picture was extremely confused. Who had fired the opening shots? Was it Captain Roberto Cimmaruta's *dubats*[*] or the Ethiopians commanded by *Fitaurari* Kiferra Balcha and the fugitive Somali, Omar Samantar? It is impossible to say which side was responsible for the flareup; even the Arbitration Commission, after months of inquiries, was forced to define the incident as "an unfortunate combination of

---

[5] A. H. M. Jones and E. Monroe, *A History of Ethiopia* (London: Oxford University Press, 1966), p. 176.
[*] Somali irregulars (TRANS.).

circumstances." [6] Not only, then, did the question of who had
provoked the fighting remain unanswerable, but it was also
extremely doubtful whether Italy had a legitimate right to Wal
Wal's 359 wells, which she had occupied in 1930 and held
ever since, thanks to the fact that as the Ethiopians were free
to use the wells, Ethiopia had no grounds for an "official
protest." [7]

Mussolini, however, did not bother his head about such
technical and juridical niceties; his mind was now wholly
engaged by the prospect of the imminent conquest of Ethiopia.
Not only would it provide Italy with a new outlet for her
shrinking export trade and a partial solution of her critical
unemployment problem by the "redeployment" of a large
proportion of the redundant labor force on the vast Amharan
uplands, but also it would furnish the Duce with what he
wanted—war. Denis Mack Smith was right when he wrote, "He
needed to justify fascism by success and prove in battle the
boasted virility of his regime and people." [8] A few months
earlier, in a speech he made in Bologna on the eve of the
grand maneuvers, Mussolini had said, "We are becoming a
military nation, we will add militaristic, and to complete it,
warlike." [9] On February 5 and 11, 1935, he ordered the mobilization of two army divisions, the Gavinana and the Peloritana, and when he received a letter dated February 13 from

[6] *Official Journal* of the League of Nations, No. 11, Document 1571
(November 1935), pp. 1351–55. The members of the Committee were
Aldrovandi and Montagna of Italy, A. de la Pradelle of France, Pittman B.
Potter of the U.S.A., and N. Politis of Greece. They reached this conclusion
September 3, 1935.

[7] Ethiopia did, however, protest to the League of Nations. (See Ethiopian
Memorandum, December 15, 1934, p. 6.) According to Addis Ababa, the
presence of Italian troops and the fortifications the Italians had erected in
the Wal Wal and Warder localities constituted "the illegal occupation of
territory over which Ethiopia has sovereign rights. Under clause 10 of the
Treaty of Friendship, Italy, a charter member of the League of Nations,
solemnly pledged herself to respect those rights."

[8] Denis Mack Smith, *Italy, a Modern History* (Ann Arbor: University of
Michigan Press, 1959), p. 448.

[9] Extract from the speech made in Bologna August 24, 1934.

poor, dear, honest General De Bono informing him that "at present the Nagusa negust is ordering too many prayers and fasts to give us reason to think that he wishes to attack us," [10] he showed his contempt for the Arbitration Commission and its conciliatory powers by replying immediately, "In case the negus has no intention of attacking us, we ourselves must take the initiative." [11] In a subsequent letter to the general, he wrote, "You ask for three divisions by the end of October; I mean to send you ten, repeat ten: five divisions of the regular army, five formations of Blackshirts. For the lack of a few thousand men, we lost the day at Adowa. We shall never make that mistake. I am willing to commit a sin of excess, but never a sin of deficiency." [12]

Mussolini was as good as his word. On April 18, the first battalion of the Gavinana disembarked at Massawa, and during the next few months, five army and five Blackshirt divisions arrived in East Africa via the Suez canal.[13] One division and a few Blackshirt battalions were assigned to General Graziani, Commander of the Forces in Italian Somaliland, but the main buildup was in Eritrea. This first expeditionary force was made up as follows: more than 200,000 men and 7,000 officers, 6,000 machine guns, 700 cannon of every caliber, 150 tanks, and 150 pursuit and bomber planes. The flood of troops and equipment that was being poured into Africa reached its height in September when General Baistrocchi, Under Secretary for War, informed the senate that from Naples alone 100,000 men, 1,000,000 tons of stores and ammunition, 200 cannon, 6,000 mules and 2,300 motor vehicles had been shipped overseas. Faced with this staggering influx of men and materials, General De Bono was compelled to ask the Duce for a 10,000 strong labor force (the figure was soon to rise to

[10] De Bono, *Anno XIII*, p. 117.

[11] *Ibid.*, p. 118.

[12] *Ibid.*

[13] These divisions were the Gavinana, Peloritana, Sabauda, Gran Sasso, Sila, and the Blackshirt divisions, "23rd March," "28th October," "21st April," "3rd January," and Tevere.

50,000), to widen the port of Massawa, resurface the Massawa-Nefasit-Asmara road, repair and construct other roads, erect barracks, hangars, etc., and carry out the huge program of work entailed by new hydrological projects. The general's request gratified various federal secretaries who rid their provinces once and for all of the chronic unemployed, but when the first squads arrived De Bono was anything but overjoyed: "Just anyone was sent out. No selection had been exercised and no warranty was given of physical or moral soundness. There were men among them who had never handled a pick or shovel; there were 12 schoolmasters, 4 chemists, 3 lawyers, 9 watchmakers and several barbers." [14] But against this he was given invaluable aid by his Quartermaster-General Dall'Ora, who dealt brilliantly with the complex problems of provisioning, billeting and transport. On October 2, the stage was set for the invasion. From his headquarters in the center of Asmara, whose every street was jammed with troops, guns, and all the equipment for war, General De Bono issued his final instructions. Five days earlier he had received a peremptory telegram from the Duce: "Order you to attack at dawn on third, repeat third October." [15] De Bono had planned to strike on October 5, but loyal servant that he was, he obeyed without demur. (Later on, however, he was to abide fearlessly by his own decisions.)

Both in Eritrea and in Italian Somaliland, all the preparations were now complete and Mussolini might well have congratulated himself on the speed and efficiency with which the expeditionary force had been organized. But the Duce was not in a self-congratulatory mood; on the contrary, he was incensed and preoccupied by the turn events had taken in Europe. For several months he had been firmly convinced that the treaty signed by Laval in Rome on January 7, 1935, and the threat to Great Britain that she would be left to face

[14] *Ibid.*, pp. 95–96.
[15] *Ibid.*, p. 220.

Hitler's Germany alone, had flattened out all the obstacles that lay in the path of his conquest. But what he had failed to take into account was the weight carried by public opinion in Great Britain. The campaign organized by anti-Fascist and pacifist groups in February and whose slogan was "Not a man, not a penny for capitalist schemes in East Africa," reached such proportions that the Conservative government, which had almost bent over backwards to "appease" the Duce with offers of valuable concessions, was compelled to adopt a very different, a far more resolute policy. From then on the British government made it absolutely plain that it fully supported the League of Nations' principles of international and democratic solidarity, and this new attitude reached its culminating point September 20, when the British fleet was dispatched to the Mediterranean.

But neither threats (and this threat did not amount to much since SIM * had managed to ascertain that the 144 ships of the fleet were not yet fully equipped for action) nor promises could now stop Mussolini from pressing on with the Ethiopian campaign, for to him it was more than a war of conquest, it was the long-awaited opportunity to prove the mettle of the generation his regime had forged. That Giuseppe Bottai, Governor of Rome, understood the Duce perfectly emerges clearly from his article in *Critica Fascista:* "The colonial war that Italy is girding herself to fight is the first war of the Fascist State . . . over and above all, the Ethiopian enterprise is the first manifestation of the might of the Fascist revolution, Mussolini's revolution, which springs from the Mediterranean basin to the shores of the Indian Ocean—European Italy, peninsular Italy, Libyan Italy, Saharan Italy, Ethiopian Italy —this is the route of our march." [16]

* *Servizio Informazione Militare:* Italian Military Intelligence (TRANS.).
[16] *Critica Fascista*, July 1935. During this period F. T. Marinetti, the founder of Futurism, wrote an open letter urging all young Italians to volunteer for the war in East Africa. Part of this letter ran, "The African

From this time forward Mussolini only listened to those voices that spurred him on, and the tone of his speeches became increasingly harsh, increasingly menacing. On September 8, to the vast crowd packed shoulder to shoulder in the Piazza Venezia, he thundered, "And now, at the end of this stirring day, I come to the words you have been waiting to hear: we shall go straight ahead." Ten days later he said insolently to John Munro of the *Morning Post*, "We have an army in East Africa which has cost us two billion lire. Do you really believe that we have spent such an astronomical sum for nothing? We are on the march: 400,000 blacks are ready to oppose our 200,000 soldiers." He continued to rant on in this manner with mounting violence and ever-direr threats right up to the day of his "mobilization speech," while the Italian newspapers vied with one another to depict the Ethiopians in the darkest colors, as a people that had forfeited every right to exist as a nation.

When Mussolini embarked on his anachronistic colonial venture, he could not be sure that the democracies would allow him to carry it through to the end, and he did not even have the full support of those totalitarian countries whose regimes closely resembled his own. If we look through the newspapers of the day, we find the *Frankfurter Zeitung* rapping the Duce severely on the knuckles, "We must take every possible step to localize this colonial war and prevent it from leading to a general flareup in Europe . . . Signor Mussolini bears an

---

War is: (1) the one true way of showing our Fascist mettle by fighting for Mussolini's New Italy; (2) the infallible measure of our spiritual worth; (3) the perfect interpretation of our country's lyrical and ardent Africanism; (4) the most glorious expression of the swiftness and spontaneity of our will; (5) the perfect interpretation of our peninsula's ardent and lyrical African rapture; (6) the game of games; and (7) the unique, passionate adventure of body, heart and soul . . . For all these reasons, poets and artists of Italy, I hope to meet you all in Africa, fighting to Italianize that archaic country, fighting to transfigure it, and so transfiguring yourselves." See *Almanacco Letterario* (Milan: Bompiani, 1936), p. 32.

exceedingly grave burden of responsibility on his shoulders
. . ." [17] But it was an article entitled, "Race Psychology and
Military Education," in *Deutsche Schule*, the official magazine
for Third Reich educators, an article that, needless to say,
never reached the Italian people, but threw Mussolini into a
paroxysm of rage: "The South Italian has always been a
pitiful sort of fighter. The North Italian is much more compe-
tent, but he, too, is inferior to both French and German
soldiers . . . In what appears to be a remarkable contrast to
accomplishment are Italy's pretensions to fame and recognition. The Italian people are consumed by a sickly striving to
pass for a nation that is great and important. Yet even the
unification of Italy was only attainable through the help of
French and German troops. And the loudly trumpeted "victory" in the World War was not gained by Italian arms. This
national pretentiousness is boundless." [18] A further dose of
unpleasant medicine was administered to Mussolini by the
Austrian Nazi Party: "They distributed tens of thousands of
leaflets in which they declared that Italy, after shamelessly
attacking Ethiopia, had another army on Austria's frontier,
ready to make the preservation of Austrian independence a
pretext for an invasion.[19] Finally Japan, who continued to
proclaim her unbounded admiration for the Fascist regime
through Yotaro Sujimura, her ambassador in Rome, received
Daba Birru, the Ethiopian envoy extraordinary, with full diplomatic honors while the 2,000 students of the fascist *Kokuryu
Ku* (Black Dragon) society, who had been invited to the
ceremony, carried placards that screamed, "Down with
Italy!" [20] Decidedly, in the eyes of the world, the Ethiopian
campaign was anything but popular!

In Italy, however, it was a very different story for complex

[17] *Frankfurter Zeitung*, October 4, 1935.
[18] *Morning Post* (London), October 16, 1935.
[19] *Sunday Times* (London), October 6, 1935.
[20] *The Times* (London), September 20, 1935.

reasons. The appearance of the British fleet in Mediterranean waters and the economic sanctions imposed by the League of Nations had only increased the people's enthusiasm for the war. As Herbert L. Matthews wrote, "The soldiers fought bravely and overcame heartbreaking climatic and geographical difficulties, and the people of Italy were overwhelmingly behind them. Here was evidence that Italians could fight if they wanted to and that the majority of them were behind Fascism—as long as it produced such results." [21] Another writer, Ruggero Zangrandi, whose work is not tainted with any Fascist sympathy, had this to say, "The vast majority of Italians, particularly the younger generation, hailed the colonial enterprise with sincere enthusiasm. They were fighting for a place in the sun that other great powers had enjoyed for years or for centuries, and to a country as poor and overpopulated as Italy, the conquest of Ethiopia meant jobs and a patch of land for millions of unfortunates." [22]

More than thirty years have passed since these events, and the present generation of Italians who have only read about them cannot bring themselves to believe that an entire nation allowed itself to be so possessed by nationalistic frenzy that when the sirens sounded and the church bells pealed, its people rushed shouting and cheering into the streets and squares in a passionate patriotic stampede unique in our history. But thirteen years of Fascist propaganda and indoctrination had made an indelible mark on the Italians, particularly on the younger generation. [23] The young soldiers when they

[21] H. L. Matthews, *The Fruits of Fascism*, p. 226.

[22] Ruggero Zangrandi, *Il lungo viaggio attraverso il fascismo* (Milan: Feltrinelli, 1962), p. 66.

[23] In an article that appeared in translation in *Servizio Stampa A.O.* (Florence: Beltrami, 1936), p. 36, the French journalist Pierre Bonardi recorded this significant "confession" made to him by a youthful Second Lieutenant: "The young men under thirty who had been too young to fight in the First World War or take part in the March on Rome, envied their elder brothers and felt that through no fault of their own they fell far short

sailed from Italy (they were to revolt against Fascism once the hideous aspects of the war showed themselves), sincerely believed that they were the champions of a proletarian nation crying out for living room and justice, or that they were the bearers of light and civilization to a race ground down by a ferociously feudal "upper class." Laborers flocked to Ethiopia because they were lured by a wage of 45 lire a day, as much as they could earn in a week in Italy. Members of the Fascist hierarchy, bored with provincial life, rushed off to Africa to win themselves easy laurels and double or treble their salaries. Industrialists gave the campaign their full support, for in wartime prices rocket. Even such lukewarm Fascists as Vittorio Emanuele Orlando, Arturo Labriola, and Sem Benelli took advantage of the war to effect a reconciliation with the regime. As for the high-ranking officers, they certainly had no cause to complain; after a few months of not very arduous fighting, they won promotion, princely titles and medals galore. Badoglio, the victor, was covered with glory and laden with honors (he was created Duke of Addis Ababa and when he left Africa was given a magnificent mansion in the Via Bruxelles in Rome, plus an annual income equal to the lordly pay he had received as commander-in-chief, tax-free for life). Badoglio, who had once warned the Duce in a memorandum not to "overtax the patience of Great Britain as Italy was in no state to fight a war against her" [24] and who, on a single occasion advised him to give up the idea of an Ethiopian campaign, this same Badoglio wrote, "When the documents came to be published, all Italy will see—and it will be a fresh motive for devotion, for gratitude, for pride—how great was the foresight of the Duce in his

---

of those who had done so much for their country. I speak from experience— I'm under thirty and until today I've suffered from a terrible inferiority complex. Now it's different. I can hold up my head when I look at the older chaps because I myself am going to do something tremendously worthwhile: *I'm going to found an Empire!"*

[24] Badoglio's letter to Mussolini will be found in *Mussolini e lo stato maggiore*, by F. Rossi (Rome, 1951), pp. 24–26.

interpretation of history, how exactly he foresaw events, how firmly he controlled the situation, with what wisdom he issued timely instructions by which all—in every field of action, in plan and preparation, in the development and conduct of the war—were guided." [25]

It is literally true that apart from the anti-Fascists who lived in exile abroad not a single Italian raised his voice to denounce the anachronistic character of the African venture. Not one of them had the courage to tell the dictator that he was acting against the interests of the country. Worse still, not one of them denounced the war for what it was, a long-premeditated, patiently prepared-for, naked act of aggression. [26]

At midday on October 2, seven hours before Mussolini announced to the world, "We have been patient with Ethiopia for forty years; now our patience is exhausted," General Emilio de Bono left Asmara and drove to the tiny hamlet of Coatit, his temporary headquarters, where barracks and tents had been put up for himself and his staff. Here, at 0500 hours on the following day, he was to give the order to attack. But even as General De Bono's car was taking him to Coatit, one

[25] Pietro Badoglio, *The War in Abyssinia*, p. 8. With regard to the Marshal's attitude toward the Italo-Ethiopian war, Marshal Enrico Caviglio wrote in his *Diario* (Rome: Casini, 1962), p. 136: "When Badoglio and Lessona saw De Bono in Eritrea, the Marshal evidently realized it would take very little to defeat the Ethiopians, hence he maneuvered so successfully that De Bono was removed in his favor. When the Ethiopian project had first been mooted, he had opposed it stubbornly; now, however, he coveted De Bono's position, for he realized that as commander-in-chief, he would win easy laurels for himself. He pursued the method that had proved so profitable in the Great War." But from evidence supplied to me by General Faldella on April 29, 1965, it seems doubtful Badoglio ever opposed the Ethiopian project. "Throughout his career, he never once expressed a personal opinion on any event. Moreover, he supported Mussolini right to the end."

[26] The attitude of the Vatican was somewhat ambiguous. While Pope Pius XI declared at Castel Gandolfo on August 28, 1935, "The very thought of this war is abhorrent to me . . . a war of conquest would clearly be a totally unjust war," a number of prelates, among them Cardinal Schuster, Archbishop of Ancona, the Bishop of Parma and the Archbishop of Brindisi gave the war their blessing.

thousand kilometers away in Addis Ababa, the Emperor Haile Selassie telegraphed to the Secretary-General of the League of Nations that Italian troops had already violated the Ethiopian frontier "in the region south of Mount Musa Ali in the province of Aussa" [27] and ordered Ras Seyoum, Commander of the Tigre army, to withdraw "a day's march from the River Mareb before the Italians cross it." [28] The negus was determined to show the world once and for all who was the aggressor. And De Bono, after a four-day march ("Just a boring route march," said some of the veterans after the war was over) was forced to admit, "We didn't have the good luck to meet the enemy in force." [29]

Right up to the last moment, the man who, according to Fascist propagandists, was a savage and bellicose tyrant, had done his utmost by appealing to the world powers, to save the peace. And at the end, when he realized that war was inevitable, he uttered these noble words in the senate in Addis Ababa, "If our repeated efforts and all the goodwill we have shown fail, our conscience remains clear and unsullied, and the Ethiopian nation, united and strong in faith, will stretch out its hand to God, who will defend the just cause of our country." [30]

[27] The telegram was sent from Addis Ababa at 1315 hours. The text appears in the *Official Journal* of the League of Nations, No. II, Document 1571 (November 1935), p. 1603.

[28] *Une victoire de la civilisation*, p. 31.

[29] De Bono, *Anno XIII*, p. 40.

[30] In a speech made at the end of September 1935. The full text appears in a pamphlet printed by the Berhanenna Selam Press (Addis Ababa: July 23, 1942), pp. 38–42.

Chapter three

In the "Enemy's" Camp

Before we cross the Mareb with General De Bono's army, let us glance briefly at the "enemy" camp of Addis Ababa to see what Ethiopia was like in those days and evaluate our "antagonists" who, according to the "Minculpop," * were ferocious savages, warring tribesmen, and traders of black ivory. Addis Ababa is rapidly developing into one of the most beautiful cities in Africa, with the splendid buildings designed by the Italian architect Mezzedimi, rising on its hills, but it is easy to trace, particularly in the eucalyptus groves and the valleys of the Kurtumi and Genfile torrents, the Addis Ababa of 1935. A few brick-built, balconied houses vaguely oriental in style, a huddle of mud *tukuls* daubed with whitewash, pens for the domestic animals, a number of shops owned by Armenians, Greeks, Arabs, and Indians—"Yes, that was Addis in those days," said Petros Giannopoulos, the Greek bookseller, "there

* Abbreviation for *MINistero della CULtura POPulare:* Ministry of Popular Culture (Trans.).

30

In the "Enemy's" Camp

was only one generator, the generator that supplied electric light and power for the 'Little *Gebbi*,' the emperor's palace, only one passable hotel, the Imperial, and only one hard-surface road, the one which had been asphalted for Haile Selassie's coronation. There were no drains, no system of waste disposal; all the refuse was simply dumped into the streets and the sky was always black with vultures and crows." [1] When John Melly, the medical missionary who was to die in the emperor's service, arrived in the capital in 1934, he was aghast at what he saw. "Conditions here are appalling," he wrote in his diary. "The country is way back in the 15th century—ruled over by feudal lords—with sanitation unheard of. This is the capital, Addis Ababa, which outstrips the rest of the country by 500 years." [2] Still, as Leonard Mosley tells us, Addis could boast of a night club run by a Greek and "staffed by a pliant mixture of Hungarian, Roumanian, Czech, and White Russian cabaret girls." Out of a total population of 100,000, no fewer than 20,000 were prostitutes. [3]

By and large the "appalling conditions" in Ethiopia were to be found in other parts of Africa, not excepting those regions where white settlers had lived for years, even centuries. An objective observer would have been compelled to admit that the task of modernizing Ethiopia which Haile Selassie had set himself seemed almost hopeless, taking into consideration the vastness of the country, the lack of roads and communications, and above all the power wielded by the reactionary and ambitious rases. Before the relations between Italy and Ethiopia broke down for good, a few Italians expressed favorable opinions of the emperor. On the day after his coronation, the nationalist review *Politica* described him as "energetic, coura-

[1] This conversation took place in Addis Ababa on March 23, 1965.

[2] Kathleen Nelson and Alan Sullivan, *John Melly of Ethiopia* (London: Faber and Faber, 1936).

[3] Leonard Mosley, *Haile Selassie, the Conquering Lion* (London: Weidenfeld & Nicolson, 1964), p. 168.

geous and progressive, a man who is deeply interested in, and greatly admires our Western civilization and who is a sincere friend of Italy." [4] Again, only a short time before the war, Africanus wrote in *Ethiopia, 1935,* "Ras Tafari is a man of unquestionable worth. He dreams of transforming Ethiopia into a modern and civilized nation and of centralizing his rule, thus leaving the rases with only a semblance of authority. . . ." [5]

But suddenly the whole picture changed. In the twinkling of an eye, Haile Selassie was transmogrified by Italian propagandists into a sanguinary and primitive despot, a kind of Cesare Borgia who, after a series of intrigues and dark crimes, had waded through pools of blood to his throne, an ignorant savage allowing himself to be sucked dry by the Coptic priests and soothsayers who succeeded one another at his court and exerted over him the malevolent influence of a Rasputin. At a single stroke he became the vilest of all the slave owners, and vicious cartoons of him appeared regularly in Italian newspapers. He was shown laden with antiquated trumpets and scabbards, his arched, Semitic nose distorted into a monstrous beak and his slightly flat feet extended to a couple of platters. In 1935, Ras Tafari, whose name lent itself to the most trivial puns, was the target for every kind of abuse and vilification. But while the Italians laughed heartily at the negus, they showed no disposition to hate him. For that matter it was

[4] Quoted by Salvatorelli and Mila in *Storia d'Italia nel periodo fascista* (Turin: Einaudi, reprinted 1964), p. 168.

[5] Africanus, *Etiopia 1935* (Rome: Edizioni Ardita, 1935), p. 77. Among others who thought highly of the emperor was Corrado Zoli (*Etiopia d'Oggi,* pp. 106–7): "As governor of Sidamo, *Dejatch* Tafari showed from the first he was a born administrator, and he won golden opinions for his natural goodness, his unfailing justice, qualities that shone out in him and have retained all their luster. . . . His endless patience, his outstanding ability, his energy, his extraordinary indulgence and humanity, his farsightedness, his grasp of the radical needs of his empire, his knowledge of men, his understanding of the people of his vast and heterogenous country, have enabled him to accomplish all this. . . ."

somewhat difficult to hate a man who lived 6,000 kilometers away, a man they had never seen in the flesh, who asked for nothing more than to be allowed to live in peace.

What does he look like, this emperor, who together with Menelik figures so prominently in Italian history? "His dark-skinned face with its delicate features and large, melancholy eyes, is strikingly handsome," wrote Hermann Norden, the explorer, "But what impressed me most were his beautiful, aristocratic hands, so tiny, so exquisitely shaped that I shall never forget them." [6] Haile Selassie is far below the average height, and has the fragility of a figurine—he cannot weigh more than 110 pounds. (He is said to be tubercular.) But the moment one looks into his eyes, and from 1960 onward I had many opportunities of doing so, one instantly forgets his air of frailty and realizes that the man one is confronting, the man seated on the edge of the great, gilded bed-throne, has a will of iron, an acute and alert mind, and the strength of purpose to move mountains. Although for fifty years he has had to contend with a long series of rivals, from the deposed Emperor Lij Yasu to Dejatch Balcha, from Ras Gugsa Wolie to Ras Hailu Tekla Haimanot, of whom he rid himself either by astute maneuvers or force of arms, it is true to say that Haile Selassie admits to only one rival worthy of him—the ghost of a dead man, the phantom of Menelik the Great. It is Menelik alone that he has striven to emulate and surpass. Today when he is in the evening of his life, it can truly be said that he has attained his goal. While Menelik extended his rule from his own kingdom of Shoon to the territories comprised by modern Ethiopia, the negus has succeeded in holding his empire together despite the secessionist activities of the rases, the disintegrating influence of the Arab-Moslem world, and the ambitious designs of grasping European powers.

But at the time when the Italians on the frontiers of Ethio-

[6] Hermann Norden, Le dernier empire africain en Abyssinie (Paris: Payot, 1935), p. 33.

pia first began to show signs of their intentions, the emperor had only reached the initial stages of his plans for centralization and modernization. In November 1930, he drew up the country's first penal code; a year later, he gave it the first written constitution and outlined a vast program of administrative reforms. To carry these out, he enlisted the help of foreign experts—Everett Colson of America, General Virgin of Sweden, de Halpert of Great Britain, and Auberson of Switzerland. Outwardly, the changes were so slow as to be almost imperceptible; this was because Haile Selassie was opposed to any sudden and radical reforms. To the French writer and adventurer Henri de Monfreid, he gave his reasons for proceeding at such a snail's pace: "I believe that certain Western institutions, provided they are assimilated by my people, can make us stronger, strong enough to follow unaided the path of progress. But these new ideas cannot be assimilated at once. You must remember that Ethiopia is like Sleeping Beauty, that time has stood still here for 2,000 years. We must take great care, therefore, not to overwhelm her with changes now that she is beginning to wake . . . We must strive to steer a middle course between the impatience of Western reformers and the inertia of the Ethiopians who would close their eyes if the light were too strong. . . ."[7]

In addition, Haile Selassie had to contend with the reactionary influence of the Coptic clergy who were averse to any kind of change, and the pressure exerted by the nobles who regarded any attempt at reform as a direct threat to themselves. As it was impossible for him to rid himself at one stroke of these two power groups, the traditional pillars of the throne, he proceeded with the utmost caution and so laid himself wide open to attack. Italian propagandists made great play of his dilatoriness, and heaped derision on him; according to them, he was a mere puppet in the hands of his greedy rases and

[7] Henri de Monfreid, *Vers les terres hostiles de l'Ethiopie* (Paris: Bernard Grasset, 1936), pp. 229–30.

quite incapable of holding his empire together. But it was above all on the question of slavery that Haile Selassie came under fire. At the beginning of the thirties, this scourge was still widespread in Ethiopia, as Robert de Beauplan, among others, pointed out: "How many slaves are there? The figure is given as a million. This is probably an exaggeration, but there must be at least half that number. All the powerful rases have hundreds, even thousands of slaves. These unhappy creatures are herded together and breed like animals—they will perpetuate themselves forever. Slavery is so deeply rooted in the customs of the country that the negus is powerless to extirpate it." [8]

Nevertheless, at the time when he was still regent, the negus had taken steps to rid the country of this evil. On September 28, 1923, he had issued a decree making the buying and selling of slaves a crime punishable by death. On March 31, 1924, he had announced in an edict that the children of slaves would be born free and that on the death of their masters, all slaves would be given their liberty. In 1934 the emperor set up a bureau in Addis Ababa for the repression of slavery, and two years later, sixty-two similar centers had been opened in the country. Unfortunately, owing to the stubborn opposition of the feudal classes and the fact that, as V. Zoppi noted, "Slavery is closely bound up with the social and economic life of Ethiopia," the results had been negligible.[9] The Italian government could flatter itself it had scored a point when the League of Nations, after an open controversy with the negus, decided on May 22, 1935, to publish the latest secret report of the Advisory Committee on Slavery, a report that came down with particular severity on Ethiopia. It was transparently clear, however, that Italy's satisfaction at these revelations was in-

[8] *L'Illustration,* special number on the Italo-Ethiopian war (Paris: July 1936), p. 25.

[9] *Cronache illustrate della azione Italiana in A.O.* See V. Zoppi, "Schiavitù in Etiopia" (May 25, 1936), p. 96.

spired by the fact that they played into her hands and not by genuine moral indignation. As Elizabeth Jones and A. H. M. Munroe rightly observed, "There were many good points in the Italian case against Abyssinia, but their effect on public opinion was neutralized by these psychological mistakes. Slavery, the wild conditions on the frontiers, the barbaric mutilations that were still the punishment for crime, the cruelty of many native customs, the lack of imperial control over outlying provinces, the primitive state of national development—all tended to be forgotten in the wave of world sympathy evoked by the tactics of the Italian Government." [10]

From 1929 onward, duly warned that Italy was showing her intentions more and more plainly, Haile Selassie had taken certain precautions. The Ethiopians serving in the King's Own African Rifles had been recalled from Kenya, the Imperial Guard were being drilled and instructed by offices of the Belgian Military Mission headed by Major Dothée, and the emperor had asked General Erik Virgin to set up at Holeta a military academy for the training of cadets who would form a cadre of officers for the army. But on the eve of the war, the army had not made much progress, a fact that was duly noted by the Italian Supreme Command in East Africa. In a manual marked "confidential" and intended only for officers, we read, "All but the human element can be discounted. The Ethiopian soldier needs little, is tough and zealous of his honor. He is such a fanatical fighter that in the heat of battle he is utterly oblivious of death." [11] But how pitifully little it was, this desperate courage, against the weight of ten divisions (it would soon be seventeen), equipped with modern arms and commanded by modern tactical experts, supported by an excellent air force, artillery of every caliber, as well as by

[10] A. H. M. Jones and E. Monroe, *A History of Ethiopia*, p. 246.
[11] Comando Superiore A. O. Stato Maggiore, Ufficio Informazioni, "Riservato," *Etiopia: Guida pratica per l'ufficiale destinato in Africa Orientale* (Asmara: July 1935), p. 50.

36

flamethrowers, and, as if this was not enough, by the deadly weapon of "special liquids."

"We did not even contemplate fighting a European-style war," Haile Selassie said subsequently. "Moreover, it would have been impossible as what we had in the way of artillery, even machine guns, was laughable." [12] The Italians estimated —overestimated, according to the Ethiopians—that on the eve of the hostilities the enemy had an army of 350,000 men (of whom only a quarter had had any kind of military training); 400,000 rifles of every type and in every kind of condition; 200 antiquated pieces of artillery mounted on rigid gun carriages; about 50 light and heavy antiaircraft guns, Oerlikons, .75 Schneiders and Vickers; and a mixed batch of Ford and Fiat-3000 armored cars. The regulars of the Imperial Guard were fitted out in the greenish khaki uniforms of the Belgian army, but their berets had been made in Japan; the rest of the troops wore the white *shamma*,* and an excellent target it proved to be.

Modest and ill-equipped as this army was, the negus waited until September 28 before giving the order to mobilize. He could not bring himself to give up hope that the dispute would be settled peacefully and placed an excessive faith in the League of Nations as well as in the sympathy extended to him by the pro-Ethiopian committees that had been set up in countries all over the world as a protest against Italy's belligerent attitude. At the end of April 1935, the Amsterdam World Congress against War, of which Henri Barbusse was president, had indeed issued a manifesto affirming its support for Ethiopia and denouncing Italy as a deliberate aggressor. In the same month Carlo Rosselli attacked Italy's policy in a series of articles that appeared in *Giustizia e Libertà*, and subsequently published in book form under the title *How to Conduct the Campaign Against the War in Africa.* Another eminent sup-

[12] *Une victoire de la civilisation*, p. 16.
* Cotton cloak worn by most Ethiopian men and women (TRANS.).

porter of Ethiopia was Victor Basch, President of the League of Human Rights. In London Sylvia Pankhurst devoted herself tirelessly to the emperor's cause and the Cuban poet Nicolàs Guillén, vented his hatred of Mussolini in the following jingle:

> What a devil of a pirate
> This Mussolini is
> With that countenance of granite
> And those greedy claws of his!

But the most vehement outburst of indignation and grief provoked by Italy's threat to Ethiopia came from the large African cities where an elite of cultured Africans was establishing itself, from the Caribbean, and from the Negroes of the United States. To the colored people of the world, Ethiopia was the last bulwark of African political freedom, the one African country that had inflicted a crushing defeat on a European nation, indeed, to many of them Ethiopia was a kind of black Zion. So great was the appeal of this "promised land" that in the twenties a prominent group of Negroes emigrated from America and established a community on the uplands of Amhara. It was during this same period that, largely due to Marcus Garvey, a number of semireligious cults came into being, chiefly in the West Indies. These cults were either known as "Ethiopianism" or took the regent's name and title, hence the Rastafarians.[13] Subsequently, various Afro-Negro committees of solidarity with Ethiopia were set up, among them the American Committee for Ethiopia and the International African Friends of Ethiopia. The latter was presided over by Prince Ismail Daoud, and among its members were Jomo Kenyatta, J. B. Danquah, and George Padmore.

[13] Vittorio Lanternari, *Movimenti religiosi di libertà e di salvezza dei popoli oppressi* (Milan: Feltrinelli, 1960), pp. 160–67.

Ethiopia, then, had many supporters, but friendship alone could not halt the mighty Fascist war machine. At last Haile Selassie realized the invasion was inevitable and at the end of the summer began to prepare his people for the struggle that lay ahead. On July 18, from the country's only radio station at Akaki, he told them he would never agree to the proposal that Ethiopia should become an Italian protectorate. He had hardly finished speaking before the Coptic clergy and Moslem clerics formed the Association of Ethiopian Patriots, and within three days they had enrolled 14,000 members. On August 12, the negus once more addressed his people over the radio: "Italy continues to pour men and arms into Eritrea and Italian Somaliland. The danger of an armed conflict increases hour by hour." [14] It was during this critical period that Dr. Hanner, the Swedish physician who was in charge of the hospital in Addis Ababa, initiated the Ethiopian Red Cross.

On September 15 after Italy had turned down the proposals for a peaceful settlement put forward by the Committee of Five, the emperor was again at the microphone: "Today, when it has been made absolutely clear that the Wal Wal incident provides no grounds for war, Italy, who has been supplied with arms and munitions by powers that have denied them to our country—which has never manufactured war materials and desperately needs them for self-defense—Italy is seeking to discredit our government and our people in the eyes of the world by asserting that we are savages whom it is her duty to civilize. The attitude that Italy has seen fit to assume will be judged by history." [15] Two days earlier the Empress Menen had made a radio appeal to the women of every country, calling for their support: "The wives and mothers of Italy are as anguished as the wives and mothers of Ethiopia at the thought of all the agony and suffering war would bring upon them.

[14] For full text of speech, see A. Gingold-Duprey, *De l'invasion à la libération de l'Ethiopie* (Paris: Dupont, 1955), p. 193.

[15] *Ibid.*, p. 199.

Women of the world, unite! Demand with one voice that we may be spared the horror of useless bloodshed." [16]

The continuous broadcasts of the emperor stirred up the people, certainly those of the capital, to a patriotic fever. In Italy flags were blessed with "holy water from the Piave" and the "Fascist Sabbath," a day devoted to furthering the military and athletic prowess of the young men, was introduced. The Ethiopians succumbed to the same temptation and indulged in an orgy of patriotic displays and speeches. Indeed the Boy Scouts actually sent a letter to their leader, the eleven-year-old Duke of Harar, bemoaning the fact that their training was not sufficiently warlike and asking for real rifles.[17] Waizero [Lady] Ababath Charkoze, the young daughter of a wealthy landowner, organized "The Battalion of Death," and was photographed in uniform clutching a rifle to her stomach. Another *waizero* told the correspondent of the *Daily Express* that she had recruited a "Legion of Amazons," and had already enrolled 3,000 recruits.[18] A redoubtable old woman, Ferlenek, who forty years earlier had fought against the Italians at Adowa, willingly posed in front of the cameras aiming a pistol threateningly at an invisible enemy. On September 25, the war fever was temporarily forgotten: the emperor's lions had escaped from their cages and the panic-stricken people rushed to take cover. As soon as they learned that the last of the animals had been shot by the Imperial Guard, out they all came, clapping and "loolooing," as the drum-major Belu Abaka, a giant of a man well over six feet tall, marched along twirling his baton with consummate skill. On September 27, the feast of Maskal,* after the emperor had attended the religious ceremony in St. George's cathedral, he seated himself

---

[16] *Ibid.*, p. 197.

[17] *Evening Standard* (London), September 12, 1935.

[18] *Daily Express* (London), September 24, 1935.

* Religious feast celebrating the finding of the True Cross, also a secular feast in Ethiopia to mark the end of the rainy season and the return of spring (TRANS.).

in the magnificent pavilion that had been erected in the cathedral square, and the military procession filed past him. It was headed by a veteran of Adowa who recalled the heroic deeds of the past as he brandished his scimitar threateningly. Then came the cavalry with a shining array of lances, the Imperial Guard with their brand-new Mausers, a detachment of infantry in khaki uniforms but barefooted, Boy Scouts, cadets of the Holeta Academy, liberated slaves, ambulances, and finally armored cars. Three tiny Potez biplanes whose maximum speed was pitifully slow, flew overhead. On the following day Haile Selassie gave the order for general mobilization. In the speech he made to his people, he said, "Our ancestors sacrificed their lives to preserve our country's independence. It is better to die free than live in bondage. Follow their example." [19]

In the last remaining days of peace, the statesmen of the five continents, realizing intuitively that the Italo-Ethiopian war would be the prologue to a second world conflict, thought of nothing else, spoke of nothing else but the imminent clash of arms. In Great Britain 3,000 young men volunteered to fight for the emperor.[20] In New York 9,000 white Americans and Negroes staged a rally in Madison Square Garden and tore a huge effigy of Mussolini to shreds. In Rome James Donahue, Barbara Hutton's cousin, leaned out of the window of his hotel and shouted, "Long live Ethiopia!"—a few hours later, he was escorted to the frontier. In Berlin cinemas were showing "Ethiopia, 1935," a film that was markedly anti-Italian, while in London, long queues formed in Coventry Street to see "The Truth about Abyssinia" at the Rialto. In Cairo the

[19] A. Gingold-Duprey, *De l'invasion à la liberation*, p. 205.

[20] *Daily Express* (London), September 4, 1935. The emperor declined this offer, giving as one reason the fact that he had insufficient funds to pay them. These were not the only men who volunteered; among those to offer their services to the negus were a number of White Russian exiles, who had fought in Wrangel's army, as well as Turkish nationalists, Hungarians, and Czechoslovakians. See *The Observer* (London), October 6, 1935.

muezzins called the faithful to pray to Allah that Ethiopia might be spared. Astrologers and seers unanimously predicted Italy would win the war, and one of them, Reginald Naish, declared no power on earth could prevent the war from breaking out because it was foretold in the Bible in Isaiah, Habakkuk and Zechariah.[21]

And in fact at 6:45 P.M., on October 2, the last, lingering hopes crumbled to dust. From the balcony of the Palazzo Venezia, Mussolini addressed the vast crowd that had been summoned to the square by the wailing of sirens and the pealing of bells: "At this moment, forty million Italians have gathered in the piazzas of every city, town and village. Never in the history of mankind has such a tremendous spectacle been seen. . . ." [22] It was the end. After the rape of Ethiopia, it would be the rape of Spain; after the rape of Spain, the rape of Poland. Thereafter, all Europe from the Urals to the Pyrenees would be ablaze.

[21] Reginald T. Naish, *1934 . . . and After!*" (London: Thynne & Co., 1935). Another astrologer, R. H. Naylor wrote an entire book on Ethiopia, *Abyssinia, What the Stars Foretell* (London: Hutchinson, 1935), in order to prove that Mussolini, who was "born under Uranus when it was in conjunction with Mars," was destined to prevail over Haile Selassie, whom he described as "a curious mixture of primitive and modern man."

[22] Benito Mussolini, *Spirito della rivoluzione fascista* (Milan: Hoepli, 1940), p. 222.

Chapter four
The De Bono Phase of the War

The Mareb is a trickle of reddish water flowing between bare foothills, and while it has the status of a river, it is no serious obstacle. But to the 100,000 men who reached it in the early hours of October 3, it was the forbidden frontier, the frontier of shame. "For forty years the Mareb has been the signature on a miserable peace treaty," General Villasanta had said to the men of the Gavinana on the previous evening. It was the frontier imposed by Menelik after the shattering defeat of the Italians at Adowa, Amba Alagi, and Makalle. It was a "cursed" frontier that the troops were impatient to cross, to put behind them, together with the memory of the failure of liberal, Umbertinian "Little Italy." As they stood there in the uncertain light of dawn while the engineers were completing the pontoons, there was not a man among them, conscript or volunteer, infantryman or Blackshirt, Fascist or apolitical, indifferent to the regime, who did not feel his heart swell in his breast. "We have reached the 'tragic frontier,'" wrote Delio Mariotti, a volunteer, "At this historic hour all Italy is with us, the dead of Adowa call us. We close ranks and await the order to advance. Forward! No one, nothing can stop us now. A new cycle is beginning for our country, the Roman legionnaires are once more on the march. This narrow, dusty track shut in by thorny hedges is the road to the empire." [1] High-flown rhetoric, yes, but we must remember that this was indeed an exalting moment. For these very young men—the oldest were those of the class of 1911—crossing the Mareb was symbolic. They were avenging the dead of Adowa, hurling defiance at the "sated" powers, the "haves," whose governments had strenuously opposed the war, and above all they were showing the world that believed the wretched southern peasant obliged to emigrate was typical of their nation, that there was a new generation in Italy, one with whom it would have to reckon.

At precisely 0500 hours the three attacking columns, covering a front of 60 kilometers, crossed the Mareb. On the right, the Second Army Corps under General Maravigna began its advance on Adowa. In the center General Pirzio Biroli's Eritrean Corps moved off toward the ambas of Enticho. On the left, the First Army Corps commanded by General Santini had Adigrat as its objective. Each man had been issued 110 rounds of ammunition, four days' rations, and two liters of water. As the sun burst forth, the three columns irrupted into Ethiopia with banners waving and trumpets blaring triumphantly. Carried away by the delirious excitement of the Italians, the Askaris of the Seraé company discharged their rifles into the air and improvised wild "fantasies." * Not another shot disturbed the utter tranquility of the first day of the war.

---

[1] Delio Mariotti, *In armi sulle Ambe* (Milan: La Prora, 1937), p. 94.

* Impromptu songs and dances in which they boasted of their valor and prowess in war (TRANS.).

There was only one drawback to the war at this stage once the Mareb had been crossed; wheels were useless for only vaguely defined paths, and the troops had to proceed on foot over the mule tracks that lay ahead. "Every now and then, a man would pick up a clod of earth and crumble it with his fingers to test its quality," wrote the journalist Cesco Tomasselli, "and those who planned to work on the land after the war spoke knowingly of cultivation." [2] It was good earth, and as they marched on they were to find it even better. It would yield two, even three, crops a year, they told one another, and their elation was almost as great as when they had crossed the "forbidden frontier." At 0820 hours, Alessandro Pavolini, who was in Ciano's three-engined plane, glanced down and saw Ciano raise the still unmounted sights and guns as if he were carrying out an exercise. But it was no exercise. Although Mussolini, to stress his contempt for the enemy had not declared war, it had already begun as Pavolini realized when the Caproni 133's of the *Disperata* squadron roared over Adowa: "The antiaircraft guns on the *gebbi* spat flak at us, and the heavy machine guns blazed away from the houses and surrounding ambas, but this didn't stop us from flying in formation three times over the town to pinpoint our targets. Our bombs landed accurately; every gun emplacement, every machine-gun nest was shrouded in thick smoke." [3]

On the second day the columns met with little resistance. "My own regiment, the first to cross the Mareb, lost only one man who was killed by a stray shot fired by one of his comrades," wrote the author Paolo Cesarini, who was in command of a detachment of heavy artillery, "Yet the country we were passing through was ideal for the enemy had he chosen to attack us." [4] Emperor Haile Selassie, however, had decided to pursue another course, that of withdrawal. His reason was

[2] *Con l'esercito italiano in A.O.*, vol. I (Milan: Mondadori, 1936), p. 77.
[3] *Ibid.*, p. 66.
[4] Information given to me by Paolo Cesarini on April 19, 1965.

twofold: In the first place he was demonstrating his adherence
to the conditions imposed on him by the League of Nations,
and in the second he was following the customary Ethiopian

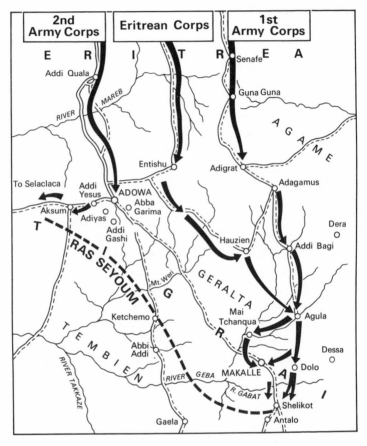

Map 2. Operations carried out by General De Bono from October 3
to mid-November 1935.

tactics of drawing the enemy deeper and deeper into Ethiopian territory and further and further away from his lines of
supply. Of this maneuver the negus said: "Contact between

our armies and the Italian army on the northern front was
delayed for several weeks because we had ordered Ras Gugsa
and Ras Seyoum to stabilize their forces at points respectively
50 and 80 kilometers from the frontier. We were determined
that the 30 kilometers of the neutral zone agreed upon with the
League of Nations should be strictly respected. It was difficult
to make the Ethiopians understand why we had taken this step
since it appeared to them as if we had already ceded part of
our territory. Later on it became even harder to convince them
that they must retreat whenever the enemy threatened to attack in force. My brave Ras Seyoum, because of his very
courage, left Adowa in tears." [5]

In actual fact Ras Seyoum had disobeyed the emperor and
had sent a few hundred men into the "neutral zone" where one
group established itself at Daro Takle and the other, still
deeper in the strip of land, at the Gashorki Pass. But they only
held out for a few hours, and on the evening of October 4, as
Colonel Konovaloff tells us, Ras Seyoum Mangasha abandoned
his modest *gebbi* on the summit of the hill that dominates
Adowa, and took refuge in a cave at Maryam Shoaitu. It was
from this temporary hideout on the following morning that he
witnessed the second wanton and bloody bombing of the
town.[6] From now on the roads were wide open for the invasion. Ras Seyoum withdrew. Ras Gugsa, as we shall see, had
turned traitor and was seeking to make contact with the
enemy. On October 5, Adigrat capitulated—not a single shot
was fired. The next day it was Adowa that, like Adigrat,
offered no resistance.

With the fall of these two cities, Toselli, Arimondi, and Da
Bormida were "avenged." The Italian soldiers were wild with
joy, but when the feverish excitement induced by the fanfares
of trumpets and ringing patriotic speeches had subsided, they

[5] *Une victoire de la civilisation*, p. 16.
[6] Theodore Eugene Konovaloff, *Con le armate del negus* (Bologna:
Zanichellie, 1936), p. 54.

realized that Adowa and Adigrat were two miserable little villages and some of them, with that commonsense that characterizes the working class, began to ask themselves whether it was really worthwhile fighting a war to occupy them. In any case they felt it was pointless to behave like conquerors to these poor Tigreans who overflowed with gratitude if they were given an empty wine bottle. Consequently, before very long, as noted by the French journalist Paul Gentizon, who was covering the Italian front: "The people have no misgiving about accepting money. Wherever I go, I find Italian soldiers fraternizing with the inhabitants. I've seen them helping the Ethiopians to pick peas and beans. The 'miles agricola' of 2,000 years ago has returned to life in Africa." [7] Italian soldiers worked in the fields for a freshly laid egg, a chicken, or simply because they wanted to show the "poor stinkers" how to get the best out of their land. They lent the Ethiopian peasants a hand out of sheer good nature and pity, thus revealing themselves in a new light, one that was to go far towards their ultimate exoneration from war guilt. General De Bono himself lost no time in establishing peaceful relations with the population, and an October 14 he issued a proclamation ordering the suppression of slavery. [8] But very little came of it, hence he was able to appreciate the difficulties that had beset the emperor in his efforts to rid Ethiopia of this evil. "If the absolute truth be told," wrote the general, "I am obliged to say that the proclamation did not have much effect on the owners of slaves and perhaps still less on the liberated slaves themselves. Many of the latter, the instant they were set free,

[7] Paul Gentizon, *La revanche d'Adoua* (Paris: Berger-Levrault, 1936), p. 219.

[8] In *Haile Selassie, the Conquering Lion*, p. 207, Leonard Mosley writes, "De Bono was, for his time and considering the regime, a civilized and decent man, and he firmly believed that he and his fellow Italians had come into Ethiopia, not just as conquerors but as civilizers."

presented themselves to the Italian authorities, asking, 'And now who gives me food?' " [9]

On the afternoon of October 11, *Dejatch* Haile Selassie Gugsa with 1,200 men and 8 machine guns, reached the Italian outpost at Adagamos. General De Bono notified Rome "where the news was very welcome, but it was improperly exaggerated so that Gugsa's men became 10,000 in number." [10] But even though the ras had only succeeded in persuading a tenth of his men to desert, this event was undoubtedly important because he was the emperor's son-in-law. His defection, as Haile Selassie himself recognized, "not only lowered the morale of our people but produced an adverse effect on the military situation. Some of our generals declared that this act of treachery had given the Italians two months' advantage over us." [11] Yet the negus had several times been warned that Gugsa was not to be trusted. Two weeks before the invasion, Wodaju Ali, the ex-consul of Asmara, had brought him proof positive that the ras was in the pay of the Italians. He showed the emperor a copy of his son-in-law's bank account, but after noting the sums that had been regularly paid in Haile Selassie merely observed, "Most of my rases take money from the Italians. It is bribery without corruption. They pocket Italian money and remain steadfast to Ethiopia." [12] Not only did he refuse to remove Gugsa from his command, but he did not even take the precaution of modifying the military plans with which the ras was familiar.[13]

In the meantime, the paternalistic policy of old General De Bono was beginning to pay off although the first results were

[9] De Bono, *Anno XIII*, p. 253.
[10] *Ibid.*, p. 262.
[11] *Une victoire de la civilisation*, pp. 17–18.
[12] Leonard Mosley, *Haile Selassie*, p. 199.
[13] It is worth recalling that at the time when Gugsa went over to the Italians there were still some 100 Italians in the capital, including the

merely of a superficial character. The Tigreans learned to sing the songs of the Italian soldiers and raise their arms somewhat clumsily in the Fascist salute. But on October 13, the chapter of the cathedral of Axum presented itself in Adowa and made a solemn act of submission that was followed two days later by the bloodless occupation of the holy city of the Copts. General De Bono entered on horseback "amidst the cheers of the population *who had been told they must applaud me. I was not so ingenuous as to think this applause sincere.*" [14] As De Bono, the ex-chief of police, sensed, the real object of this ovation was to mitigate the rigors of the occupation, and was not, as Italian propagandists asserted, a gesture of servility or the clear evidence that the people of the Horn of Africa were utterly devoid of love of country. Indeed, the falsity of these too facile assumptions was proved by the desertion, even at this stage of the war, of dozens of Eritrean Askaris who went over to the Ethiopians, thus forfeiting their pay and signing their own death warrants. Naturally, the Italian people were never informed of this defection or of others that occurred later on the southern as well as the northern front (in the Negelli area, 904 Askaris deserted in a single night), hence they asked themselves in vain what had driven *Shumbashi*

Italian ambassador, Vinci-Gigliucci. Far from carrying out reprisals on them, the emperor treated them extremely well, and even asked the ambassador to accompany him on the occasion of the state opening of the capital's first model prison. When the Italians were on the point of leaving for Jibouti, the emperor sent for Castagna, the architect, and said, "Stay in Addis, Castagna, you're an old man and you're not involved in the war." Castagna, however, had made up his mind to leave with the rest. "Go if you must, but remember that the door of Ethiopia will always be open for you," the negus told him.

[14] De Bono, *Anno XIII*, p. 266. Paul Gentizon tells us (*La rivincita di Adua*, p. 209) that "on the following day, in honor of the general, the Coptic priests performed their traditional dances, 'the Dance of the Lion,' for instance, which celebrated the killing of a king of the forest by an Ethiopian, and 'the Dance of the Passion,' which it seemed had not been performed for more than a hundred years."

Wandom Tesfazien and thousands of Askaris to desert. They did not know that for a number of years hundreds of Eritrean exiles had been given asylum in Addis Ababa. Moreover, if they heard Omar Samantar and the Sultan Herzi Bogor mentioned, they merely gathered that these two men were common bandits. Instead, as will appear later, notwithstanding the Italian policy of fanning the traditional flame of hatred between Somalis and Ethiopians, Eritreans and Ethiopians, Moslems and Copts, not only the Tigreans and Shoans but also Samantar's Somalis and Tesfazien's Eritreans fought beneath the banner of the Lion of Judah in a desperate stand against the most powerful invasion force Africa had ever seen.[15]

General De Bono, however, barely had time to sense that the defection of the Askaris might become a serious problem, for his days as commander-in-chief were numbered and Rome had already decided upon his successor. In the eyes of Mussolini, stung as he was by the increasing disapprobation of the League of Nations, the general, immersed in logistics, was moving far too slowly. "Lightning advances" and "glittering victories" were what he needed, and like all dictators who fight campaigns miles from the scene of battle, he would not hear of obstacles or delays. He decided, therefore, to send Alessandro Lessona, Colonial Secretary, and Marshal Badoglio, Chief of Staff, on a "mission" to Eritrea. Accordingly, he summoned Lessona and said to him confidentially, "Marshal Badoglio will accompany you. General De Bono will certainly be displeased, hence your presence is required to prevent any friction." Lessona recorded this conversation in his *Memoirs*, commenting: "It was plain that the Duce had no faith in De

---

[15] We lack details about this common stand against the enemy, but it may well be one of the most significant moments in Africa's nascent nationalism. Most of these Eritreans were captured and executed by the Italians in the months that followed the end of the war. One of the surviving Eritreans rose to the rank of general and is still serving with the Ethiopian army.

Bono and that, in sending him to Eritrea, he had allowed himself to be ruled by party considerations. He regarded De Bono as merely a fair-weather pilot; in other words, substantially incapable." [16] While Lessona and Marshal Badoglio were carrying out their mission in Eritrea, Mussolini wired De Bono, "By the middle of November all Tigre, to Makalle and beyond, ought to be ours." [17] A few days later he sent another telegram ordering the General to begin the advance on November 5. In his reply De Bono pointed out the difficulties and dangers that such an operation involved, stressed the great risk that would be incurred if the supply lines were lengthened by another 90 kilometers, and added acidly, "This, my dear Leader, I feel it my duty to tell you in order to put you on your guard against any frivolous statements that may have been reported to you by Lessona and even Badoglio." [18] Mussolini's only answer was to order the advance to be made two days earlier: "To synchronize the political exigencies with the military, I order you to resume action Makalle-Takkaze on the morning of November 3. On October 3 all went well, now it will go better." [19]

In the face of this pigheadedness, this dilettantism, De Bono was forced to yield. The advance took six days and was uneventful, except for a brush with the enemy on the slopes of Mount Gundi. At dawn on November 8, the first patrols sighted their objective. "The great plain of Makalle lay before us," reported Alfio Russo. "It made a harmonious picture with waving rows of yellow corn, dhurra that had not yet ripened, graceful white teff and the tender green of sprouting barley. The men of the patrol I was attached to were the first to shout 'Makalle!' 'Makalle!' roared Gugsa's band, and the rough

[16] Alessandro Lessona, *Memorie* (Florence: Sansoni, 1958) pp. 184–85. He was appointed Colonial Minister June 9, 1936.

[17] De Bono, *Anno XIII*, p. 276.

[18] *Ibid.*, p. 281.

[19] *Ibid.*, p. 283.

male tones were softened by the soprano voices of the Tigrean women chorusing 'Makalle! Makalle!' " [20] The people of Italy were wild with joy when they heard that Makalle had been taken and needed no urging from party orators to commemorate to the full "Galliano's heroic resistance." Nevertheless, from the military point of view, the advance had been a grave mistake because it had left the flank of the Italian army completely uncovered.[21]

But Mussolini's appetite for victories was still unsated, and barely three days after the occupation of Makalle, he telegraphed General De Bono to "resume the march on Amba Alagi without delay." [22] This time, De Bono revolted; exasperated beyond measure, he forgot his long-standing loyalty to the Leader, and wired back a terse reply, giving him a lesson in military tactics, "Note lastly that apart from painful historical memory which, to my thinking, needs no vindication, position of Amba Alagi has no strategical importance and is tactically defective because it can be completely surrounded." [23] It was the last telegram he was to send as commander-in-chief. Six days later, Mussolini informed him that his "mission" had been completed and that he would be replaced by Badoglio. To sweeten this bitter pill, the Duce promoted him from general to marshal of Italy.

"Mussolini deluded himself into believing that by substituting Badoglio for De Bono the advance would be rapidly resumed and carried through uninterruptedly to the end," wrote the military historian, General Emilio Faldella. "The truth was that the reports sent to him by Lessona and Marshal Badoglio made no mention of the fact that a temporary halt was absolutely essential in order to prepare for the final thrust.

[20] *Con l'esercito Italiano in A.O.*, vol. I, p. 112.

[21] Badoglio realized this advance was a mistake forty days later when the Ethiopians threatened to cut his army in two and he was forced to make plans for the possible evacuation of Makalle.

[22] De Bono, *Anno XIII*, p. 305.

[23] *Ibid.*, p. 306.

These reports dwelt on the spirit of the troops who were 'panting to push on,' and Badoglio wrote that the difficulties were 'invariably' exaggerated and that to proceed south was a straightforward tactical problem that could easily be solved." [24] So easily solved, indeed, that Badoglio, who had arrived in Eritrea on November 26, 1935, was unable to resume the initiative until January 20, 1936. Hence there can be no doubt that General De Bono was the victim of intrigues hatched in Rome, and that he was not removed for incapacity as is generally believed. "True, he had his limits," General Faldella told me, "but with the means at his disposal, it would have taken him no longer to reach Addis Ababa than it took Marshal Badoglio." [25]

The "changeover" completely altered the character of the war. De Bono had conducted the first phase more in the role of a pacifier than in that of a conqueror. Badoglio, as we shall see, had only one end in view—to wipe out the enemy—and to achieve his purpose, he made use of every weapon he possessed, legal and illegal. As Leonard Mosley justly observed, "From this moment, the character of the war changed . . . everything Ethiopian was to be bombed—open towns, encampments, roads, hospitals, even those plainly indicated by the Red Cross and the flags of the nations which ran them." [26] De Bono had refused to avail himself of "special liquids." Not so Badoglio, who soon gave the Ethiopians their first dose of yperite (mustard gas), and other poison gases. The war that had begun as a campaign of conquest in the romantic spirit of the *risorgimento* degenerated into a bloody affair of wanton and brutal destruction. The brash lyrics of Alessandro Pavolini, who was enjoying such success in those days, have an ugly ring of bitter truth:

[24] *Storia Illustrata*, May 1963, p. 620.
[25] This conversation took place in Turin, April 29, 1965.
[26] Leonard Mosley, *Haile Selassie*, p. 207.

Life, be our friend, death, be our lover,
Ciano is our leader, with him we will fly over—
Bombs away—craters gape
And a new landscape
Far below us suddenly takes shape.

Chapter five

Conscripts, Volunteers, and War Correspondents

"Before the beginning of the advance on Makalle," wrote General De Bono, evidently with some amusement, "H.R.H. the Duke of Bergamo arrived in the colony to take part in the operations as vice-commandant of the 'Gran Sasso,' and also H.R.H. the Duke of Pistoia, who assumed command of the '23rd March' . . . other arrivals were Senator Suardo, several deputies and Fascist functionaries, and also the academician, Marinetti (who came to me on the first night of the advance with only a briefcase for all his luggage)." [1] Some of these personages remained in Ethiopia till the end of the war, some

<hr>

[1] De Bono, *Anno XIII*, p. 288.

stayed for a few days, others only spent a few hours in the country; just long enough, in fact, to give them a whiff of the war. During the seven months of the hostilities and during the year that preceded them, some 500,000 Italian troops disembarked at Massawa and Mogadishu and went into action on the northern and southern fronts. This expeditionary force, unique in colonial history because of its magnitude and the variety of its human elements, deserves a chapter to itself, particularly as there are a number of questions to be answered —how high was the morale of the army, how many of those who served in it were volunteers, how many conscripts, how much reliance can be placed on the reports and in the books of the three hundred journalists and writers who covered the Italo-Ethiopian War?

First, almost all the men who fought in the war came from the class of 1911 and had already done their two years' compulsory training in Italy. These conscripts outnumbered the volunteers by five to one, consequently, as Paolo Cesarini told me, "the morale of the army was not very high. Furthermore, the dread inspired by the Dark Continent and the fame of the Ethiopian warriors which, strange to say, forty years had not dimmed, was hardly calculated to raise it." [2] Not all these young men, however, were afraid of unknown Africa; some of them indeed, among them Giovanni di Modica, an officer in the Pusteria division, found it utterly fascinating: "Africa, the Dark Continent, with its wild life, cannibals [sic], forests and lions; Africa, with its dangers, its promise of new vistas, the possibility it held out of living an adventure—perhaps the last, before I became a staid citizen moving uneventfully towards the evening of my life, gradually cast an irresistible spell over me." [3]

The low morale of the army was mainly attributable, how-

[2] In the course of a conversation with the author.
[3] Giovanni di Modica, *Cinghia* (Turin: Libreria R. Mariano, 1937), pp. 9–10.

ever, to the relations between the conscripts and the Black-shirts, which were not always easy. "We conscripts underwent an iron discipline," stated Giovanni Montagna, "but the Blackshirts weren't put through it as we were. They got far better rations than we did and higher pay as well. Naturally, this caused a lot of bad blood between us and often led to blows." [4] Those who resented this disparity of conditions most bitterly were the Alpini [Alpine troops] who on more than one occasion (at Amba Aradam, for instance, as will appear in a later chapter) bore the entire brunt of the enemy attack and were subsequently compelled to divide the honors with the Blackshirts. But in some divisions, I learned from Cesarini, "the conscripts and Blackshirts were on excellent terms. The soldiers sympathized wholeheartedly with the latter (many of whom were only nominally volunteers) when they complained justly or unjustly that their officers were a poor lot. To men who are fighting a war, an incompetent officer is the worst nightmare of all." [5]

Genuine volunteers, then, were a minority. As boys, most of these had experienced the exciting atmosphere of the *Balilla* and the "Dux" camps, and when they were old enough many had become *squadristi*. Others had lived abroad and conse-quently felt a greater need than the rest for a "strong" and "respectful" Motherland. The heroic ardor of this compara-tively small group was so infectious that it spread through the ranks of the army, and even conscripts were inspired to pen such high-flown stuff as this: "Even more implacable than our dead, we are prepared, for our Fascist faith, to strike to the

[4] Statement made in France by Giovanni Montagna and published in the *New Times and Ethiopia News* on May 8, 1937. In a letter sent to me on May 18, 1965, Nino Giuseppe, who had fought in a Blackshirt division during the Italo-Ethiopian war, wrote: "For a time, we shared quarters with the men of the regular army, but we were never on good terms, there was no feeling of comradeship. There was even a certain coolness between their officers and ours."

[5] Evidence given to the author.

hilt as our Duce commands. Always, everywhere." [6] On the whole, as even Salvatorelli * was forced to admit, the Black-shirts, incorporated in divisions named for the most important dates in Fascist history, gave an excellent account of themselves from a strictly military point of view.

There were three other groups of volunteers, men who had offered their services for state, party, or dynastic reasons. In the first category were Mussolini's sons, Vittorio and Bruno, and his young son-in-law, Count Ciano, then minister for propaganda. These three arrived in Eritrea as the final preparations for the invasion were being made, with the C.A.-133's of the *Disperata* and *Quia Sum Leo* squadrons, and took part in all the indiscriminate bombing raids of the war. Vittorio, the intellectual member of the Mussolini family, has left us a record of his experiences, the crude and brutal *Flight over the Ambas*, which was translated into many foreign languages shortly after it appeared. And quite rightly, for there is no other book as authoritative and circumstantial on the terrorist activities of the Fascist air force. Here is one of its pearls chosen at random: "I was always miserable when I failed to hit my target, but when I was dead on, I was equally upset because the effects were so disappointing. I suppose I was thinking about American movies and was expecting one of

---

[6] Delio Mariotti, *In armi sulle Ambe*, see preface. See also Adriano Grande, *La Legione Parini* (Florence: Vallecchi, 1937), in which the poet writes, "I wasn't old though I was certainly past my first youth, but when I put on my uniform I felt as though I were once more in my teens . . . it wasn't the intoxication of enthusiasm that gave me this feeling, it stemmed from the fact that I was participating in an adventure way above myself—a supreme adventure that had captured the attention of the whole world . . . in short, the sensation that the years had rolled away came from the joy I experienced of being able at last to play an active part—even if it was only the infinitesimal part of a Chosen Blackshirt—in the making of history, instead of being, as I had been up till then, a mere spectator" (pp. 14–15).

* Although not politically active, Salvatorelli, former professor of history at the University of Turin, detested the Fascist regime, and co-authored a book on the period (TRANS.).

those terrific explosions when everything goes sky-high. Bombing these thatched mud huts of the Ethiopians doesn't give one the slightest satisfaction." [7] Further on, as if he were telling us that eating one cherry makes him yearn for more, Vittorio remarks, "War fills a man with the longing to fight another." [8] On reading the book, Francesco Stanco, a professor of Latin, was so filled with admiration that in his incredible little primer for elementary schools, he included the following, *"Digni qui laudentur sunt Bruno et Victorius Ducis filii, qui cum administro G. Ciano audactur hostium propugnacula demoliti sunt, dum plumbeis glandibus ferrisque globis excipiuntur."* ["Worthy of praise are Bruno and Vittorio, the sons of the Duce, and the minister Galeazzo Ciano, who daringly destroyed the enemy fortifications amidst a hail of shot and shell."] [9] It is nauseating to think that I, and thousands of other eleven-year-olds, were forced to toil away at construing this utter balderdash.

The first members of the hierarchy to arrive in Africa were Parini, who took command of a "legion" on the southern front; Attilio Teruzzi, who led a Blackshirt division; Roberto Farinacci, Giuseppe Bottai, Carlo Scorza, Gherardo Casini, and Nino Dolfin. But none of them, endowed with authority and fertile imaginations though they might be, succeeded in equaling the exploit of Achille Starace, Secretary-General of the Fascist Party, who had always been determined to outshine the rest in Italy and had made up his mind to be the leading light in Africa. With his own small, completely mechanized army of 3,400 men, he left Asmara on March 14, 1936, and reached his objectives Gondar and Lake Tana fifteen days later, thanks to the fact that *Dejatch* Ayelu Birru who should have blocked the road of the "epic march" had been suborned.

[7] Vittorio Mussolini, *Voli sulle ambe*, (Florence: Sansoni, 1937), p. 28.

[8] *Ibid.*, p. 152.

[9] Francesco Stanco, *Epitome di Cultura Fascista* (Turin: SEI, 1936), p. 84.

As Starace tells us in *The March on Gondar,* the infernal sun beating down on the plains had turned the scrub to tinder, and had Ayelu Birru set fire to it, not a single man would have escaped from the fiery furnace. "If the enemy had planned such a treacherous act, it would have been the work of a moment to annihilate the entire column. He had only to strike a single match," wrote the irresponsible secretary-general of the Fascist Party.[10] Unbelievably vain, Starace asked Gabriele D'Annunzio to write the preface for *The March on Gondar,* and instead of giving his true opinion of this wretched work, the aged poet replied with nauseating sycophancy, "Your book is a model for future commentators; the conciseness of your style makes what you have to say all the more forceful." [11]

As the House of Savoy had given its wholehearted blessing to the African undertaking, it was essential that a few personages of royal blood should grace the theater of war. Princess Marie-José of Piedmont went out as a Red Cross nurse; the Dukes of Bergamo, Aosta, Spoleto, and Pistoia (Filiberto of Savoy-Genoa) took command of various divisions. Of these five, the last-named seems to have been the most enthusiastic, the most convinced that this was a war of high purpose. "When the Duce decided to put an end to the intolerable state of barbarism in Ethiopia . . . I knew that I had to go to Africa where the fate of our people was at stake," he wrote in his extremely modest little book of memoirs.[12] The Duke was in command of the "23rd March," and the men more than forgave him for his effeminate ways and the fact that the caramels distributed to them daily were wrapped in paper stamped with his family crest when they saw him on several occasions, a tall, spare figure with a pallid complexion, break

[10] Achille Starace, *La marcia su Gondar* (Milan: Mondadori, 1936), p. 84.

[11] *Ibid.,* see preface by Gabriele D'Annunzio.

[12] Filiberto di Savoia-Genova, *La prima divisione Camicie Nere "23 marzo"* (Milan: Bompiani, 1938), p. 10.

CHAPTER FIVE

away from his bodyguards, seize a rifle, and hurl himself into the fray.[13]

Mussolini who, for the first time since he had become dictator was spending vast sums ungrudgingly, was anxious that the war should be covered by the largest possible number of Italian reporters, Italian writers who were loyal to the regime, and foreign correspondents. "Before we left Italy," wrote Bruno Roghi in *Green Press Card in Africa*, "we were received by the Hon. Dino Alfieri, then Under-Secretary of State, who greeted us, wished us luck, and gave us the exhortation that our press cards warranted: we were to be lively and concise in our reports so as to bring out in our style of writing the latest prerogatives of the Italian undertaking, vibrant with youth, unshakable determination, and singlemindedness of purpose." [14] In other words this was an invitation to glorify the war, to exalt every incident into a shining example, to give voice, in fact, to a paean of unqualified praise, unmarred by the faintest shadow of doubt, the least trace of criticism. For the rhetoricians and writers who made it their profession to laud the party with loyal effusions, this was a chance to have "a real ball." Salvatore Aponte managed to transform the Italian defeat at Dembeguina into a decisive victory.[15] Ivon de Begnac extolled the "derring-do" of the Blackshirts; Federico Valli, in his description of the bombing of Harar, asserted that "when I saw the bombs fall, I wanted to fling my heart after them"; [16] while Mario Appelius continued for months to turn out such incredible purple passages as, "It became a heroic struggle, a sublime game of death. The battle broke up into countless incidents, crumbled into stardust. As the corpses piled up higher and higher, as the fixed bayonets glittered, as

[13] Evidence given to the author by Lt. Roscigno.

[14] Bruno Roghi, *Tessere verde in Africa Orientale* (Milan: Ed. Elettra, 1936), see preface.

[15] See "Lo scontro di Mai Timchet," in *Con l'esercito italiano in A.O.*, pp. 215–18.

[16] *Ibid.*, vol. 2, p. 463.

the scimitars flashed through the air and embroidered on white flesh the lurid scarlet tracery of death, I heard, like a salvo of guns, the voice of a legionary who was opening up a way with his bare fists through a hundred heaped-up bodies. 'By God!' he thundered, 'you won't kill me! I'll put paid to the lot of you!' " [17] The only writer to outdo Appelius was the founder of the Futurist movement, the academician Marinetti, with his "spontaneous" poems. One, dedicated to the ambas, runs:

Siete lo credo dichiaro confermo mense sterminate offerte dalla Patria ai giganti Galliano Toselli De Cristoforis si sollazzino finalmente con vivande e liquori celestiali senza scatolame politica mediocrista. [18]

[You are I believe declare confirm the immense tables offered by the Motherland to the giants Galliano Toselli De Cristoforis who divert themselves at last with nectar and ambrosia without tin-can utterly mediocre politicians.] *

Of the two hundred accredited Italian reporters and writers who had been given the task of glorifying the war, only a handful possessed real talent, good taste, a sense of proportion and, above all, a feeling of shame. Naturally these men found it extremely difficult, conscientious as they were, to reconcile their own individual style of writing with the extravagant demands of the "Minculpop." However, the most honest and intelligent members of this group found various ways of extracting themselves from their embarrassing position. Enrico Emanuele, for instance, the correspondent of the Genoa news-

[17] *Ibid.*, vol. 1, p. 305.
[18] F. T. Marinetti, *Il poema africano della divisione "28 Ottobre"* (Milan: Mondadori, 1937), p. 71.
* Marinetti's poems can only be translated into "Spontaneous" English! (TRANS.)

paper *Il Lavoro*, steered clear of the rocks by confining himself to delicate water-color sketches of the daily life of the Italian soldiers, depicting them on the march or in their quarters, and attempting to give an impression of their psychology. Much the same course was followed by the Neapolitan reporter Gian Gaspare Napolitano, though his pen was more lively: "It was night, and the *dubats* lay asleep outside their *tukuls*, their women clasped in their arms. Only the hard, dry coughs of the tubercular broke the silence, painful sounds that made themselves heard throughout the village. One evening during an improvised 'fantasy,' a *dubat* was suddenly possessed by a djinn, a demon." [19] Others like Luigi Barzini, Jr., entrenched the true facts in a hard, gemlike prose: "At 0130 hours we became aware of a sound that was to torment us throughout the day till the final burst of gunfire at sunset. Hidden from sight on the summit of Derdega someone was blowing a horn, the kind of horn used to give the "right of way" signal to branch-line trains. Its long-drawn-out, mournful note made itself heard above the roar of the guns. 'What does it mean?' I asked a *bulukbashi* who was standing near us. 'Courage and strength, Ethiopians—that's what it means,' he told us." [20]

After the war almost all the Italian journalists and writers, as well those members of the hierarchy and the House of Savoy who had taken part in the campaign, produced books about their experiences, but not one of them was a masterpiece. Sem Benelli, the poet and playwright, failed to reach this standard with *Myself in Africa*, as did Adriano Grande with *The Parini Legion*. Indro Montanelli's *The Twentieth Eritrean Battalion* is only a mediocre work although the author had aimed high. He had gone to Africa, he wrote in the preface "for literary reasons, among others: not to seek for

[19] *Con l'esercito italiano in A.O.*, vol. 1, p. 242.
[20] *Ibid.*, pp. 133–34.

'color' but to try and find for you the conscience of a man." [21]
The scenery of Ethiopia was majestic and there was an abundance of material, but what these writers lacked was a valid justification for the war—a moral justification. Despite their diligent attempts to present it in a favorable light, despite the tricks they used, despite all their talent, it remained a war of conquest. Yet they themselves did not regard it as such. For Montanelli it had been a "long and marvelous holiday, a reward given to us by 'Big Daddy' for thirteen years of work at our school desks." [22] Or it had been, as Beonio-Brocchieri wrote in *Ethiopian Skies*, a personal adventure "to be jumped at with all the enthusiasm of a true sportsman." [23] Or as for Gino de Sanctis, "the chance to breathe in all the fragrance of Africa when the rainy season comes to an end and Maskal marks the return of Spring." [24]

In addition to the specially invited Italian reporters and journalists who covered the northern and southern fronts,[25]

[21] Indro Montanelli, *XX Battaglione Eritreo* (Milan: Panorama, 1936), see preface.

[22] *Ibid.*, p. 226.

[23] V. Beonio-Brocchieri, *Cieli d'Etiopia* (Milan: Mondadori, 1936), p. xiv.

[24] Gino de Sanctis, *La mia Africa* (Milan: Mondadori, 1938), p. 16. Sem Benelli, however, seized on the opportunity provided by the Ethiopian campaign to reinstate himself with the Fascist regime. On his return to Italy, he wrote a book on his experiences, *Io in Africa* (Milan: Mondadori, 1937), from which the following poem, "The Toast," is taken:

> Black people of the world, black not in face
> But in spirit, purify yourselves,
> Cleanse your hearts as you put your lips,
> Even if they are feathered with gold, to the tin mugs
> Our soldiers offer you.
> If you disdain to drink a toast
> From these crude vessels, you will never sense
> The mighty breath of the world to come:
> For you, all the seers, all the prophets
> Will have lived on this earth in vain.

[25] Among the Italian journalists and writers invited to report on the war were Monelli, Tomaselli, L. Barzini, Jr., Zappa, Fattarappa Sandri, Volta,

there were some forty foreign pressmen, the personnel of twelve film units and the correspondents of six agencies. But while they held the "green card," not all were genuine journalists. The Paris correspondent of the important right-wing *Le Temps,* for instance, went under an assumed name and was less engaged in journalistic activities than in "what was discreetly known as *gathering information,* a field in which he was so successful that, two years later, he was appointed head of the *Deuxième Bureau.*" [26] This pseudo journalist's real name was Raoul Salan, a name that, twenty years after the Italo-Ethiopian War, the French either loathed or revered. Then there was Captain Roland von Strunk of the *Volkischer Beobachter,* who was a Nazi spy, and Henri de Monfreid of *Petit Soir,* who purveyed information to the Italians and other interested parties, and who carried on a lucrative traffic in guns and slaves. Among the most respected of the foreign correspondents were Mortimer Durand, Paul Gentizon, General Fuller of Great Britain, and Herbert L. Matthews of *The New York Times,* who confessed a few years later, "I too was an enthusiastic admirer of fascism once, but I saw in the travail of Spain under the bombs that brought misery and death to an unoffending people, what fascism meant to me and to all of us." [27]

These, then, were the actors "on stage" just before the curtain fell on General De Bono: great and small, conscripts

---

Max David, Tomajùoli, Roghi, Emanuelli, Napolitano, Chiarelli, Serra, Orsino Orsini, Perbellini, Massai, Beonio-Brocchieri, Patti, Aponte, Russo, Poggiali, Zamboni, D'Orazio, Cesarini, Crepas, Bassi, Appelius, Artieri, Baroni, Benedetti, Cipolla, Maratea, Orano, Pianca, and Sandri.

[26] Declaration made by Pierre Stibbe at the Salan trial held at Turin on April 2, 1962, in the Alfieri Theater. See publications of the "Comitato di solidarietà con il popolo algerino" (Turin: 1962), pp. 16–17.

[27] H. L. Matthews, *The Fruits of Fascism,* p. 2. Among the foreign correspondents who had been invited to cover the war was Marie Edith de Bonneuil of *L'Illustration,* who was awarded a medal for bravery—I have not been able to discover what she did to earn this medal.

and volunteers, members of the Fascist hierarchy and the House of Savoy, writers and journalists, both genuine and false. Now that we have assessed the morale of the army and glanced briefly into the minds of some of the Italian war correspondents, let us turn to Italy and see how the country reacted to the "iniquitous sanctions." Today it is agreed by all, even by English historians, that the decision arrived at in Geneva on November 2, 1935, to apply economic sanctions to Italy (only three of the 54 member states voted against the resolution) played straight into Mussolini's hand. As Denis Mack Smith commented, "The sanctions seemed to show that Italy was encircled and persecuted, that the nation itself, not only the regime, was in danger, and the campaign of austerity envisaged by the autarchy was not pure caprice, but a vital national interest." [28] The sanctions, then, helped to consolidate Italy's home front and, as they were full of loopholes and not properly enforced, they had no serious effects on the Fascist economy; in any case, they did not slow down the military operations in Africa. If the powers responsible for the sanctions had enforced the threatened embargo on oil, if Great Britain had closed the Suez canal to Italian shipping, it would have been a very different story. But as Roy MacGregor Hastie commented, "There was a great display of verbal humanity in Geneva, but little in the city of London or on Wall Street." [29] Hence, for paltry financial considerations and strange and absurd political calculations, the sanctions became farcical, as the Fascist regime was quick to point out to the nation.

All the same, austerity became the order of the day and the people were exhorted to eat less meat, use less gasoline and electricity, and buy fewer woolen goods. The economist Luigi Federici wrote, "With that courageous candor that characterizes the strong, we must admit that if sanctions are applied

[28] Denis Mack Smith, *Italy, a Modern History*, p. 450.
[29] Roy McGregor-Hastie, *The Day of the Lion* (New York: Coward-McCann, 1964), p. 233.

over a long period our economy will be seriously affected. On the one hand, the application of sanctions is destroying our normal trade links with other countries; on the other, they will compel us to reorganize our industries on an autarchic basis." [30] The press launched a "Buy Italian" campaign, the production of synthetic materials made of home-grown fibers such as hemp, flax, and juniper was stepped up, the processing of lignite was intensified, and the drive for scrap metal was begun.

Some of these measures were highly unpopular, some merely gave rise to jokes about the regime of which there was already a rich collection. But the "harvest of gold," as Ruggero Zangrandi observed, "was one of the very few ceremonials thought up by the Fascist regime that won the hearts of the people." [31] On December 18, 1935, while Ras Imru and Ras Seyoum were counterattacking in Shire and in Tembien, several million Italians participated in the "rite of faith" and handed over their gold wedding rings to their country, receiving rings made of steel in exchange. "Years later, when the climate of the country had completely changed," wrote Zangrandi, "a woman who had taken part in this 'act of faith,' hesitated, wavered and went through agonies before she could bring herself to criticize or condemn Fascism because in a certain way this meant the repudiation, the annulment of her generous, heartfelt gesture." [32] But when the eyes of the people

---

[30] Luigi Federici: *Sanzioni* (Turin: Einaudi, 1936), p. 131.

[31] Ruggero Zangrandi, *Il lungo viaggio attraverso il fascismo*, p. 69.

[32] *Ibid.*, p. 69. The sacrifice of the wedding rings inspired many lyric writers and composers. The following example appeared in the weekly *Illustrazione del Popolo*, in the issue of February 2–8. The words by Mario Fraenza were set to music by Vincenzo Fiorillo:

"The Day of the Wedding Rings"

When we are old and bent and gray-headed,
We'll tell our grandchildren how, long ago, there were
Sanctions against us, and so in the evenings
The supper table was almost bare.

were finally opened, they felt they had been cheated of their most precious possession and they could not forgive the regime for the most ingenious of all its rituals—the sacrifice of the wedding rings.

But there was a Queen, so loving and giving,
She was the first wife and mother to bring
To her dearest country, Italy, the lovely,
Her gold, her faith, her own wedding ring.
From every mansion, every lowly cottage
Came women eager to play their part,
Their wedding rings for steel rings gladly exchanging
That their country might be strong, they hurried along:
"Our motherland will conquer!" sang every heart.
Once upon a time, there was a Leader,
Once there was a King who was mighty too—
Long, long ago when we were children,
When we were little ones as small as you.

Chapter six

The Ethiopian Counter-offensive

At the end of November 1935, when Marshal Badoglio assumed command of the Italo-Eritrean expeditionary force, the huge Ethiopian army began to move by forced marches toward the northern front, then held only by Ras Seyoum Mangasha's 30,000 men. Ras Kassa, the emperor's second cousin, with an army 40,000 strong, advanced on the Dessie-Makalle line. The ras was more of a churchman than a warrior, but he was reasonably well supported by his three sons, Asfa Wossen, Aberra, and Wondewossen. Within a few days' marching distance of this force was the considerably larger and better equipped army of Ras Mulugeta. In his day Mulugeta had been a magnificent fighter and had put down a number of revolts, but he was now over seventy and, as Leonard Mosley tells us, had become a confirmed alcoholic.[1] While these two

[1] Leonard Mosley, *Haile Selassie*, p. 201.

armies were advancing with the intention of linking up at Makalle, another of the emperor's cousins, Ras Haile Selassie Imru, had left his province of Gojjam, and with his 40,000 warriors, was moving toward the River Takkaze; by delivering a sudden and overwhelming surprise attack, he hoped to outflank the enemy army.

None of these commanders was an eagle of war. None of them had been to a military academy, had read Clausewitz, or studied Napoleon's campaigns. "Ras Seyoum was always extremely courteous to me, but I could not understand why he had sent for me," wrote Colonel Konovaloff. "When I showed him the topographical maps, he said, 'Don't bother about them —I don't need them. It's Ras Kassa who's interested in maps —he's prepared to study them for hours on end. But they don't mean a thing to me, so don't put yourself out on my account.' " [2] The emperor chose these four men as commanders for dynastic reasons, or because they were related to him, or because he knew he could rely on their loyalty. Furthermore, apart from a few very young officers who had graduated from St. Cyr, he had no trained military experts in reserve. In the book he wrote after the war, Badoglio dismissed the four rases with contempt: "They had no qualities of commanders at all . . . they were absolutely incapable of appreciating a situation or of thinking out a maneuver. . . ." [3] Possibly the Piedmontese marshal would not have pronounced this overhasty and arrogant judgment in January 1936, when, despite his vast superiority in men and materials, Ras Kassa and Ras Imru were threatening to drive him out of Makalle. In view of this fact, it is worth recalling the opinion, either more accurate or more chivalrous, expressed by General Quirino Armellini, one of Badoglio's closest collaborators: "The Rases Kassa, Mulugeta, Seyoum and Imru undoubtedly possessed the necessary qualities for fighting a combat—I say combat rather than

[2] T. E. Konovaloff, *Con le armate del negus*, p. 36.

[3] Pietro Badoglio: *The War in Abyssinia*, p. 39.

battle—in which a furious assault by a massive body of men is the predominant factor. I do not believe, however, that their military training—that is, military training as we understand it—was such as to enable them to conduct a battle against modern formations armed with modern weapons and commanded by modern tacticians. This was the cause of their defeat." [4] Nevertheless, for two months in the winter of 1935, the Ethiopian army forced the Italians to fall back from the Takkaze to Axum and from Amba Tzellere right to the Warieu Pass. At this period the combined action of the four commanders had all the aspects of a genuine counteroffensive.

Of the rases who fought on the northern front, the sole survivor is Ras Imru, and it is thanks to his courteous collaboration that I have been able to reconstruct the various phases of the "Christmas offensive," which became known in the very few informed circles in Italy as the "black period." Ras Imru, who is in his late seventies, lives in a *gebbi* in Arada, a quiet suburb of Addis Ababa. He is of medium height, with a round, pleasant face, very clear, almost sky-blue eyes, and a shock of white hair worn in the fashion of Einstein. He received me in his study and as soon as the Abuna who had been visiting him had taken his leave, he put on a gray, double-breasted smoking-jacket made in London and a black tie. Ras Imru is the soul of cordiality, and his polished manners, his mode of expressing himself are eloquent of his long postwar diplomatic career when he became a well-known figure in Washington and New Delhi. In view of Starace's brazen description of him as a brutal and avaricious tyrant, Italians would find it hard to believe that this serene, benign old man is none other than Ras Imru, who has become a living legend not because of the part he played in the war (which he himself says was modest), but because he has distributed so much of his land and wealth to his needy countrymen.[5]

[4] Information given to me in a letter dated April 27, 1965.

[5] Ras Imru, who was greatly loved by the poor—the compound of his *gebbi* was always packed with humble petitioners—was probably the emper-

"Tell me," I asked, "Is it true, as the air force pilot Hilaire du Berrier stated, that while you were in Shire, you made four incursions into Eritrea?" He smiled. "I never even attempted to invade Eritrea," he said. "I reached the Mareb at several

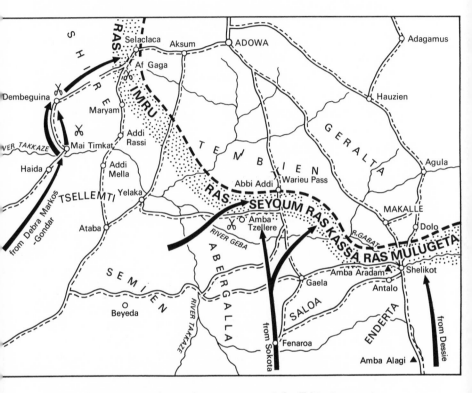

Map 3. The arrows indicate the movements of the Ethiopian armies during the "Christmas offensive," December 1935.

points but that was all." The rest of his account was characterized with the same modesty, the same determination to be meticulously accurate. "Shortly after the war," he told me,

---

or's most trusted friend. Haile Selassie always listened to what Ras Imru had to say.

"the emperor ordered me to march into Shire and converge on Adowa. The *kitet* [mobilization order] raised 25,000 men in my own province, *Dejatch* Ayelu Birru raised 10,000 more in Begemder, and a further 5,000 were raised by minor chiefs. Therefore, I could count on 40,000 men, but the main body of this force was based at Debra Markos and the region of Lake Tana 1,000 kilometers from the front. Thus, I had to undertake a difficult and exhausting march that lasted for weeks.[6]

"At the beginning of December shortly after we had reached Dabat, we were spotted from the air and subjected to an intensive bombing attack. It was our first experience with this kind of warfare and threw us into such confusion that not until it was all over did I discover that *Dejatch* Gassassa had turned tail and fled back to Gojjam. He was not the only chief to desert and I was seriously alarmed, the more so because I knew I could not rely on Ayelu Birru with his 10,000 men. I was aware that he was negotiating with the Italians, and when we held our counsels of war, his attitude was invariably defeatist. By the time I reached the Takkaze fords, therefore, I could only count on about half the number of men who had made up my original force."[7]

At dawn on Sunday, December 15, Ras Imru's advance guards crossed the Takkaze at the fords of Mai Timkat and Addi Atcheb. It was the first day of Italy's "black period," the period that had been predicted a month earlier by the soothsayers of Addis Ababa. As one Ethiopian column advanced on

[6] Ras Imru told me his story when I interviewed him in Addis Ababa on April 13, 1965. The men of the Gavinana and the Third Eritrean Brigade learned for themselves how wild and broken was the region through which Ras Imru had made his way when they penetrated it from the opposite direction a few months later. The barely visible track rose steeply upward to a height of some 3,000 meters, plunged down into deep ravines, climbed vertiginously upward once more to the ambas and rocky pinnacles of Woggera, descended precipitously to the Wolkefit Pass, and wound more and more tortuously among the mountains of Semien and Tsellemti, till it reached the Takkaze fords.

[7] See *Daily Telegraph* (London), November 20, 1935.

Mai Timkat, held by 1,000 native irregulars, the other column, 2,000 strong, marched rapidly toward the Dembeguina Pass to cut off the Askaris commanded by Major Criniti, who, informed of Ras Imru's movements, withdrew from his "observation post" on the Takkaze, and, protected by nine light tanks, made hurriedly for the Pass. This defile was the sole route leading from Shire to the Italian lines at Selaclaca. But when he emerged from the tortuous valley of the Takkaze and reached the plateau, he found Dembeguina already occupied by the Ethiopians.

When the battle began the sun was at its zenith and the heat was unbearable, although it was only a few days to Christmas. The Ethiopians had drawn themselves up in a horseshoe formation on the crests of the ambas from Mount Asar to Amba Manamba. In order to force a way through the threatened encirclement, Major Criniti ordered the squadron of L.-3 tanks to advance, but they were soon put out of action by wave after wave of Ethiopians who rushed down on them from the heights and tore off the chains. "The tanks might have been animals," the emperor said subsequently, "It was an incredible spectacle: men in flimsy cotton *shammas* attacking these steel monsters with their bare hands."[8] Criniti ordered his Askaris to fix bayonets and charge, and although he succeeded in forcing an opening in the direction of Selaclaca, when dusk fell almost half his men lay dead or wounded on the field of battle. The casualty figures according to the Italians were 9 officers, 22 Italian soldiers, and 370 Askaris killed or wounded. The most reliable of the Ethiopian bulletins put the number of dead or wounded at 150 Italian soldiers and 200 Askaris.[9]

[8] *Une victoire de la civilisation*, p. 31.

[9] The first of the Ethiopian bulletins, bulletins invariably exaggerated as the principal aim was to keep up the morale of the people, was transmitted on November 14, 1935. This bulletin and those that followed were printed in the official newspaper *Berhanenna Selam*, and the semi-official *Courrier d'Ethiopie*, edited by L. De Robilland, a Frenchman.

CHAPTER SIX

Let us see how the generals of both sides viewed this battle. First, Ras Imru: "It was important, not only because we captured 50 machine guns and a huge quantity of rifles, but also because we had routed the enemy so completely that our advance-guards sent in pursuit succeeded in occupying Enda Selassie and, shortly after, Selaclaca. With this feat of arms, we won back much of the ground we had lost in Shire and were thus in a position to hammer the flanks of the Italian army." Now for Badoglio: "The episode was of little importance in relation to the general situation; however, it constituted a failure on our part that the enemy, as could reasonably be foreseen, had sought to exaggerate." [10] But this opinion of the defeat at Dembeguina was not expressed until a year later when, as Duke of Addis Ababa and laden with honors, the marshal could manipulate the facts of the campaign to suit himself. At the time of the setback, however, he was far less confident; indeed, he was so shaken, as we shall see later, that he seems to have resorted to panic measures.

In reality it was not only Ras Imru's thrust toward the gates of Axum that caused Badoglio deep concern. The initiative appeared to have passed to the Ethiopians who had made contact with the Italians along nearly the entire front. Indeed, on the day that Ras Imru crossed the Takkaze, Ras Kassa linked up with Ras Seyoum in Tembien, while in the Makalle sector, Ras Mulugeta's advance-guards had established themselves on the right bank of the Geba. As the emperor explained subsequently, "The main object of our maneuver was to isolate Makalle by operating against the enemy's right flank, attacking along the entire length from those positions he held in the extreme south to those on the Eritrean frontier." [11] In his book and therefore a posteriori, Badoglio wrote that he doubted "the enemy's capacity to carry out a strategic plan on

[10] Pietro Badoglio, *The War in Abyssinia*, p. 37.
[11] *Une victoire de la civilisation*, p. 31.

so vast a scale," [12] yet he appears to have been far from skeptical in December 1935, because he sent an urgent wire to Italy asking for two more divisions (Mussolini sent him three), and dispatched two massive columns to halt the advance of Ras Imru and the combined armies of Ras Kassa and Ras Seyoum. On December 22 and 25, two bitter hand-to-hand engagements took place, at Af Gaga and Mount Tzellere, and it was only after hours of violent fighting that the Italo-Eritreans gained the day. But these victories were ephemeral; during the next few days, the Ethiopians forced them to abandon the positions they had succeeded in occupying, and they were compelled to fall back as far as the entrenched camp of Axum in the north and the Warieu Pass in the south, leaving Abbi Addi, their headquarters in Tembien, in the hands of Ras Kassa's warriors.

Four years later Raffaele Ciasca wrote of the "black period," "The situation remained very delicate. The Ethiopian press transformed every partial success into a resounding victory. Europe, far too ready to sympathize with Ethiopia, welcomed the news and gave it ample coverage. Foreign military experts who had noted the dismal state of our military balance sheet, already prophesied woe for us." [13] Needless to say the man who was most perturbed by the "black period" was Mussolini. His anger was fomented by General Baistrocchi, Under-Secretary for War, who hoped that his friend, General Graziani, would replace Badoglio as commander-in-chief. "Mussolini, who cannot bear the slightest setback, thunders that he intends to get rid of Badoglio immediately," wrote General Emilio Faldella.[14] Badoglio, indeed, had been a bitter disappointment; not only had he failed to move an inch since replacing General De Bono, but he had actually allowed much

[12] Pietro Badoglio, *The War in Abyssinia*, p. 39.
[13] Raffaele Ciasca, *Storia coloniale dell'Italia contemporanea* (Milan: Hoepli, 1940), p. 659.
[14] *Storia Illustrata*, May 1963, p. 633.

of the territory taken by his predecessor to be torn from his grasp. There is not the slightest shadow of doubt that the "Roman rages" of which Badoglio was only too well aware were responsible for his unspeakably grave decision to use poison gas. It must be said, however, in his partial exculpation, that he did not make up his mind to resort to this illegal weapon without the highest authority. As Commander-in-Chief of the Forces in East Africa, he knew of the telegram General Graziani had sent to the Duce a few days before he had reached his decision—on December 16, to be exact—"I ask the maximum liberty for the use of asphyxiating gases," [15] and of Mussolini's reply, "The use of gas is admissible when Your Excellency considers it necessary for supreme defense reasons." [16] A few days after the arrival of the Duce's telegram, on Badoglio's orders, the Takkaze fords were drenched with mustard gas, while Graziani—in his own words—"terrorized the inhabitants" of the villages scattered round Jijiga by dropping on them container after container of poison gases. [17]

Ras Imru told me of his own experience. "It was a terrifying spectacle," he said, "I myself narrowly escaped death. On the morning of December 23, shortly after we had crossed the Takkaze, we saw several enemy planes appear. We were not unduly alarmed as by this time we were used to being bombed. On this particular morning, however, the enemy dropped strange containers that burst open almost as soon as they hit the ground or the water, releasing pools of colorless liquid. I hardly had time to ask myself what could be happening before a hundred or so of my men who had been splashed by the mysterious fluid began to scream in agony as blisters broke

[15] From the official history edited by the Chiefs of Staff of the Armed Forces of Italian Somaliland, *La guerra italo-etiopica—Fronte Sud*, vol. III Ufficio Superiore Topocartografico del Governo Generale dell' AOI (Addis Ababa, 1937), document no. 262, p. 274. The telegram was addressed by Graziani to Lessona and is dated December 1935 (telegram no. 1475).

[16] *Ibid.*, document no. 262, p. 274, telegram 14551.

[17] Rodolfo Graziani, *Fronte Sud* (Milan: Mondadori, 1938), p. 220.

out on their bare feet, their hands, their faces. Some who
rushed to the river and took great gulps of water to cool their
fevered lips, fell contorted on the banks and writhed in agonies that lasted for hours before they died. Among the victims
were a few peasants who had come to water their cattle and a
number of people who lived in nearby villages. My chiefs
surrounded me, asking wildly what they should do, but I was
completely stunned. I didn't know what to tell them, I didn't
know how to fight this terrible rain that burned and killed." [18]

The "mysterious fluid" was yperite—mustard gas—or, to
give it its chemical name, dichlorodiethyl sulfide
$S(CH_2CH_2Cl)_2$. By the end of the first few months of the
summer of 1936, several tons of this gas had been dispatched
to Massawa, as well as large quantities of other gases—tear
gas, sneezing gas, and various asphyxiating gases. [19] This was a

[18] From Ethiopian sources, it appears that asphyxiating gases were (a)
fired in shells by the artillery; (b) dropped in containers from planes; and
(c) diffused by planes fitted with sprayers. On June 30, 1936, the emperor
described these gas attacks: "In the early days of the war, toward the close
of 1935, the Italians dropped containers of tear gas on my troops. These
attacks soon proved ineffectual, for once our soldiers discovered that tear gas
was rapidly dispersed by the wind, they immediately scattered when it was
dropped. The enemy then began to drop containers of yperite, but this was
almost equally unsatisfactory as comparatively few of our soldiers were
affected, and furthermore, they avoided those areas in which containers were
dropped. It was when we were threatening to encircle Makalle that the
Italian High Command adopted a method which it is our duty to denounce
to the world. The planes were fitted with sprayers in order to contaminate
vast areas with mustard gas. Wave after wave of planes in groups of nine,
fifteen and eighteen, sprayed the deadly vapor so that it formed one
continuous pall. From the end of January 1936 onward, this lethal rain fell
unceasingly on civilians as well as soldiers, on men, women and children, on
animals, on rivers, lakes and pasture lands. The gas was sprayed unremit-
tingly on order of the Italian High Command as the surest way of killing us
off. The enemy also made certain that our rivers and lakes were contaminated. Poison gas was his principal weapon of war." *Official Journal* of the
League of Nations, Special Supplement no. 151 (1936), pp. 22–25.
[19] General Fidenzio Dall'Ora tells us in his book, *Intendenza in A.O.*, that
Unit K (the chemical-warfare unit) was set up in July 1935, and that the
equipment for chemical warfare was assembled in magazines at Ala (Soro-

top-priority secret for on June 17, 1926, at Geneva, Italy had solemnly signed the document that prohibited the use of gas as a weapon of war. According to General Faldella, who was then responsible for the Ethiopian section of SIM, it was quite by chance that he and Roatta, the chief of SIM, learned that poison gas was being used in Ethiopia: "When planes touched down at Centocelle on the Cairo–London flight, our agents took advantage of the short stopover to scrutinize the contents of the mailbags. One day, in a package addressed by a press photographer to a London agency, they found several photographs of Ethiopians whose bodies were covered with sores. These photographs struck them as extremely suspect and a few minutes later they were on my desk. I looked at them and took them straight to Professor Castellano, then the leading authority on tropical diseases. He examined them and confirmed what I had suspected—there could be no doubt, he said, that the sores on the bodies of these Ethiopians had been caused by mustard gas. We stared at one another in deep embarrassment. After an awkward silence, Castellano added, "Still, leprosy produces almost identical sores," and he handed me a few photographs of lepers so that I could compare them with the others. As I could not even spot the difference, I suddenly made up my mind: I would substitute the pictures of the lepers for the original photographs and let the package go on its way. The "tragic" pictures appeared in the newspapers a few days later, and our ambassador, Dino Grandi, who of course knew the truth, pointed out with great indignation that the "victims" were, in fact, lepers, and that the publication of these falsely captioned pictures was a contemptible trick thought up by the anti-Fascist press to bring discredit on the

---

doko); flamethrowers, sprayers, vaporizers, gas masks, and protective clothing. But, says Dall'Ora, "Throughout the war we never made use of poison gases and the Ethiopian allegations were completely false. The activities of Unit K were restricted to supplying the chemicals for the flamethrowers . . ." (pp. 217–21).

regime." [20] Nevertheless, on December 30, the emperor informed the League of Nations that the Italians were using poison gas in Ethiopia: "On December 23, in the region of the River Takkaze, they attacked our troops with various poison gases. This violation by Italy of an international agreement must be added to the long list of those she has previously contravened." [21]

Faced by a world-wide wave of indignation, the Italian government began by strenuously denying that gas had been used, then went on to speak of "legitimate reprisals" against the Ethiopians who were firing dum-dum bullets. Finally, a partial admission was made: gas *had* been employed, but it was not of a lethal type, it merely produced a paralyzing effect that wore off after a few hours. But gravest of all, while Rome was refuting the accusations, poison gas attacks were being systematically carried out in Ethiopia. One asks how Alessandro Lessona could have brought himself to write in his memoirs, published in 1958, that gas was only used on a single occasion to "avenge" the death of Minniti, the air force pilot. "When General Graziani received absolutely reliable information of what had been done to Minniti, he decided to strike terror into the enemy and, as a legitimate act of reprisal, drop three, I repeat three, very small gas bombs on the encampment that had been the scene of such barbaric savagery. No other gas bombs but these were ever dropped on the Ethiopians." [22]

[20] Information given to me by General Faldella.

[21] *Official Journal* of the League of Nations, *Anno XVII*, document 1587 (February 1936), p. 241.

[22] Alessandro Lessona, *Memorie*, p. 292. In a letter to me dated June 16, 1965, subsequently published in the *Gazzetta del Popolo*, Anna Vailati protested strongly against certain charges of brutality I had made against Badoglio in the articles that appeared in this newspaper. In her account of her interview with the marshal after World War II, she unintentionally provided me with a new piece of evidence on the use of gas in Ethiopia: "When I told the marshal that in the course of postwar polemics, he was accused inter alia of having used gas in Ethiopia, he replied, 'After the battle of Enderta, I did in fact order shells of tear gas and sneezing gas to be

CHAPTER SIX

Yet Lessona could not possibly have been ignorant of the fact that the most damning evidence of poison-gas attacks is to be found in the actual documents of the Italian Military Command. On page 406 of the third volume of *The Italo-Ethiopian War: Southern Front,* compiled by the General Staff of the Armed Forces of Italian Somaliland and printed in Addis Ababa in 1937, we find the following telegram dated February 2, 1936, and signed "Bernasconi": "At 0600 hours, departure of bombers began and continued until 1200 hours at intervals of about thirty minutes. About 24 aircraft took part, 6 with gas load. Released 1,700 kilograms of gas and 7,000 bombs of various sizes. Gas released over Bandu ford and right bank Ganale Doria as far as Wadi Bakkara." [23] Not only was gas used throughout the war, but afterward as well to break down the resistance of the Ethiopian patriots, as we know from a telegram dated September 11, 1936, sent by Graziani to General Pirzio Biroli—"Today our air force will carry out reprisals, dropping various asphyxiating gases between those who have submitted and those who have not in the zone where it is presumed Wondewossen [son of Ras Kassa] had led his armed forces without distinction. Be assured, Your Excellency, that I act in perfect accord with His Excellency, the Head of the Government." [24]

Even when the war was raging, however, our "enemies" were able to make the vital distinction between the fanatical supporters of the regime and the vast majority of the Italian

fired for a couple of hours to drive out the Ethiopians who had lodged themselves in caves. These were the only gases I ever used, although on one occasion an experiment was carried out with mustard gas; it was fired in shells well outside the lines and it was found that it evaporated almost immediately.'"

[23] From the official history edited by the Chiefs of Staff of the Armed Forces of Italian Somaliland, *La guerra italo-etiopica—Fronte Sud,* document no. 316, p. 406.

[24] *Documents on Italian War Crimes Submitted to the United Nations War Crimes Commission* by the Imperial Ethiopian Government (Addis Ababa: Ministry of Justice, 1949), p. 59.

troops who behaved humanely to the Ethiopians and were completely unaware that poison gas was being used against them. Even today, for motives that can easily be understood, they are not wholly convinced that such attacks were actually made. Not long after the war when the emperor was in Geneva, he told the anti-Fascist Mario Rietti (who was killed shortly after fighting with the Spanish Republicans on the Aragon front), that he harbored no bitter feelings against the Italian people. Indeed, he said, he sympathized with them for "To destroy Ethiopia's independence, Fascist regime resorted to the same violent means it has used in the past, and is still using, to destroy liberty in Italy." [25]

[25] See the *New Times and Ethiopia News*. There is plenty of evidence in the Italian official military documents that poison gases were used. Here is further testimony provided by a number of foreign journalists and doctors. Let me quote a few of them. In *Half a Life Left* (London: Eyre & Spottiswoode, 1937), James Strachey Barnes, a pro-Fascist, wrote that the Italians never denied using mustard gas as a legitimate means of reprisal against those Ethiopians who violated the international conventions by mutilating prisoners, firing dum-dum bullets, and misusing the Red Cross. The Italians, he said, first used gas toward the close of 1935 (see p. 206). Herbert L. Matthews, who was pro-Fascist during this period, wrote in *Eyewitness in Abyssinia* (London: Secker & Warburg, 1937), "Mr. Harrison [the correspondent of the *New York Times*], who was a chemist with experience in poison gas, recognized the smell of mustard gas, which had been dropped between Allomata and Kobbo . . ." During the three weeks that Harrison spent in Quoram in March, he "witnessed almost daily bombardments and spraying of mustard gas by Italian planes . . ." (see p. 257). In *Le conflit italo-éthiopien devant le droit international* (Paris: A. Pedone, 1938), Professor Charles Rousseau has this to say: "Jérôme and Jean Tharaud, writers known to have no anti-Italian feelings, who were covering the Ethiopian front for a Paris newspaper, stated in their articles that Italian planes flying almost at ground level sprayed the fields continuously with mustard gas, destroying crops and grassland; animals died of starvation, and the deadly gas burned the feet and seriously affected the lungs of the terrified people." (See p. 169.) Now for a few extracts from reports made by doctors to the League of Nations (*Official Journal*, no. 6, June 1936). Dr. Schuppler of No. 3 Field Hospital: "I beg to bring to your notice that on January 14, 1936, containers of mustard gas were dropped for the first time by the Italian Air Force. Twenty peasants were killed, and I dealt with some fifteen gas cases, two of whom were children. Their burns

were caused by mustard gas (Senfgas) which was dropped south of the Alagi hills. . . ." John Melly: "Between March 7 and March 22, we had 200–300 cases of mustard-gas burns. Most of the victims had been temporarily blinded and we had to set up a special clinic. . . ." Dr. Gunnar Ulland of the Norwegian Red Cross: "At 0800 hours this morning, two Italian bombers flew over Yirgalem. At 1700 hours, two casualties were brought in; both were suffering from violently watering and inflamed eyes and acute irritation of the nose and throat; one of them had extensive burns on the soles of his feet. We immediately drove off in the ambulance to Yirgalem as we had learned that there were other gas cases. We found four Ethiopians with exactly the same symptoms. These six victims, who were in agonies of pain, were treated at our field hospital and eventually cured. . . ."

Chapter seven

Under the Banner of the Lion of Judah

Once the war was over Italian propagandists, whose duty it was to deny the Ethiopians even the virtues they manifestly possessed in order to maintain the thesis that they were hopelessly incapable savages, asserted that if the Ethiopians had managed to put up a certain measure of resistance, the credit was entirely due to the "white mercenaries" who had fought in their ranks. In actual fact these mysterious personages were military advisers, air pilots, and doctors, and although there were never more than a hundred of them, they became thousands so that the regime could account for the virtual standstill of the Italian army after the rapid advance of the first few weeks. All the war correspondents wrote of the "brilliant foreign tacticians" in their reports, all the serving generals mentioned them in their dispatches. Every maneuver carried out by the Ethiopians was attributed to one or other of these

85

elusive characters. In reality the effect of the European military advisers on the course of the war was negligible, particularly on the northern front where its outcome was decided. As we shall see, it was not always through any fault of theirs that they achieved so little.

A few members of this foreign contingent had lived for a number of years in Ethiopia, the rest arrived on the eve of the invasion. "Each week," wrote Patrick Balfour, war correspondent of the *Evening Standard*, "a further trainload of journalists, photographers, adventurers, arms peddlers and doctors of fortune was spilled into Addis Ababa from Europe, Asia and America . . . there was an airman from Cuba, an airman from Harlem and an airman from Monte Carlo . . ." [1] Intriguers predominated among these new arrivals, closely followed by opportunists who hoped to make their fortunes without running too many risks; and the smallest group consisted of men with genuine motives for supporting the Ethiopians. The doctors had come to Ethiopia for humanitarian reasons; Wehib Pasha was there because of his long-standing Italophobia; Dr. Schuppler, an Austrian who had taken part in the Nazi *putsch* against Dollfuss, offered his services because Mussolini had earned his undying hatred by acting as the "protector" of the Catholic Chancellor; John Robinson, the American Negro airman, had come to Ethiopia to testify to the solidarity of the colored peoples; the rest were anti-fascists, pacifists, and philanthropists. All these men united under the banner of the Lion of Judah, but apart from the doctors, their motives for rallying round it were so diverse that it was impossible for them to make any appreciable contribution.

In order to present the main protagonists of the foreign contingent, let me begin by splitting it into three categories: (a) military advisers, (b) airmen, and (c) doctors. In the

[1] *Abyssinian Stop Press*, edited by Ladislas Farago (London: Robert Hale, 1936), pp. 48–80. Patrick Balfour was in Addis Ababa as war correspondent for the *Evening Standard*.

first category the most prominent figure was unquestionably
Mehmed Pasha, the Turk, better known as Wehib Pasha, a
seasoned campaigner and the one military adviser who possessed real talent. Graziani, who knew that most of the difficulties he encountered in the Ogaden were the work of Wehib
Pasha, described him as "a soldier who is thoroughly experienced in mobile warfare," and indeed Wehib Pasha had
fought against the Italians in Libya in 1911, against the
Anglo-French in the Dardanelles in 1917, and had played an
important role in Kemal Ataturk's victorious revolution in
1923. In the Ogaden he was Ras Nasibu Zamanuel's chief of
staff, and the architect of the "Hindenburg Wall," a series of
fortifications and entrenched camps thought for some time to
be impregnable. In 1936, when Badoglio had routed the last
Ethiopian army on the northern front and had begun his
advance on Addis Ababa, Graziani decided to launch an attack on the Wall. The full story of this attack will be told in a
later chapter, but let it be said here that although the Italians
brought extreme pressure to bear on both flanks of Nasibu's
army, Graziani was forced to send his picked troops to storm
the barricades of Janagobo and Gunu Gadu and take the
armed camps of Daggahbur, Sassabaneh, and Jijiga. When
Wehib Pasha returned to Europe, he wrote in a German
review devoted to military subjects that the Italians won the
war not so much by force of arms as by subversive activities,
and went on to say that the performance of the much-vaunted
Fascist air force was greatly overrated: "I never saw them fly
below some 7,000 feet, at an altitude, that is, that prevented
them from making effective use of their machine guns, and
they even had difficulty dropping their bombs on target. The
only casualties caused by the massed bombing attacks in the
Ogaden were ten Ethiopians killed or wounded." [2]

The largest group of military advisers was made up of

[2] *Deutsche Wehr*, no. 27 (Berlin), July 1936.

Belgians led by Colonel Leopold Ruel, who had replaced Major Dothée at the beginning of the war. Anxious to avoid giving offense to Italy, the Belgian government had, in fact, recalled its military mission, but raised no objection to the setting up of another composed of volunteers, some of whom had already seen action in the Congo.[3] The Belgian military advisers, of whom there were not more than a dozen, were distributed as follows: Colonel Ruel and Lieutenant De Fraippont were attached to the emperor's headquarters at Dessie; Captain Armand Debois and Lieutenant Gustav Witmeur to Ras Nasibu's army in the Ogaden; and Captain Cambier (who met his death in mysterious circumstances shortly after the war had begun), and Lieutenant Frère to Ras Desta's army in Sidamo Borana; Major Delery and others remained at the base as instructors. It was Lieutenant Frère, the most junior of these officers, who achieved the most notoriety. Graziani, during his advance on Negelli, found traces of him here, there, and everywhere—papers, decorations, and even his pajamas. He gave much valuable advice to Ras Desta who had been subjected to devastating attacks in which Graziani had employed illegal, as well as legal, weapons. A note he had written, warning Ras Desta of the dangers following gas attacks, fell into Italian hands, a note that Graziani was naive (or brazen) enough to include in *Fronte Sud*, "Do not approach the craters made by gas bombs for one hour after they have exploded. Fill in these craters immediately with earth or sand. Avoid all contact with the contaminated ground, and keep away from any area where gas has not been dispersed; inhaling the fumes will cause death."[4]

[3] Some of these mercenaries were engaged in Paris. They were paid 15,000 francs per month and in the contract they signed provision was made for their families, who would receive 500,000 francs as compensation in the event of their death. See *The Morning Post* (London), September 17, 1935.

[4] Rodolfo Graziani, *Fronte Sud*, p. 222. At the end of the war, Lt. Frère returned to Belgium and issued a statement to the Stefani agency in

The Swedish mission had broken up when General Erik Virgin handed in his resignation, but three of its members volunteered to remain in Ethiopia to run the cadet school at Holeta. The senior member, Captain Tamm, was asked by the Ethiopian government to organize the defense of the capital when the news came that the last Ethiopian army on the northern front was on the point of defeat. Captain Tamm decided to await the enemy at the Termaber Pass, where he established himself with the only two mechanized detachments the Ethiopians then possessed. He blew up a thirty-meter section of one of the steepest, most difficult roads the Italians would be obliged to take in their advance on the capital (this immobilized Badoglio's mechanized column for two days), recruited the largest possible number of irregulars from the neighboring villages, and fortified his positions, but at the eleventh hour the government changed its mind and ordered him to withdraw.[5] According to Pierre Ichac, correspondent of *l'Illustration*, who had been invited by the Ethiopian government to report on the war from the Ethiopian side, the nation had too much pride to rely completely on its white advisers: "The mercenaries, no matter how much they may have wished to do so, were never allowed to take command of the Ethiopian troops in action. The Ethiopians did not trust them because they were *ferenji*—foreigners. The Belgians were *ferenji*, hence the Ethiopians paid no attention to their plans; furthermore, when they were ordered to rejoin this or that army on the front, the Ethiopians refused to supply them with provisions and mules, and finally they were left behind the lines with nothing better to do than a few vague duties in the way of police work and censorship! *Ferenji* was that soldier of out-

---

Brussels in which he declared that the Ethiopians made frequent use of dum-dum bullets and that Ras Desta had allowed his men to mutilate a number of captured Eritreans. See *Gazzetta del Popolo*, June 20, 1936.

[5] See Corrado Zoli, "March of the Iron Will," *La Tribuna* (Turin), May 4, 1937.

standing merit, Wehib Pasha, remembered with respect by the French whose forces came up against him twenty years after the Italo-Ethiopian War, when they landed at Sedd ul Bahr. . . . To get rid of him, the Ethiopians sent him to fortify Jijiga, an utterly futile operation as was proved later, since they had no heavy artillery, pursuit planes or gas masks." [6]

Ichac was not one-hundred percent correct. One European, the Greek Musa Saba Karavasilis, was given the command of one of Ras Desta's columns during the abortive attempt to break through into Italian Somalia. Major Wittlin, a Swiss, was appointed commander of all the troops in the region of the River Awash, but from all accounts it seems he merely acted as an observer, being stationed with a battery of Oerlikons at the iron railway bridge across the river on the Addis Ababa-Jibouti line. Duties of an equally unimportant nature were assigned the Cuban, Captain Del Valle, who had been engaged in London and was attached to Ras Mulugeta's army. The fact was that the reluctance of the Ethiopians to make full use of their white advisers was due not only to pride but also to the suspicion that some of them might be spies in the pay of Rome. Colonel Konovaloff, for example, may well have been an enemy agent. What are we to think of this man who had enjoyed Ethiopian citizenship for ten years and had been the recipient of many favors from the emperor, who actually dedicated his book of memoirs "To the Italian soldier who proved to a skeptical and hostile world that he possessed the heroic virtues of the Roman legionary, heightened and enhanced by the new climate of Fascism"? [7]

---

[6] *L'Illustration*, p. 186. In "La Legione Parini," by Adriano Grande, we learn that "a letter from Wehib Pasha to Nasibu fell into our hands. It was written in excellent French. The Turk complained to the *dejatch* that the directives and orders he had issued to his army were not strictly carried out and that Nasibu did not keep him informed of his troop movements."

[7] T. E. Konovaloff, *Con le armate del negus*, see dedication. Konovaloff had served in the Imperial Army of the Czar as an officer in the Engineers and later as a colonel in the air force regiment. He fled from Russia at the

In the second category, the skein was even more tangled as can be seen from this valuable piece of evidence provided by General Faldella. "In February 1936," he told me, "our intelligence bureau in Cairo informed us of an extraordinary proposition that had been made to them. One of Haile Selassie's personal pilots, the Frenchman Drouillet, who had gone to Europe to purchase a Beechcraft plane, had offered for a fee of fifty million lira to abduct the negus and fly him to Asmara. Roatta and I came to the conclusion that it would be unwise to accept this offer, but Mussolini, on the contrary, never able to forget he had been a journalist, bubbled over with enthusiasm. 'What a scoop it would be!' he exclaimed. 'It would set the tongues of the whole world wagging!' and he ordered us to follow the matter up. As it turned out it never came to anything. Our zealous air intelligence agent in Paris, aware the Beechcraft was intended for the emperor and ignorant of our negotiations with Drouillet, succeeded in sequestering the plane at the Villacoublay airport. Drouillet protested vehemently and did everything in his power to get the authorities to remove the seals, but by April 25, when he finally got away from Paris and touched down at Centocelle, it was too late. Badoglio was already at the gates of Addis Ababa, and the project had to be abandoned." [8]

To compensate for such double-dealers as Drouillet, the emperor could rely on the absolute loyalty of many airmen. There was Mischa Babitcheff, for instance, whose father, a White Russian, had married a *waizero* of royal descent. Babitcheff, who had trained at the flying schools of Istres and Le Bourget and held a pilot's license, directed the operations of

---

time of the Bolshevik Revolution, found sanctuary in Addis Ababa, and eventually took Ethiopian nationality. The emperor appointed him to an important post in the Ministry of Works. He left Ethiopia after the defeat of the negus, and subsequently fought for Franco during the Spanish Civil War. An old friend, Colonel Stefano Micciché, encouraged him to write his book.

[8] See also *l'Illustration*, p. 181.

the Ethiopian Air Force, that is, as long as there was an air force to direct, for one after another the aircraft were shot down by Italian pursuit planes. There was also Count Carl von Rosen of Sweden who hit the headlines when he took off from Stockholm for Addis Ababa in the plane he had fitted out as an ambulance (the first flying ambulance, I believe), and offered his services to the emperor. During the war he made flight after flight to evacuate the wounded and take doctors to the areas where they were most needed on both the northern and southern fronts. Count von Rosen's plane was finally destroyed by the Italian Air Force who repeatedly bombed and machine-gunned it on the landing strip of Quoram despite the fact that the Red Cross was prominently marked on both wings. There were the two American Negro pilots, John Robinson of Chicago, who flew the few Ethiopian planes that were airworthy, and Hubert Eustace Julian of Harlem, better known as "The Black Eagle." There was Count Hilaire du Berrier who had made an unsuccessful attempt to raise a company of volunteer pilots in Europe, captured by the Italians on May 4, 1936, fifty kilometers from Addis Ababa. There were the French aviators Corriger, Maillet, and Demissié, and lastly, there was the German pilot Weber, who remained in the capital at the risk of his life during the sacking of the city and finally managed to fly to the safety of the Sudan. But the flights made by these men did not affect the course of the war in the slightest degree; the obsolescent aircraft could not be used as pursuit planes, and the ancient Fokkers and Potez biplanes merely served as a transport service to carry the emperor and the doctors to various destinations and to ferry light cargoes of ammunition.

It is abundantly clear, then, that the one valid and concrete contribution made by the foreign contingent was that of the doctors. They were the only members of this body to suffer for their devotion. Some were brutally treated by the victorious Italians, others like Melly, Burgoyne, Lindstrom, and Hockman were killed at their posts. Theirs is the epic story still to be written of a handful of men, short of everything they needed, working ceaselessly under unimaginably difficult conditions to ease the sufferings of the wounded, many of whom were civilians, tragic victims who had been trapped in the meshes of the enemy's pitiless dragnet. These heroic doctors carried out their mission of healing in regions that had become shambles of bombed and burned-out villages without roads and even the simplest amenities were unobtainable, regions that were infested with *shiftas* * and stalked by the specter of famine.

The first five field ambulances to make their appearance in Ethiopia after De Bono and his men, thrilled with the memory of Adowa, had crossed the Mareb, were those of the Ethiopian Red Cross. Each was handed over to a doctor and dispatched to the northern and southern fronts:

Ambulance 1: Dr. Robert W. Hockman of America. Dispatched to Ras Nasibu's army in the Ogaden.

Ambulance 2: Dr. George Dassios of Greece. Dispatched to Dessie with the Imperial Guard.

Ambulance 3: Dr. Schuppler of Austria. Dispatched to Ras Kassa's army.

Ambulances 4 and 5: Dr. Hooper of America and Dr. Balau of Poland. Dispatched respectively to the Negelli and Makalle fronts.

Later, when the news of the indiscriminate bombing to which the Ethiopians had been subjected roused the democratic countries to white-hot indignation, a number of Red Cross organizations sent out more field hospitals. The first to arrive was the Swedish unit, which reached Ethiopia as early as November 1935; it consisted of two ambulances, and the medical team was led by Doctor F. Hylander. This unit was

---

* Bandits (TRANS.).

attached to Ras Desta's army. A month or so later, at the time when the Ethiopians were carrying out their offensive in Shire and in Tembien, the Dutch Red Cross unit, with Doctor Winckel in charge, made its appearance and immediately set up its field hospital near Dessie. By far the largest and most lavishly equipped unit was BASE,* whose team of two doctors, Percy James Kelly and Robert Blackwood Anderson, was led by John Melly. Of its two field ambulances, one was set up in the region of Lake Ashangi, the other near Gondar. At the beginning of 1936 when Badoglio launched his series of devastating attacks designed to annihilate the Ethiopians, the Egyptian Red Crescent and the Norwegian and Finnish Red Cross sent out medical teams, led respectively by Prince Ismail Daoud, Doctor Gunnar Ulland and Professor Faltin. Some dozen other doctors, among them Hanner of Sweden, Loeb and Stadin of America, and Argyropoulous of Greece, treated the wounded in the military hospitals of Addis Ababa, Dessie, and Harar.

Fifty doctors for an army of half-a-million men! It was like bailing out the ocean with the proverbial teaspoon or attempting to rid India of the plague of famine. Furthermore, as the emperor said subsequently, "We have seen what happens to most of the European and Ethiopian field hospitals. The Italians bomb them into a heap of twisted metal beneath which the wounded and sick, doctors and orderlies are buried. When I tell you that just as an officer in wartime has to keep a constant watch to ensure the safety of his men, the doctors have to be continually on the alert for air-raid warnings in order to evacuate the casualties in time, you will realize for yourself that their situation is desperate." [9] Men like Dassios,

* British Ambulance Service in Ethiopia. When John Melly, who had worked as a medical missionary in Ethiopia in 1934, realized that war was inevitable, he went to London and raised the money for this splendid unit (TRANS.).

[9] *Une victoire de la civilisation*, p. 29. See also the *Official Journal* of the League of Nations, no. 4 (April 1936), pp. 369–70, for the list of nineteen aerial bombardments of field hospitals and ambulances. This list was

Balau, Medinski, and Gingold Duprey remained at their posts while the battle raged around them, and when it was over were surrounded by victorious Italians who booed and threatened them. Dr. Balau was taken prisoner after the battle of Amba Aradam, brutally beaten, and haled before a firing squad several times, because the Italians were determined to make him confess that he had been one of the six signatories of a telegram sent to the League of Nations condemning the blanket bombing of Dessie. A few years later, just before he entered the Swiss sanatorium where he was shortly to die, Dr. Balau spoke of his ordeal to Marcel Junod, who had been the Red Cross delegate in Ethiopia during the war. "You've no idea of the lengths they went to in order to drag an admission out of me. They hammered my hands with rifle butts . . . and when I couldn't stand anymore, when I was in a delirium of pain—yes, I did stammer out that I'd signed some sort of document. . . ." [10]

When Haile Selassie regained his throne, he did not forget the men who had served him so devotedly. He appointed Dr. Dassios head of the Menelik II Hospital in Addis Ababa, Dr. Hylander Chief Medical Officer of the Ministry of Health, and Count von Rosen Director of the Flying School at Bishoftu. But for John Melly, almost certainly the most selfless, the greatest of them all, there was no reward. Melly refused to leave Addis Ababa on the train carrying the emperor and his suite to the safety of Jibouti and remained at his post in the hospital. When the capital was given over to looting and violence, Melly drove out as soon as it was safe to do so, to pick up the wounded in a truck. As he sat at the wheel while the doctor who had accompanied him was attending to a casualty, an Ethiopian thrust a pistol into the cab and fired at Melly; the bullet penetrated his lung and he died two days

---

presented to the secretary-general of the League of Nations by the International Commission of Jurists on April 18, 1936.

[10] Marcel Junod, *Le troisième combattant* (Paris: Payot, 1936), pp. 36–37.

later. The murderer little knew he had caused the death of Ethiopia's greatest friend, the heroic medical missionary who had saved countless lives on the bloody battlefields of the northern front.[11]

In addition to the polyglot band that united beneath the banner of the Lion of Judah, prompted by their ideals, the spirit of adventure, or by purely mercenary motives, men and women of every nationality voiced their sympathy for the emperor. I can vouch for this as I was shown a hundred or so letters that had been moved to a safe place in the first week of May 1936, when it was feared that the imperial *gebbi* might be looted. Here is a small selection. "Mussolini's intention to turn your country into a battlefield fills me with anguish," wrote an army officer from Costa Rica. "As one who fought in the 1914–18 war, I respectfully offer you my humble services. . . ."[12] A group of Greeks in the Dodecanese sent him a copy of the newspaper *Voie de Karpathos*, which contained an article urging the Ethiopians to defeat the Fascists and "avenge the victims of the Dodescanese." A Peruvian, revolted by Mussolini's belligerence, wrote that he hoped to initiate a movement of solidarity with Ethiopia in South America.[13] A Puerto Rican offered to put his newspaper, *El Combate*, and his printing press at the emperor's disposal.[14] A young American from Topeka, realizing the Ethiopian army was no match for the Italians, pointed out, "It seems to me that a head-on clash with the Italians would be disastrous. In my opinion the

[11] When the emperor spoke to me of these men who had served under his flag, he said, "The world denounced Mussolini's act of aggression and upheld our cause, hence many Americans and Europeans came to our support. To show our gratitude, we have named several of our streets after them."

[12] Letter from San José, Costa Rica, dated August 18, 1935, signed (Capt.) G. E. Cuzak.

[13] Letter from Lima, dated August 28, 1935, signed Carmelo Clumpitàzi de Zocotioco.

[14] Letter from Caguas, dated September 17, 1935, signed Valentin Castilio.

right course would be to allow them to advance into the difficult and mountainous country where their heavy equipment would bog them down and engage them in what we call guerrilla warfare, the kind of tactic American Indians used to drive back the far better equipped pioneers." [15]

An Englishman suggested the Ethiopian soldiers should be fitted out with bulletproof waistcoats, which could be obtained quite cheaply, and ornamented his letter with ingenious sketches of the waistcoats. A woman living in New York advised the emperor to adopt the tactics employed by Lawrence of Arabia against the Turks, and sent him an article on the subject by Liddell Hart.[16] A manufacturer from Pennsylvania advised him to become a member of the British Commonwealth and so assure for his country the immediate armed protection of Great Britain.[17] In addition to letters such as these, there were many from women, both black and white, who wrote to tell Haile Selassie they were praying for him. "God is full of pity and compassion," ran one of these missives from Finistère. "Ethiopia must not lose courage, for He will fight on her behalf and send His angels to protect her." [18] And a Negro woman from California had this to say: "I pray that you will deliver yourself from crucifixion and show the whites they are not as civilized as they loudly assert themselves to be. . . ." [19]

[15] Letter from Topeka, Texas, undated, signed Alfred Taeger.

[16] Letter from New York, dated September 6, 1935, signed Elizabeth C. Morris.

[17] Letter from Haverford, dated August 23, 1935, signed Archer Griffin Dean.

[18] Letter from Quimper, Brittany, dated September 27, 1935, signed Fanny Ursula Jones.

[19] Letter from Los Angeles, dated October 26, 1935, signature illegible. In addition to these letters from humble sympathizers, there were a good many that had obviously been written by rogues, bogus astrologers, and charlatans. A Mr. Frank Fox of Monterey, for instance, offered to send the emperor his pamphlet containing the secret of eternal life for the sum of five dollars. He added that if the negus ordered large quantities of this pamphlet, a handsome price reduction would be made!

Chapter eight
The First Battle of Tembien

Today all that remains of Marshal Badoglio's headquarters at Enda Yesus are a few heaps of stone. There is not even a trace of the armed camp that extended from Makalle to Kwiha. The weather wreaks its ravages far more swiftly in Ethiopia than in any other country. Torrential rains beat down on the walls crumbling them, and seedling trees soon cover the debris with a tangle of matted roots. Violent winds sweep across the plateaus tearing foundations loose, and grass springs up, burying them from sight. In a few years' time, not a vestige will be left to mark the passage of the Italian army. Even now it is difficult to distinguish a graveyard from a quarry.

Marshal Badoglio arrived at Enda Yesus toward the middle of December and set up his headquarters at the foot of the hill crowned with Galliano's old fort.[1] He had no time for report-

[1] Two weeks before Badoglio's arrival at Enda Yesus, the deposed

ers. He was in a somber mood. As he subsequently admitted, the formidable massif of Amba Aradam, swarming with Ethiopians silhouetted against the sky, "weighed heavily on my chest." The despised rases, so ignorant they could not even read a topographical map, had nevertheless succeeded in establishing themselves with 160,000 men on the heights overlooking the Italian positions, and frequently swooped down to attack them. As if the sight of Amba Aradam was not bad enough, Mussolini, in a speech he made in Pontinia, gave a glimpse of the future when he said that the war in Ethiopia would be long and hard-fought, adding in order not to convey his own pessimism to the country: "Time is not the important factor. All that counts is our ultimate victory." [2] Nevertheless, the Duce had made it clear that he lacked faith in Badoglio, a fact of which the general was aware. On the other hand, the Italian people waited confidently for him to advance, shatter Amba Aradam with his mighty battering ram, and swoop upon Amba Alagi to "avenge" Toselli.

Badoglio, however, showed no signs of haste. As he wired to the ever-impatient Mussolini, "It has always been my rule to be meticulous in preparation so that I may be swift in action." [3] Sem Benelli, who saw him during this period, neatly summed up the General's personality: "He wore a beret, a flannel-lined cape, and the thick socks and heavy boots of a mountaineer. . . . His hands, feet, shoulders, neck were evoca-

---

Emperor *Lij* Yasu, who had been exiled to Garamulata, died in somewhat mysterious circumstances. According to Henri de Monfreid (see *L'avion noir*, pp. 83–103), he had been slowly poisoned by Abba Hanna, one of Haile Selassie's ministers. In September 1938, the following statement appeared in the Abyssinia Association's pamphlet entitled, *Notes for a Reply to Propaganda Against the Emperor of Abyssinia:* "On November 25, 1935, the ex-emperor *Lij* Yasu died at the age of forty of an illness from which he had suffered since childhood. *Lij* Yasu had obstinately refused to undergo the appropriate treatment prescribed by doctors of every nationality."

[2] Benito Mussolini, *Scritti e discorsi dell' Impero* (Milan: Hoepli, 1936), p. 31.

[3] Pietro Badoglio, *The War in Abyssinia*, p. 71.

tive of the primeval earth. . . . [4] In other words, apart from his physical appearance, Badoglio's mind was cast in the same mold as the Piedmontese peasant to whom discretion is the better part of valor—"Don't open your mouth too wide. Don't try to go faster than your legs will carry you. Don't do anything in a hurry or you'll live to regret it." Accordingly, before giving the order to advance, he reinforced his positions, doubled the strength of his artillery, completed the network of roads for his lines of supply and communication, and continually harassed the enemy with air attacks. At length, at the beginning of January 1936, he was ready to march against Ras Mulugeta, who had established his 80,000 men in fortified positions on Amba Aradam,[5] but because of the increasing pressure that Ras Kassa and Ras Seyoum were exerting in Tembien, he was compelled to change his plans. On January 11, he telegraphed the Duce that he would have to "hold up the projected southward offensive," [6] and immediately took steps to deal with the Ethiopian offensive.

The "Christmas offensive" had made it clear that the main objective of the Ethiopian plan was to isolate Makalle by cutting the Italian army in two. While Ras Mulugeta engaged the Third Army Corps, Ras Kassa and Ras Seyoum were to force an opening through the Tembien region, occupy the Abaro and Warieu passes, push on to Hauzen, and breach the enemy lines to open up the road for Ras Imru who, after he had retaken Adowa, was to thrust forward into Eritrea. The plan was excellently conceived, but it was on too vast a scale, altogether too ambitious for an army operating on a front of more than 200 kilometers, an army that possessed few field radios, whose ammunition had to be strictly rationed, and

[4] Sem Benelli, *Io in Africa*, pp. 58–59.

[5] I have given the Italian figures as I could not always rely on those of the Ethiopians. However, the accuracy of the Italian figures must not be taken as absolute, since, as General Faldella told me, they were almost invariably overstated for reasons of security.

[6] Pietro Badoglio, *The War in Abyssinia*, p. 45.

whose supplies could only be brought up at night because of the incessant daylight air attacks. The sole advantages the Ethiopians could boast of were their extreme mobility and speed, but they were unable to make use of them because of the heavy ground barrage and the constant bombing. To avoid

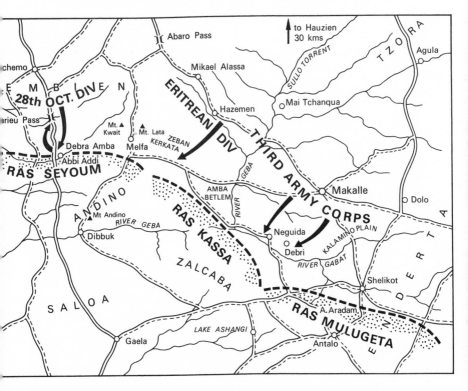

Map 4. Movements of Italian divisions and Ethiopian armies during the first battle of Tembien.

heavy losses, they were forced to proceed with the utmost caution, and Badoglio took good care not to afford them any chance of rushing his positions.

Two courses were open to the General—he could either

stand fast and wait for the enemy to attack, or he could take the offensive. In the hope of throwing the Ethiopian plan of campaign into confusion, he chose the latter. On the morning of January 19, he ordered the Third Army Corps, commanded by General Bastico, to leave its positions at Makalle and occupy those of Nebri and Negeda, so as to close the road to Ras Mulugeta and prevent him from sending reinforcements to Ras Kassa. On the following day he launched his offensive in Tembien. On the left, the 2nd Eritrean Division advanced in two columns; on the right, a column of Blackshirts of the "28 October" division, which held the Warieu Pass, pushed forward toward the Beles torrent. The Eritreans were stubbornly opposed by the enemy and fierce fighting continued throughout the day; when dusk fell, however, the Eritreans succeeded in dislodging the Ethiopians from their positions on the heights of Zeban Kerkata and the lower slopes of Amba Salama. In this first encounter with the Ethiopians, the Italo-Eritreans had the best of it, and Ras Kassa was forced to admit in his radio communiqué to the Emperor that "the men I sent to cut off the Italians were surrounded." [7]

Twenty-four hours later, however, the situation was completely reversed. An army detachment commanded by General Diamanti made a sortie from the Warieu garrison, advanced too far, and consequently found itself in imminent danger of being surrounded and wiped out by the troops of Ras Seyoum. General Diamanti was obliged to fall back, but, emboldened by success, an ever-increasing number of Ethiopians forced him to fight every inch of the way. The Diamanti detachment finally reached the outer defenses of the Warieu Pass, but it was not until sunset that the survivors (335 men had been killed or wounded during the retreat) managed to rejoin the garrison. But an extremely dangerous situation had arisen: the Ethiopians had succeeded in infiltrating the outer defenses and

[7] *Ibid.*, p. 53.

were pushing on toward Zebandas and Dembela on the Adowa road. Worse still, the beleaguered garrison could not expect any help from the 2nd Eritrean Division, which had failed to realize the threatening nature of the enemy's movements and consequently made no move from the positions it had occupied on the previous evening. For three consecutive days the Ethiopians blazed away at the Italians with their machine guns and rifles, inflicting heavy casualties on them and forcing them to abandon their peripheral fortifications. As a result Addis Ababa was able to issue a bulletin announcing an authentic victory even though its claims, particularly with regard to the amount of war material captured, were as usual exaggerated: "The Diamanti detachment and, still more important, the "28 October" brigade have been annihilated. The three fortified positions of Shum Abera, Erbawassa and Kassa Damba have been occupied by our troops. On January 20, our victorious soldiers brought to our headquarters the arms captured from the enemy—29 cannon, 175 machine guns, 2,764 rifles, many mules carrying loads of ammunition, and various other materials of war. They also brought in a number of prisoners." [8]

The siege of the Warieu garrison lasted from sunset on January 21 till sunrise on January 24. Ras Kassa, who had been appointed Commander-in-Chief of the forces on the northern front, aware that the Italians could not hold out much longer as they were short of food, ammunition, and, above all, water, sent an urgent message (he had a field radio operated by two Czechs) to Ras Mulugeta asking for reinforcements to crush the garrison's final attempts at resistance then push on to Adowa and Hanzen. Ras Mulugeta, however, possibly because he resented the fact that Ras Kassa had been promoted over him, avoided giving a direct promise of help on

---

[8] This bulletin and various others will be found in *Annali dell' Africa Italiana*, II, no. 1, March 1939 (Milan: Mondadori), p. 142.

the pretext that his forces were heavily engaged with the Third Army Corps, and so allowed precious hours to slip away. As for Ras Imru, he did not possess a field radio and therefore knew nothing of what was happening in Tembien. (He told me in the course of our interview that it took his runners fourteen days to complete the course between Ras Kassa's headquarters and his own.) Thus, instead of attacking the fortified camp of Axum, Ras Imru withdrew from his positions at Af Gaga. Despite these predictable contretemps, the Ethiopian manuever still presented such a threatening aspect that had it succeeded, "the course of the campaign would have been very different," as Badoglio observed in his extremely reticent book.[9]

A few provisions were dropped by air to the stubborn defenders of the Warieu garrison, but they had almost run out of water. By January 3, only a few hundred liters remained, and the "consul," Biscaccianti, in order to economize the precious liquid, dampened a pad of cotton and moistened the parched lips of his men. Around the fortifications the battle raged furiously. Wave after wave of Ethiopians led by Aberra and Wondewossen, Ras Kassa's sons, and Bajirond Latibelu and *Dejatch* Admasu, surged forward relentlessly and engaged the Italians in hand-to-hand combat, urged on to fresh feats of daring by the wailing notes of the hornblowers. Among those who fell beneath their *gurade* (long swords), was the Dominican chaplain, Padre Reginaldo Giuliani, who was struck down as he was administering the last rites to a dying officer. "I found his body on the battlefield on the morning of January 25," wrote a doctor. "He was still wearing his black shirt, which was soaked with his generous blood. His left clavicle had been split in two. The weapon had been driven through the red cross on the pocket of his burnoose, the cross that is the

[9] Pietro Badoglio, *The War in Abyssinia*, p. 53.

distinguishing sign of an army chaplain." [10] Among the besieged was the *doyen* Marinetti,* whose vision of the battle was chaotic, fragmented, crepitating, as harsh as his poems. Here is one intended to extol the stoicism of the Italian troops:

> Signor maggiore guardi questo liquido è
> l'orina dei compagni cotta bevuta da noi
> ma l'acqua delle mitragliatrici intatta
> brilla magnetizzare la bocca.[11]

> [Great God look at this liquid it is the
> boiled urine of our comrades that we are drinking
> but the intact water of the machine guns
> glitters magnetizes our mouths.]

Another poem celebrated the last day of the fighting when the horns of the Ethiopians wailed incessantly:

> *Suomando per carnevale o per Natale una altra*
> *tromba infantile fa biba bo bo*
> *il generale Somma gambe incrociate*
> *nell'arenaria grida*
> *—si sfotta subito quel suono del nemico con*
> *una nostra tromba caricaturante*
> *bi bo bo baaaa.*[12]

> [Sounding for carnival or Christmas, another
> toy trumpet squeaks biba bo bo

---

[10] Episode related by Dr. Alberto Lixia in *P. R. Giuliani, per Cristo e per la Patria* (Salani, 1937), p. 335.

* Marinetti was then fifty-eight (TRANS.).

[11] F. T. Marinetti, *Il poema africana*, p. 191.

[12] *Ibid.*, p. 190.

general Somma cross-legged
on the sand shouts
the hell with the enemy's horn answer it straight away
with one of our mocking trumpets
bi bo bo baaaa.]

While the battle was raging at the Warieu Pass, Badoglio, at his headquarters in Enda Yesus, could not conceal his anguished state of mind. He had dispatched two battalions to reinforce the garrison, sent the 1st Eritrean Division to the Abaro Pass and ordered the 2nd Eritrean Division to fall back to Abaro Pass, from which point it could proceed to the Warieu Pass to relieve the beleaguered Italians, but these movements would take time and the situation in Tembien was critical. The general made no secret of his anxiety; he questioned the pilots the moment they returned to base from a bombing raid on the enemy, and he scarcely left the radio tent. On the afternoon of January 22, when Ras Kassa had unleashed the full fury of his attack, he ordered "a study to be made of the possible procedure in the event a retirement from Makalle became necessary. A force of some 70,000 men, 14,000 animals, 300 pieces of artillery of various caliber, munitions for two or three days, supplies for six days . . . will have to be sent by one single road. . . ." [13] To make this measure appear less grave than it actually was, Badoglio is careful to add in *The War in Abyssinia*, "I could not disregard the thought of worse possibilities, slight though the risk of them might be. To think of the worst and to prepare to confront it and overcome it is the part of strong men." [14] In reality those four days in January 1936, were among the worst in his life. "It might have been a second Adowa," wrote Ciasca.[15] Possibly, General Badoglio was thinking less of

[13] Pietro Badoglio, *The War in Abyssinia*, p. 56.
[14] *Ibid.*
[15] Raffaele Ciasca, *Storia coloniale dell' Italia contemporanea*, p. 664.

Adowa than of Caporetto where, on October 24, 1917, thanks to his flagrant blunder, the Austro-German army breached his lines at Tolmino and Plezzo and forced the Italian troops to retreat in disorder all the way back to the Piave. The memory of this calamitous defeat must have been ever-present in his mind during these hours when he had every reason to be gravely anxious. Even though Ras Mulugeta had failed to send reinforcements to Ras Kassa—and Badoglio may well have asked himself what the outcome would have been had he done so—the combined armies of Ras Kassa and Ras Seyoum were fighting, as he himself acknowledged later, with "such courage and determination" [16] that he could not overlook the possibility of their hurling themselves against him at any moment and cutting his army in two.

Badoglio's state of tension was graphically described by Paolo Monelli: "That night, January 23, he refused to go to bed. Fully dressed, still wearing his cap, with his cape spread over his knees like a blanket, he sat on a stool in his tent beside the telephone. On the few occasions when it rang, he lifted the receiver and listened in silence, his face a mask of stone in the crude light of the acetylene lamp. The sun was beginning to rise when it rang once more, and at last he heard the news for which he had been so anxiously waiting. His set expression relaxed, the shadow of a smile played about his lips. He rose, went outside, and took his customary morning exercise, pacing to and fro among the sleeping tents." [17] The "news" that had restored the general's calm was that the relief column commanded by General Vaccarisi had reached the Warieu Pass. Caught in a deadly cross fire, "the enemy gradually relaxed his pressure and withdrew." [18] This is Badoglio's version. Ras Kassa, however, told a very different story. It was not, he said, the arrival of the relief column that forced him to

[16] Pietro Badoglio, *The War in Abyssinia*, p. 66.
[17] *Storia Illustrata*, May 1963, p. 651.
[18] Pietro Badoglio, *The War in Abyssinia*, p. 56.

retire from his positions, but the impossibility of exposing his forces any longer to the deadly clouds of mustard gas: "The bombing from the air had reached its height when suddenly a number of my warriors dropped their weapons, screamed with agony, rubbed their eyes with their knuckles, buckled at the knees and collapsed. An invisible rain of lethal gas was splashing down on my men. One after another, all those who had survived the bombing, succumbed to this new form of attack. I dare not think of how many men I lost on this one day alone. [January 23] The gas contaminated the fields and woods, and at least 2,000 animals died. Mules, cows, rams, and a host of wild creatures, maddened with pain, stampeded to the ravines and threw themselves into the depths below. On the next day, and the next and the next, the Italian planes subjected my army to gas attacks. They dropped it on any spot where they detected the slightest movement."[19]

Ras Kassa accompanied the emperor to London and made this statement immediately after his arrival in July 1936. I read it carefully, taking into particular consideration the state of mind of the defeated commander-in-chief, and came to the conclusion that so vitiated as it was by Ras Kassa's bitter feelings, I could not honestly accept it as a proof that Badoglio had authorized the use of this illegal weapon. Ras Kassa was no longer alive when I went to Ethiopia, but I sought confirmation from the supreme commander himself, Haile Selassie. Was it an incontrovertible fact, I asked him, that the Italians had used mustard gas against the Ethiopians? He replied as follows: "The Fascist army made use of poison gas from the early days of the war right up to the last. We were present in person when this toxic gas [mustard gas] was used on the northern front. The Italians employed it not only to cause panic among our troops but, far worse, to injure them so

---

[19] *Une victoire de la civilisation*, pp. 37–39.

seriously that they would never be able to fight again." [20] A few years ago, General Faldella wrote, "It is probable that gas was used after the first battle of Tembien and the battle of Enderta, but certainly not to the extent that Ethiopian propagandists wished to make the world believe." [21] In the document on war crimes presented to the League of Nations, the Ethiopians alleged that mustard-gas attacks were made on twenty occasions. [22] According to Linton Welles, correspondent of the *New York Herald Tribune*, 250,000 Ethiopians were killed or seriously affected by mustard gas. [23] After so many years it is well-nigh impossible to verify this figure, but from statements made to me from various eyewitnesses, I can state with *absolute certainty* that the Takkaze fords, the locality of Amba Alagi, and the lower region of Tembien were drenched with yperite on several occasions, and that the town of Quoram and the country around Lake Ashangi were subjected to mustard-gas attacks on at least six occasions. But the exact number of times it was used is not important. Twenty times or

[20] Statement made to me by the emperor while I was interviewing him.

[21] *Storia Illustrata*, May 1963, p. 635.

[22] In a letter dated April 13, 1936, the Ethiopian delegate to the League of Nations wrote to the Secretary-General, "The Ethiopian delegation has the honor to transmit to Your Excellency the telegram dated April 12, 1936, which it has received from the Ethiopian government in order that its contents may be made known without delay to the Committee of Thirteen, the Committee of Eighteen, the Council and all the members of the League of Nations. The following regions and cities have been subjected to poison-gas attacks: Takkaze, December 22, 1935; Amba Alagi, December 26, 1935; Borana, December 31, 1935; Sokota, January 10, 1936; Makalle, January 21, 1936; Megalo, February 1936; the Woldia road, February 27, 1936; Quoram, March 16, 1936; Ilanserer, March 17, 1936; Quoram, March 17, 18; Yirgalem, March 19, 21; Enda-Mahoni, March 29, 30; Quoram, April 4, 5, 6, 7. During these last four attacks on Quoram, the city was literally enveloped in asphyxiating gases. The gas most frequently used was mustard gas." See *Official Journal* of the League of Nations, no. 4, document 1592, (April 1936), pp. 479–80.

[23] The figures given by Linton Welles, author of *We Cover the World*, appeared in the report of the Abyssinia Association for May 1943.

only ten times—what difference does it make? That the Italians resorted to mustard gas is the damning fact and nothing can lessen the guilt of the generals and politicians who decided to authorize chemical warfare.

On the morning of January 24, the first battle of Tembien came to an end and with it, notwithstanding the progress that Ras Imru was still making in Shire, the heroic but doomed Ethiopian counteroffensive. Badoglio had "won the day," even though, as he admitted, he had not accomplished his "final purpose of forcing the enemy back to the south of the River Geba," [24] and was thus compelled to abandon all the positions that had been taken during the four days of the battle. He had won because the Ethiopians sustained 8,000 casualties and "almost exhausted their supply of ammunition," [25] hence they were unable to reap the fruits of their initial success. In a telegram to Rome dated January 28, a telegram Badoglio took good care not to include in his book, he informed Mussolini that "we did not escape unscathed." Indeed, as the Ethiopians had used no artillery in this battle and had no bombers, no mustard gas with which to attack the enemy, the Italian losses were extremely heavy—60 officers, 605 nationals, and 417 Eritreans killed or wounded. Even General Armellini, when I questioned him about this first major clash with the Ethiopians, admitted that the victory had not been easily won. "From the strategical and operational point of view, none of the battles of the war presented or could present us with any problems," he told me, "But certain difficulties did arise in the first battle of Tembien and that of Lake Ashangi. In the former they were caused by the speed and overwhelming onrush of the enemy and the visible weakening of our troops who were not inured to fighting in such wild and unknown country." [26]

[24] Pietro Badoglio, *The War in Abyssinia*, p. 57.
[25] *Ibid.*
[26] Evidence given to me during an interview.

But the "black period" did not come to an end with the first battle of Tembien, the proof being that Mussolini had not regained his assurance and chose this moment to authorize General Roatta, chief of SIM, to make contact with the Palestinian Shukry Yasr Bey, who had offered to act as an intermediary and sound out the emperor as to a possible peace of compromise. The conditions stipulated by Mussolini for such a peace were the cession of the provinces of Tigre, Danakil, and Harar, and the setting up of two Italian missions in Addis Ababa, one military, the other economic. On February 24, General Roatta flew to Athens to meet Shukry Yasr Bey and acquaint him with the Italian terms.[27] In February 1936, therefore, five months after invading Ethiopia, the Duce was not yet altogether certain that the empire would reappear on the "fatal hills of Rome." [28]

[27] Evidence supplied by General Faldella when I interviewed him.

[28] There is evidence to show that at the close of 1935, few men in the highest circles believed in an Italian victory. As we learn from Ruggero Zangrandi (*il lungo viaggio*, p. 451), Vittorio Mussolini wrote on October 25, "I have always maintained that at the opportune moment an Italo-Ethiopian agreement would be greatly to our advantage. If we treat with Ethiopia now, we shall avoid cutting an ugly figure in the eyes of the world." A few days later, Ciano talked about the war to Lessona and made no secret of his pessimism, "In any case, I shall keep a plane at my disposal so that I can fly back to Italy if the worst comes to the worst." Lessona himself took an equally gloomy view. When General Faldella told him Italy was prepared to make peace provided the emperor agreed to her terms, he exclaimed, "If the negus does agree, we'll jump so high with joy that our heads may hit the ceiling!" (See *Storia Illustrata*, May 1963, p. 623.)

Chapter nine

The Occupation of Negelli

"When we journalists, Italian and non-Italian, entered the room, he rose to his feet. He was a giant of a man. Clad in a white burnoose and dark trousers, he was the personification of the classic hero; he seemed to be not a mere creature of flesh and blood but a mythical being conjured up by an entire nation to symbolize the glories of its past. Homer must have had such a figure in mind when he wrote of his heroes." [1]

The personage who inspired Sandro Volta to pen this effusion and about whom there was nothing in the least Homeric, was General Rodolfo Graziani. He was an extremely debatable figure even at this time, but thanks to the renown he had won for himself in Libya and his bold and insolent air of an all-conquering hero, he had succeeded in capturing the popular imagination. We boys were as ardently pro "good old Graziani" and anti "rotten old Badoglio" as we were pro "good old Guerra" and anti "rotten old Binda," pro "good old

---

[1] Sandro Volta, *Graziani a Neghelli* (Florence: Vallecchi, 1936), p. 33.

Carnera," and anti "rotten old Paolino." True it was alleged that he had suppressed the Senussi uprising in Libya with the utmost brutality, but as only a few voices rose in protest, the charge remained almost as vague as the rumor regarding certain mutilations he was said to have inflicted, and the story that he had murdered the members of his own family to save them from falling into the hands of the Senussi. All this talk, far from damaging Graziani's reputation, actually reinforced his legendary image, that of a man as fearless as he was ruthless, as brilliant as he was implacable. We schoolboys, horrid little beasts that we were, pictured the war in Africa as a kind of super sporting event, an Ethiopian *Grand Prix,* so to speak, in which the two contestants were Graziani and Badoglio. Naturally all our money was on Graziani for we were quite convinced that he would be the first to pass the finish line of Addis Ababa!

In actual fact this hero of ours had feet of the basest clay. Thirty years before the advent of Raoul Salan, and other generalissimos of his type, Graziani waged a war without quarter in Libya and set up "flying tribunals," concentration camps, and barbed-wire entanglements hundreds of kilometers long. On his orders thousands of Libyan patriots were shot or hanged—in his opinion there *were* no Libyan patriots, patriotism being strictly confined to Europe.[2] Graziani's brutality became so notorious that when he was appointed Commander-in-Chief of the forces on the southern front of Ethiopia, he was quoted as saying (and even if the words were put into his mouth, he might very well have uttered them in view of his past), "The Duce shall have Ethiopia, with the Ethiopians or without them, just as he pleases." [3] Graziani himself was convinced, however, as he told Paolo Orano, that "history"

[2] Graziani's methods of dealing with the rebel Senussi in Libya are recorded in *The Senussi of Cyrenaica* by E. E. Evans-Pritchard (London: Oxford University Press, 1954). See in particular pp. 157–229.

[3] Rodolfo Graziani, *Fronte Sud*, p. 44.

would "absolve" him as it had absolved every conqueror. In his palace by the sea at Benghazi where he spent five years, he went on to say, "At times I search my conscience to see if I can find any justification for the charges of brutality and savagery that have been brought against me, and believe me, never do I sleep as soundly as when I've spent the evening in such self-scrutiny. I know from the history of every era that in order to rebuild, the past or that part of the past that bears no relation to the present must be destroyed." [4] Graziani expressed this concept of history in 1937 so we can see how narrowly the Amhara population of Ethiopia escaped total liquidation.

Graziani arrived at Mogadishu on March 7, 1935. His mood was anything but serene. During the long sea voyage on the *Vulcania,* he had tried to console himself with the thought of the magnificent apartment worthy of a "Wall Street financier" which he had rented for 60,000 lira,[5] but he could not banish from his mind the fact that he had been relegated to the command of a secondary front, and worse still, allotted a purely defensive role. As it had been foreseen that the decisive battles of the war would be fought in the north where the Ethiopians had concentrated most of their forces, almost the whole of the Italian expeditionary force had been assembled on the Eritrean frontier. To be merely the protector of an armed camp—nothing could have commended itself less to a man as ambitious as Graziani, this "taciturn, fiercely energetic Roman soldier," as Orano called him, "gazing with eagle eyes toward the far-distant sources of the great equatorial rivers that he dreamed of linking to the sand hills of Cufra in one vast continuous stretch of territory over which it was Rome's destiny to rule." [6]

[4] Paolo Orano: *Rodolfo Graziani, generale scipione* (Rome: Pinciana, 1936), p. 16.

[5] Rodolfo Graziani, *Fronte Sud,* p. 23.

[6] Paolo Orano, *Rodolfo Graziani,* p. 41.

Shortly after his arrival at Mogadishu, burning with resentment because he had only one Italian division, the Peloritana,
whereas De Bono had ten, and because his orders were to dig
himself in and await a hypothetical attack, Graziani hatched
out various schemes to convince Mussolini that the plans of
the Supreme Command needed modifying and that he should
be allowed to launch an offensive on Harar, a project that the
Duce himself cherished. With the tacit and later the open
consent of the Leader, Graziani began to make preparations,
not for the defense of the colony but for transforming it into
an operational base. He opened up new roads, improved the
facilities of the ports, solved the difficult problem of water
supplies, stocked up the provisions that would be needed for

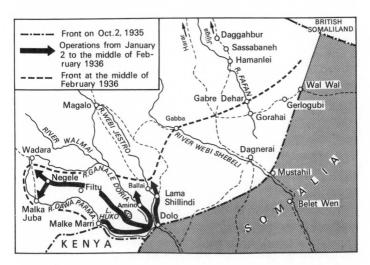

Map 5. The southern front.

an army on the march, and bought hundreds of motor vehicles
from British car dealers in Mombasa and Dar-es-Salaam ordered from car manufacturers in America. When the war broke
out, Graziano had at his disposal 51,000 rifles, 1,585 machine
guns, 112 pieces of artillery, 1,800 motor vehicles, 7,857 pack

animals, and a mixed bag of armored cars and tanks, 70 in all, and 38 planes, figures that he more than doubled during the first few months of the war. Furthermore, he assiduously wooed certain Somali chiefs, Olol Dinle and Hussein Ali, for instance, who, provided with arms by the regional government of the colony, had provoked the Ethiopians from 1933 onward by continually attacking their frontier posts.[7] As Ciasca wrote, Graziani "subtly fanned the traditional flame of hatred between the Somali shepherds and the agriculturists of Harar, between the nomads of the plain and the settlers on the uplands."[8]

When the war began, Graziani was confronted by an enemy 80,000 strong. Of these, 40,000 under the command of Ras Desta Damtu were massed in the provinces of Sidamo and Bale; 30,000, commanded by Ras Nasibu, manned Wehib Pasha's Hindenburg Wall and garrisoned the fortified towns of the Ogaden and Hararge; while the remaining 10,000, commanded by *Dejatch* Amde Mikael, were concentrating in Arussi. The two principal armies on the southern front were better trained and equipped than those in the north, and their commanders were young, progressive and absolutely loyal to the emperor. They were men of a very different type from the other four rases, three of whom were old—only Ras Imru was still under forty. Ras Desta had married the emperor's daugh-

---

[7] In *Fronte Sud* (see p. 50), Graziani wrote, "Olol Dinle, probably because he had become convinced that owing to the presence of Ethiopian frontier posts he could not continue to dominate the country as he had in the past, completely changed his policy toward the government of Italian Somaliland, which thereupon sent him fresh supplies of arms and ammunition and even persuaded a number of Somalis to join his forces. From 1933 onward, reinforced by the government, Olol Dinle waged a ceaseless guerrilla war against the Ethiopians and finally succeeded in occupying Gorahai, held by a strong Ethiopian force commanded by a *fitaurari*. Olol Dinle, who had scored a brilliant victory, gave no quarter: the armed camp was burned to the ground and its defenders put to the sword." All this took place a year before the Wal Wal incident.

[8] Raffaele Ciasca, *Storia coloniale dell' Italia contemporanea*, p. 660.

ter, Tenagne Worq, the firstborn of his children. Ras Nasibu had traveled extensively abroad, spoke several European languages, and was considered to be the most advanced of the "Young Ethiopians."

On October 3, when De Bono crossed the Mareb, Graziani activated the "Milan Plan," whose objective was to make a series of thrusts all along the southern front in order to eliminate the most troublesome of the Ethiopian frontier posts and gauge the strength of the enemy. These preliminary attacks, hindered though they were by three weeks of incessant rain, resulted in the occupation of Callafo, Dagnerai, and Gerlogubi and, even more important, Gorahai, which fell on November 7. Gorahai had been fortified by the brilliant *Gerazmatch*, Afewerk, who was posthumously promoted to the rank of *dejatch* by the emperor. The Italians attacked Gorahei mainly from the air and Afewerk sustained these bombing raids virtually single-handed. With the one antiaircraft gun that Gorahai could boast of, an Oerlikon .37 mounted on one of the turrets of the Mad Mullah's fort, he fired burst after burst of flak at the twenty bombers that appeared over the town every half-hour till he was struck in the leg by a heavy splinter of shrapnel. It was a serious wound, but his life could undoubtedly have been saved had he allowed himself to be driven to the military hospital at Daggahbur. But Afewerk refused to leave his post for he knew that if he did so the resistance of his men would crumble. He ordered those who were standing near him when he was hit to say nothing about it to the rest, and for the next two days continued to fire at each successive wave of bombers. The wound became gangrenous, and on November 5, he collapsed unconscious across his gun. Afewerk died a few hours later as he was being taken to hospital and, as he had foreseen, once his Oerlikon had fallen silent, the defenders of Gorahei panicked and fled.[9]

[9] For the story of Afewerk, see *Caesar in Abyssinia* by George Steer (London: Hodder & Stoughton, 1936).

Graziani sent a flying column commanded by Colonel Maletti in pursuit of the Ethiopians of the Gorahai garrison. Colonel Maletti followed them along the valley of the Fafan to Hamanlei, as it turned out an unwise move for the Ethiopians, who had recovered from the shock of the incessant air raids, had dug themselves in, and were waiting for the enemy. The battle was joined on the dry scrub under a pitilessly hot sun. The Ethiopians, commanded by *Fitaurari* Gongol (and not by "four white officers in khaki uniforms, high-peaked caps, brass spurs and international belts")[10] attempted to surround Colonel Maletti's *dubats*, hampered though they were by the deadly machine-gun fire of the escorting tanks. The battle lasted the entire morning, and both sides suffered heavy losses. In the afternoon fighting shifted to the banks of the Jarar torrent. There, however, the Italian tanks met with some difficulties. Two of them bogged down, and two others were immobilized by fire from the Ethiopians. "It was the first time I'd seen a tank," *Fitaurari* Gongol said later, "and I asked myself how it was possible to kill the men inside them. The tanks were sealed fast at the back and on both sides, but as I looked at them closely, I saw two small openings in front that enabled the occupants to see where they were going and aim their machine guns. We were quite near the tanks and hidden from sight and we began to fire into these openings. We knew we had killed our invisible enemies when the two machine guns ceased to fire and slowly tilted downward till their muzzles touched the ground. . . ."[11] When the *dubats* saw what had happened to the tanks they panicked, but they finally succeeded in breaking out of the encirclement and fell back toward Gabridihari. Graziani had the audacity to claim Hamanlei as an Italian victory in *Fronte Sud*, but in actual fact, after this encounter

[10] Sandro Sandri, *Sei mesi di guerra sul Fronte Somalo* (Ancona: Bertarelli, 1936), p. 130.

[11] This episode was related to Pierre Ichac by *Fitaurari* Gongol, who was in the hospital of Addis Ababa. See picture and story in *l'Illustration*, p. 171.

118

with the enemy he made no move from Gorahai, and it was not until five months later that he resumed his offensive in the Ogaden.[12]

The initiative now passed to the Ethiopians just as it had passed to them at this time on the northern front. In order to relieve the pressure on Harar, Ras Desta left the Bale plateau, assembled his army at Negelli and, splitting it into three columns, advanced toward Dolo with the obvious intention of forcing his way into Italian Somaliland. But this plan of campaign was far too ambitious; in addition to the fact that there was nothing new about it, and like all Ethiopian maneuvers was openly boasted about, it did not take into account the vast distance the army would have to cover from Dolo to Negelli (over 400 kilometers), the difficulty of provisioning such a large force on the march, and the devastating role that the Italian Air Force might play. Indeed, although they only advanced during the night and concealed themselves in the scrub by day, the Ethiopians were soon spotted by reconnaissance planes and subjected to incessant bombing. By the time Ras Desta's army reached the first Italo-Somalian outposts, it had completely lost its impetus; the air attacks, the long march through the pitiless desert, the epidemics that swept through its ranks, completely shattered its morale. Lieutenant Frère was forced to advise Ras Desta to give up all thought of attacking the Italian positions and confine himself to guerrilla warfare. Junod, the Red Cross delegate, was deeply shocked by what he saw when he visited Ras Desta's encampment. "The last defenders of the southern front are fighting and dying under appalling conditions . . . the strength of the Sidamo army was greatly overstated to me in Addis Ababa; in actual fact, it never consisted of more than some 15,000 men. There are only four or five thousand survivors, and as no more than three oxen are slaughtered daily, their meat ration is

[12] Rodolfo Graziani, *Fronte Sud*, p. 191.

almost nonexistent. . . . Their allowance of flour is a cupful a week, but they cannot count on receiving even this pitiful amount as the two trucks that bring up the supplies often break down or are pounced on by *shiftas*. The men are so weakened by hunger they go down like flies with dysentery and malaria. . . ." [13]

At the end of November, Graziani began to assemble troops, artillery, rifles, provisions, and motor vehicles at Dolo to attack this famished horde, but on December 7, his immediate superior, Marshal Badoglio, reminded him in a telegram that his role was strictly defensive. Graziani feigned compliance but while he was urging Rome to authorize an offensive on the southern front he continued his preparations, amassing at Dolo 14,000 men, 26 pieces of artillery, 700 motor vehicles, 3,700 pack animals and a few dozen armored cars and tanks. Finally, Mussolini yielded and gave permission for "a limited attack in the case of absolute necessity." [14] By forcing the Duce's hand, Graziani took a grave responsibility on himself, but it did not perturb him in the least since he had all that the enemy lacked: abundant provisions, a plentiful water supply, a swift, mechanized force, and ample air cover.

The massacre that was to become known as the battle of Ganale Doria began at dawn on January 12, 1936, with the dropping of 1,700 kilograms of mustard gas and various asphyxiating gases on the enemy positions. Graziani split his force into three columns: the first, under General Morelli di Popolo, advanced through the valley of the Ganale Doria toward Bander; the central column, under General Bergonzoli, proceeded toward Filtu via Bogol and Magno; and the third, under General Agostini, followed the course of the Dawa Parma toward its objective, Malka Murri. It took only three days to decide the battle, after which it became a swift game

---

[13] Marcel Junod, *Les troisième combattant*, p. 33.
[14] Rodolfo Graziani, *Fronte Sud*, p. 231.

of "Hunt down the Ethiopians" for the Italians. At first, the Ethiopians attempted to hold out in the positions they had so hurriedly fortified, but bombed incessantly, threatened by the enemy on every side, they were forced to abandon their positions and begin their tragic retreat. Driven away from the wells, pursued by the flying columns across the camel-thorn and burning sand of the desert, their provisions almost exhausted, and their lips cracked and parched with thirst, they sought desperately to escape from the inexorable dragnet and reach the rivers. But those who had not collapsed during the terrible retreat were mowed down by machine guns almost as soon as they reached the river banks. "The scene last night was indescribable," wrote Sandro Volta, who was with the Agostini column, "The Ethiopians went mad and rushed toward certain death for a gulp of water. It was no longer a question of fighting a war, all they could think of was water, water, water. The machine gunners had only to aim a few inches above the ground to slaughter them by the hundreds. Despite their instinctive feeling of compassion, they were obliged to continue firing, faced as they were with a horde that outnumbered them five to one—a horde of crazed animals so desperate it would have stopped at nothing. The Italians were obliged to massacre them, one after another." [15] Once this holocaust was over, the road to Negelli lay open. It took the three columns from January 15 to January 20 to converge on the capital of Galla Borana. As Paul Gentizon testified, they occupied the city "without meeting any resistance—not a shot was fired." [16] This was hardly surprising since, as almost 40 tons of high explosive had been dropped on Negelli, it had virtually ceased to exist.

Although Graziani's tactics showed a certain amount of intelligent foresight and his victory was indisputable, it need hardly be said that he owed much of this success to the vastly

---

[15] *Con l'esercito italiano in A.O.*, vol. I, p. 269.

[16] Paul Gentizon, *La conquête de l'Ethiopie* (Paris: 1936), p. 30.

superior organization and administration of his army and the decisive role played by the air force. Hence, his slighting comments in *Fronte Sud* on Ras Desta and his army, that small army whose fire had been completely extinguished by starvation and sickness, are all the more ungenerous. But Graziani did not enjoy his triumph to the full: the fact that halfway through the battle one third of the 4th Eritrean Division, attached to the Agostini column and commanded by Colonel Moramarco, had deserted, rankled in his mind. As has been said in a previous chapter, 904 Askaris deserted in a single night, some of whom crossed over into Kenya, while the rest made their way to Irgalem and joined what remained of Ras Desta's army.[17] A few days later, by an odd coincidence, a number of Askaris deserted on the northern front. At the end of a fierce day's fighting, *Shumbashi* Andom Tesfazien was ordered to bury the Italian dead and leave the Eritreans to lie where they had fallen. Filled with indignation, Tesfazien insisted that these men who had fought side by side with the Italians had an equal right to a grave. Sentenced to punishment for insubordination, the *Shumbashi*, with a hundred Askaris, went over to the Ethiopians; other Eritreans followed this example and on the eve of the battle of Mai Chew, Tesfazien's band was over a thousand strong.[18]

When the emperor spoke to me of these desertions, motivated by racial solidarity and love of country, sentiments which, according to the Fascist regime, the people of East Africa did not possess, he said: "Although the enemy intensified his attacks on us on the very frontier of Eritrea, many Eritreans, not only civilians but Askaris in the Italian army, came over to us and joined our ranks. The part played by the Eritrean people in the Ethiopian resistance movement was

[17] Information given to me by Vincenzo Franchini in Asmara, April 5, 1965.

[18] See *Chi è dell'Eritrea?* by Giuseppe Puglisi (Asmara: Regina Agency, 1952), p. 16.

extremely important." [19] At the end of 1939, after four years of continuous guerrilla warfare against the occupying forces, Andom Tesfazien was killed at Armachaho. He never knew that on the eve of his death he had been promoted to *dejatch* by the emperor.

[19] In the course of my interview with the emperor.

Chapter ten

The Battle
of Enderta

From Amba Gadam, the vantage point from which General Badoglio directed the battle of Enderta, let us look at the mountain, Amba Aradam. So level is its summit, so sculptured are its peaks that it seems to be less the work of nature than that of man; we might, in fact, be gazing at one of the vast ziggurats of Mesopotamia. If we can picture this cyclopian bastion, we can understand why it "weighed so heavily" on the general's chest, and why the Alpini of the Pusteria division sang:

> We must ascend this Amba or
> We'll never reach Ashagi's shore.

With its rocky, precipitous sides, Amba Aradam appears to be an impregnable fortress, one that recalls another celebrated natural stronghold, Massada, on whose heights the Jews fought to the last man in their final bloody battle against the Romans. But Massada held out for months, Amba Aradam for a mere

124

three days, and the men of the Sila division, which formed part of the Third Army Corps, chanted gleefully and derisively:

> Poor old Mulugeta-o,
> He's gone to tell the Emperor,
> "The Third's reached Amba Aradam,
>   There's nothing to be done!"
> The Emperor's sent his messengers
> To tell the Ethiopians:
> "The Third's reached Amba Aradam
>   So run, run, RUN!"

On February 9, 1936, a few days before an unknown Italian soldier had strung these bragging lines together, Badoglio held a press conference at his headquarters in Enda Yesus, and announced that he was about to rid himself of the mighty obstacle of Amba Aradam that blocked the road to Addis Ababa. A man of few words, he was voluble on this occasion. Indeed, he was in high spirits. Here is part of his speech as it was jotted down by Cesco Tomaselli: "I have decided to attack Ras Mulugeta. I shall proceed as follows. Tomorrow, Monday 10th, the First Army Corps will transfer to positions farther forward than those it now occupies. On the 11th, the First Army Corps and the Third Army Corps will advance in two columns toward Antalo, south of Amba Aradam, where they will coverge.* I do not expect any enemy reaction on the first day, but this will be an action on a very large scale, indeed a tremendous scale. I shall be directing the movements

---

* To follow this maneuver, it should be explained that the Italian Air Force had thoroughly mapped Amba Aradam. Its northern face (the face that confronted Badoglio) was almost impregnable, so were its east and west faces. On the south, however, it could be penetrated by five valleys rising from the plain of Antalo. Note also that Amba Aradam was riddled with caves in which Mulugeta and his forces took shelter during the bombardment (TRANS.).

of 70,000 men." [1] Tomaselli did not take down the concluding sentences of Badoglio's speech, possibly because he could not stomach them, but fortunately for us, Luigi Barzini, Jr., did: "You will have the privilege of witnessing a tremendous, indeed a stupendous spectacle, gentlemen. We shall win this war with a campaign of the utmost brilliance, a campaign unequaled since the days of Napoleon. In less than two months, beneath the weight of our assault, you will see the Ethiopian empire crumble to dust." [2]

Only three weeks had elapsed since General Badoglio, a prey to the utmost anxiety, had stood hour after hour by the radio at his headquarters in Enda Yesus. What, then, had filled him with such overweening, almost insolent confidence? In the first place he had succeeded, by using means of which we are aware, in putting an end to the Ethiopian counteroffensive; in the second, he had reorganized his front; and thirdly, his superiority over the enemy was so overwhelming that he could take the initiative without running the slightest risk. To rid himself "of the weight of Amba Aradam," Badoglio disposed of seven divisions, 280 cannon, 170 planes and thousands of trucks that during the five days of the battle brought up 500,000 cans of meat, 150,000 cans of condensed milk, 150,000 bottles of mineral water, 990 hundredweights of jam, 500 hectolitres of cognac and anise, and 700,000 lemons to sustain the morale of the 70,000 men in the front line. This expeditionary force, the mightiest ever to take part in a colonial war, was five times larger and better equipped than the army General Baratieri had commanded at Adowa. As for Ras Mulugeta, according to the Italians who always exaggerated as a precautionary measure, he had a force of 80,000 men, 400 machine guns, 10 .47 cannon, and a few antiaircraft Oerlikons.

Before sunrise, on February 10, the First and Third Army Corps began to advance across the undulating Calamino Plain

[1] Cesco Tomaselli, *Con le colonne celeri dal Mareb allo Scioa* (Milan: Mondadori, 1936), p. 128.

[2] *Con l'esercito italiano in A.O.*, vol. 2, p. 692.

and by evening established themselves on the left bank of the Gabat. On the following day they resumed their march under torrential rain; the enemy had not yet given any signs of life.

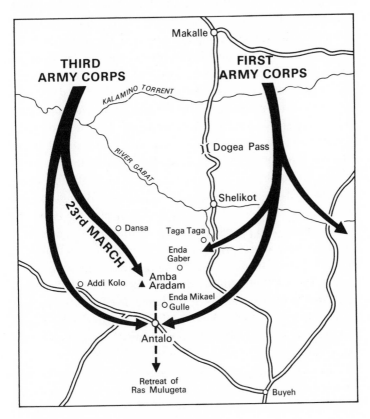

Map 6. The trap around Amba Aradam.

Badoglio, who was following the movements of the troops from Amba Gadam, turned to the war correspondents to whom he had allotted an observation post. "Well, gentlemen, are you satisfied?" he asked. "Have you a good view of what's going on? You are watching a drama that will unfold itself in several acts. This is the prologue. Our troops have made excellent

127

progress. This morning, at 0900 hours, they occupied all the forward positions.[3] On February 12, when it became clear to the Ethiopians that the Italians were executing an encircling movement, they reacted at last and launched a furious attack on the Blackshirts of the "3rd January" division on the slopes of Enda Gaber. The Ethiopians engaged the Blackshirts so heavily that they were unable to advance, and the Alpini of the Pusteria were ordered to move forward. Unfortunately for the Ethiopians, however, their onslaught, "though carried out with the greatest determination, gave no sign of any homogeneous plan or any efficient exercise of command." [4] As we know from George Steer who was reporting the war from the Ethiopian side, old Ras Mulugeta had lost his head during the first days of infernal bombing. To avoid all danger of his troops being overwhelmed by an avalanche of Ethiopians, Badoglio, even before he had launched his attack, had subjected the enemy to "a continuous and persistent air bombardment . . . comparable to the pounding, harassing artillery in the Great War . . . to affect the morale of the enemy and lower his fighting spirit. . . ." [5] During the battle of Enderta, Badoglio's 280 cannon fired 23,000 shells and his 170 planes dropped 396 tons of high explosive on Amba Aradam. Paul Gentizon of *Le Temps* was staggered by the intensity of this attack: "Throughout the entire battle, the light artillery continuously shelled the enemy. At times, 200 guns, ranging in caliber from 75 to 149 mm. pounded him simultaneously. At Enderta, the Italian Air Force furnished yet another proof of its efficacy . . . It was a tremendous advantage to the Italians that the Makalle airport was only fifteen miles from the Amba—one bomber had hardly taken off for the base than another appeared. . . ." [6]

---

[3] Cesco Tomaselli, *Con le colonne celeri*, p. 133.

[4] Pietro Badoglio, *The War in Abyssinia*, p. 82.

[5] *Ibid.*, p. 78.

[6] Paul Gentizon, *La conquête de l'Ethiopie*, pp. 55–60. The Fascist air force also managed to wipe out a good many Italian soldiers. As we learn

This kind of war was exactly suited to Badoglio's taste. It was a war carried out with twice—often four times—the strength that it called for, the swift, deadly, and effective war of a modern, industrial nation. A war of annihilation designed to prove, once and for all (and not only to the Ethiopians) that the Italians had waited far too long for their "slice of African cake" and that, impatient to enjoy it, they were not going to waste any more time. As the general conducted the battle from Amba Gedem, the eyes of all the "historians," reporters, and journalists, were fixed upon him. "A few paces from our observation post, he stood watching the development of the battle," recorded Bruno Roghi diligently. "He issued brief orders and smoked one cigarette after another. He did not remove the mosquito veiling that covered his white hair." [7] Marinetti, disdainful of facts, sought to transform Badoglio into a legendary hero and immortalize him in verse:

> *Forte un po' curva come un antico arco*
> *di guerra o meglio come una delle sue*
> *balestre d'autocarro il Maresciallo Badoglio*
> *agguante nelle lente del suo cannochiale*
> *tutta la sua battaglia.*[8]

[Mighty a little bent like the bow
of an archer or better like one of the
springs of his armored car Marshal Badoglio
watched through the lenses of his field glasses
the entire course of his battle.]

---

from General Bastico's book, *Il ferreo Terzo Corpo in A.O.* (Milan: Mondadori, 1937), p. 112, "An Italian plane dropped five bombs on a section of the 28th Medical Corps, which was almost wiped out. A hundred men were either killed or seriously wounded."

[7] Bruno Roghi, *Tessere verde in Africa Orientale*, p. 115.

[8] F. T. Marinetti: *Il poema africana*, p. 221.

On February 13 and 14, the 70,000 Italo-Eritreans halted, having reached their objectives, and in preparation for the final attack regrouped themselves, completed their lines of supply and communication, and moved their artillery to pre-arranged positions. During these two days the Ethiopians remained inert, but for two extremely violent attacks on the two battalions of the Sabaudi which held the key positions of Addi Akeiti and Addi Sembat on the left flank of the Italian army. During these attacks the Ethiopians, supported by a few detachments of cavalry, were successful at a few points, but these small gains were almost immediately wiped out by the artillery, brilliantly commanded by General Garavelli and General Pitassi-Manella. "All the might of our artillery was now displayed," noted Tomaselli. "It was so stupendous that even we were amazed. Imagine then the effect produced on the Ethiopians by this vast mass of metal." Being a scrupulously honest writer, Tomaselli added, "The Ethiopians attacked the Italians with obsolescent rifles charged with black powder and a few machine guns—hopeless. They should have hurled themselves en masse against our troops and cut them down with their scimitars; in other words, if they had fought in their traditional manner, they might have achieved much." [9]

While Ras Mulugeta in the cave on Amba Aradam that served as his headquarters was trying to puzzle out Badoglio's maneuver and halt the Italian advance, 400 kilometers to the south at Dessie the emperor was vainly attempting to coordi-

---

[9] Cesco Tomaselli, *Con le colonne celeri*, p. 137. Poorly armed as they were, however, the Ethiopians were certainly not lacking in courage and loyalty to their leaders. On p. 114 of General Bastico's book (see note 6), we read, "During the interrogation of a number of Ethiopian prisoners, an Italian officer lost his temper, and, striding up to one of them who had been wounded in three places, shouted at him in order to frighten him into speaking, that if he refused to answer the questions put to him, he would not be given any medical treatment. But the prisoner remained silent, and when the interpreter repeated what the Italian officer had said, he burst out: 'Soldier, like dog, faithful to master.'"

nate his four armies on the northern front. He had established himself and his staff in the Italian consulate, and as Stuart Emeny reported, "every morning he was up by 5:00 A.M. and usually spent half an hour in the little chapel adjoining his headquarters . . . after breakfast, he would dictate letters simultaneously to his three secretaries. The rest of the morning was taken up by audiences and almost every day he held a council of war with his closest collaborators and occasionally with some European expert." [10] Haile Selassie was informed of General Badoglio's offensive on February 11, and on the following morning, after he had spoken to Ras Mulugeta over the radiotelephone, he wired Ras Kassa, informing him of the situation and ordering him to "send with all possible speed the strongest force of his finest warriors to the aid of the ras" by launching an attack on the enemy flanks "which would force part of the Italian troops who were fighting well forward of their positions to fall back, thus relieving the pressure on Ras Mulugeta." [11] This was an excellent plan, but for some mysterious reason the telegram did not reach Ras Kassa until 2030 hours on February 15, when Ras Mulugeta had decided it was impossible to defend Amba Aradam and had given the order for a general retreat to the mountain passes of Amba Alagi. As we know, Ras Imru had no radio and was completely unaware of what was happening on the rest of the front, hence he continued his slow advance toward the Mareb, sending patrols ahead to Addi Abo, Medebai Tabor, and Addi Arbate.

While Haile Selassie was doing his utmost to bring about a concerted action on the northern front, Sir Sidney Barton, the British Ambassador in Ethiopia, sent note after note to the Foreign Office, urgently requesting that licenses be issued to Vickers and Soley Arms for the export of arms to Ethiopia. But the British government, strongly in favor of the arms

[10] *Abyssinian Stop Press*, p. 187. Emeny was the correspondent of the *News Chronicle*.

[11] Pietro Badoglio, *The War in Abyssinia*, p. 94.

embargo, only allowed very limited supplies to be sent out, and refused to provide the negus with the six airplanes he so desperately needed. It was Hitler who dispatched a massive consignment of rifles to the emperor, possibly because he had been enraged by the Fascist intervention in Austria and the stationing of two Italian divisions at the Brenner Pass. It was not until June 1937, that the British journalist, Ladislas Farago, revealed the fact that the Führer had sent arms to Ethiopia.[12] This was confirmed by the emperor himself: "Yes, we received arms from Hitler in exchange for other goods, but whether he supplied us with them to oppose Mussolini or for other reasons of his own is not clear."[13] But the Führer's rifles could not halt the advance of an army that became mightier, more dynamic day by day. Above all they did not furnish the Ethiopians with sufficient strength to continue fighting the enemy proudly face to face. It was probably the battle of Enderta that showed the emperor he was using the wrong tactics and that instead of allowing the Italians to batter him to bits, he would do far better by continually harassing them with guerrilla warfare. On February 19, when he learned of Ras Mulugeta's defeat, he ordered Ras Kassa and Ras Imru to abandon their positions in Shire and in Tembien and fall back as speedily as possible on Amba Alagi. But the order came too late, for General Badoglio, as we shall see, had succeeded in bottling up the two commanders.

But let us return to the battle, which had now reached its bloody epilogue. At 0700 hours on February 15, the Italo-Eritreans under the cover of dense cloud began to encircle Amba Aradam. At 0100 hours, however, a violent wind cleared the sky and the Ethiopians saw the full extent of the danger that threatened them. Led by Ras Gabriel Mikael and the *fitauraris* Auraris, Wolde Maryam, and Kidane, they attacked the

[12] *Sunday Chronicle* (London), June 5, 1937.
[13] In the course of my interview with the emperor.

132

enemy repeatedly during the entire day on the slopes of Addi Kolo (where Giuseppe Bottai won a silver medal for gallantry), Enda Mikael Gulla, and Edahara, but all their furious onslaughts were swiftly terminated by the barrage put up by the medium-caliber artillery and the bombing from the air. The Italians had now reached the foot of Amba Aradam, and while a few detachments of Alpini of the Pusteria and Blackshirts of the "23rd April" began to ascend it, the two Army Corps continued their encircling movement toward the rear of the Amba where they would converge. "On the right, the formidable Amba descended to the yellowish plain in a series of foothills," wrote Delio Mariotti. "On the summit of one slope, a village was ablaze. I caught glimpses of white *tukuls* and bright green pepper bushes amidst the soaring flames and the dense billows of sulphur-colored smoke. The awe-inspiring scene was violently lit up by the sun . . . the terrible Amba was finished; its doom had been sealed by the implacable maneuver of the Condottiero." [14]

Before the sun had set the battle was practically over, but owing to the "obstinate resistance encountered"—Badoglio's words—the First and Third Army Corps had not succeeded in linking up, and the Ethiopians were thus able to fall back through this gap "hurriedly and in disorder" [15] toward Amba Alagi and Sokota. There remained in the Italian dragnet only the few hundred men who had been left on Amba Aradam to cover the retreat. The task of killing off these men who had concealed themselves in the caves was allotted to the Alpini, but for political reasons, the honor of hoisting the Italian flag on Amba Aradam was given to the Blackshirts of the "23rd March." Naturally, this did nothing to improve the relations between the conscripts and volunteers; indeed, as Marshal Dante Bonaiuti told me, it led to bloodshed and the repatria-

[14] Delio Mariotti, *In armi sulle Ambe,* p. 190.
[15] Pietro Badoglio, *The War in Abyssinia,* p. 84.

133

tion of a number of men.[16] The following jingle dates back to the battle of Enderta:

> Marshal Badoglio
> Wrote to Mussolini:
> "If I'm to win in Africa
> I must have the Alpini!"

General Badoglio ordered the First and Third Army Corps to halt and entrusted the air force with the business of pursuing and finishing off the routed Ethiopian army. For four consecutive days every single plane on the northern front took part in the bombing of the hapless fugitives. "The Fifth Army was merciless," wrote Paul Gentizon. "The Italian planes made real 'aerial charges' over the hills, the fords, the tracks, on the flanks of the Ethiopian columns. In five hours they dropped forty tons of high explosives on the enemy." [17] Let us leave the last word on these "aerial charges" to General Badoglio: "At first the Ethiopians had put up a lively reaction to the action of our airmen; later, finding there was no escape, they resigned themselves to their fate, passively enduring the continuous hammering onslaught that went on without a pause from dawn till sunset. . . ." [18]

But horror was piled on horror for Ras Mulugeta's hapless army. The Azebu Galla hated the Shoan overlords who were paid and armed by the Italians (later on they were commanded by Italian officers), and ambushed the fugitives at the passes and fords and, charging them furiously on horseback, threw them into even worse confusion.[19] It was during one of

[16] Evidence given to me at Dekamere on April 4, 1965.
[17] Paul Gentizon, *La conquête de l'Ethiopie*, pp. 55–60.
[18] Pietro Badoglio, *The War in Abyssinia*, pp. 84–85.
[19] At the outset the Italians provided the Azebu Galla with 3,000 rifles, but after the battle of Enderta they increased the number to between six and seven thousand. In the various guerrilla actions on the northern front, the Azebu Galla sustained losses of 1,600 dead and 3,000 wounded.

134

these surprise attacks that Ras Mulugeta's son, who was in command of the troops at the rear, was killed (and hideously mutilated according to Galla custom). When a messenger brought him the terrible news, the old ras instantly turned back to avenge his son, but as he and his bodyguard stormed toward the Galla horde, the gunner of a low-flying plane spotted his khaki uniform, opened fire on the melee, and Mulugeta fell mortally wounded.[20] On February 19, the battle of Enderta came to an end, and Badoglio could reckon the losses both sides had sustained. The Italian casualty figures were 36 officers, 621 soldiers and 145 Eritreans killed or wounded, against 6,000 Ethiopians killed and almost twice as many wounded. On Amba Gedem, the war correspondents were addressed by General Badoglio who, as Tomaselli noted, was "extremely animated, in high good humor, and looking twenty years younger." He had to shout to make himself heard above the shriek of the cutting wind: "Amba Aradam, which weighed so heavily on my chest, is ours. If it were not covered with cloud, you would see the tricolor waving on its summit. . . ."[21]

When I visited the scene of the battle, the weather conditions were those that had prevailed on February 19, 1936. A biting wind blew on Amba Gedem, cloud enveloped the ziggurat, Amba Aradam, the mountain that has become part of our iconography. But except for these climatic coincidences, there was nothing, absolutely nothing, to recall Badoglio's first African victory. The trenches, the dry-built walls, the fortifications, the graveyards have all vanished beneath tangled thickets of thorn bushes. Indeed, the battle of Enderta is almost completely forgotten. Ask any of the young men seated at the tables of Makalle's hundred *tej-beits* * and they have never

[20] Leonard Mosley, *Haile Selassie*, p. 212.
[21] Cesco Tomaselli, *Con le colonne celeri*, p. 144.
* Ethiopian drinking houses where a particularly potent form of mead is served (TRANS.).

even heard of it. All they think about is the car they mean to buy with the money to be made in the Danakil salt trade or the contraband traffic in hard liquor. Question the old people and they stare at Amba Aradam confusedly, scratching their heads as they try in vain to recall some memory. It is well-nigh impossible, in fact, to keep records alive in a country where 90 percent of the population is illiterate, a country, moreover, where except for a couple of memorials to the fallen in Addis Ababa, nothing remains, not even an ossuary or a gravestone to mark one of the bloodiest wars in colonial history.

Chapter eleven

The Second Battle of Tembien

No sooner had he dealt with Ras Mulugeta than General Badoglio decided to liquidate the armies of Ras Kassa and Ras Seyoum (against which he had measured himself without any decisive outcome), and that of Ras Imru, which had now taken up a defensive position in Shire. "I therefore lost no time in making preparations for a second important battle . . . for the first time in colonial military history, there were to be employed simultaneously, in a general attack, five corps on a front 250 kilometers long. . . ."[1] In plain figures Badoglio had an army of 200,000 men, whereas the combined armies of the three rases only totaled 60,000. The Ethiopian forces, moreover, had already been hard tried in battle, their supply lines poorly organized, and their medical services exiguous. If at the time when Badoglio assumed the command his

[1] Pietro Badoglio, *The War in Abyssinia*, pp. 98–99.

superiority in men and means had been striking, it was now overwhelming. Not only had the extra divisions he had asked for been sent out, but he had had time to complete the network of roads for his lines of supply and communication. He was able, for example, to assemble at Hauzen with the greatest rapidity for the second battle of Tembien alone, 48,000 shells and 7 million rounds for small arms.

As his opening move, the general decided to attack Ras Kassa and Ras Seyoum in Tembien and, to ensure the annihilation of their armies, dispatched the Third Army Corps toward Gaela to cut off Ras Kassa's principal line of retreat. Once it had established itself in this position, Badoglio had only to move the Eritrean Corps southward from the Warieu and Abaro passes to close the trap. Ras Kassa, however, sensed Badoglio's intentions; accordingly, as Colonel Konovaloff tells us, "he sent a wireless message to the emperor asking for leave to withdraw from Tembien, which he regarded as a death trap." [2] As the negus (convinced, as has been said, of the futility of meeting the enemy face to face) had several times ordered him to fall back to the Alagi Pass and link up with the survivors of Ras Mulugeta's army, this request was superfluous. But something—what, we do not know—made Ras Kassa change his mind. The wireless messages between Haile Selassie and Ras Kassa, messages intercepted and decoded by Badoglio's brilliant intelligence service, and which appear in mutilated form in his book, afford no clue.[3] What we do know is that on the morning of February 27, when the Eritrean Corps came down from the mountains and the Third Army Corps issued from the valley of the Geba, both Ras Kassa and Ras Seyoum were ready to confront them, their armies drawn up in battle formation. On this same morning, a hot, sunny morning in East Africa, thousands of miles away, in Turin, a group of anti-Fascists that included Augusto

[2] Konovaloff, *Con le armate del negus*, p. 115.
[3] Pietro Badoglio, *The War in Abyssinia*, pp. 92–97.

Monti, Vittorio Foa, Michele Giua, and Massimo Mila, appeared before a special tribunal. All were sentenced to long terms of imprisonment, for Tringali, the Chief Judge, had been subjected to pressure from Mussolini, who found it intolerable that in the midst of the war when all eyes were fixed on

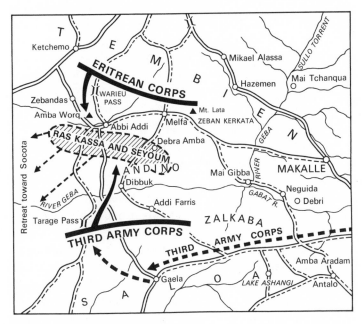

Map 7. The second battle of Tembien.

Italy, dissident intellectuals dared to murmur and conspire against the regime.

The second battle of Tembien was fought in country that was rugged and difficult to a degree, a region of forests, torrents, and ravines, where small tracts of level land alternated with rocky pinnacles. It was the sort of country, in fact, that favored the defending force. On the right flank of the Ethiopian armies was Amba Worq, the "mountain of gold," a solid bastion on which the Ethiopians had established a garrison and had even hauled up a cannon. Amba Worq blocked the road to Abbi Addi where the Third Corps and the Eritrean Corps were to converge, hence, in order to initiate their encircling movement, it was vital for the Italians to take it. Under cover of darkness, 150 Alpini and Blackshirt rock climbers, armed with grenades and knives, were entrusted with the immensely difficult and dangerous task of scaling the peak. They found the Ethiopians sound asleep when they reached the summit, flung their grenades among them and routed them completely. This brilliant exploit were kept alive by the traditional storytellers of Tigre:

> Amba Worq, Amba Worq, Mountain of Gold,
> When Mussolini's warriors climbed to your peak
> The Ethiopians fell like leaves.[4]

By daybreak of February 27, the Italians had captured the northern peak of the Amba, and two strong columns of Eritreans, leaving the protection of the Warieu Pass, had already made their way around the mountain and were pushing on toward Zebandas and Worrega. At about 0800 hours the wail of horns, the roll of the *negarait*, the war drum, filled the air, when suddenly and unexpectedly, thousands of Ethiopians armed with rifles, the regulars in khaki, the irregulars in white *shammas*, burst out of the dense woods covering the slopes of Debra Ansa and flung themselves at the Italians. "From that moment until four in the afternoon, wave after wave of Ethiopians made desperate attempts to break the line of the Alpini and Blackshirts," wrote Tomaselli. "The first to fall on our troops were the irregulars, who were sent forward under cover of the fire of the regulars. Armed with cudgels and scimitars, they hurled themselves with mad frenzy on our machine guns. At times, the Italian line wavered dramatically, but the Ethio-

---

[4] Quoted by Bruno Roghi in *Con l'esercito italiano in A.O.*, p. 37.

pians were driven back by bayonet charges and it was once more stabilized. Only a few meters of ground separated the combatants." [5] The aim of the Ethiopians was to encircle the attacking columns and, as we know from General Badoglio, they counterattacked with such overwhelming fury that they succeeded in reaching the outworks of the Warieu Pass, compelling General Pirzio Birolli who was in command of the Eritrean Corps, to throw in all his reserves. At this moment, as Badoglio admitted, "the situation was delicate." [6] Mowed down by machine guns, pounded by artillery, hammered relentlessly by bombers that dropped 195 tons of high explosive on the Ethiopian positions, Ras Seyoum's warriors, with their futile "clubs and scimitars," continued to fling themselves into this inferno of fire, and it was not until evening when they in turn were threatened with encirclement, that they withdrew. They left behind them a thousand dead, among them *Dejatch* Mashasha Woldie and *Dejatch* Beyene, who was killed as he spurred his white charger into the thick of the melee.

Once his right flank had collapsed, Ras Seyoum ordered his forces to retreat toward Amba Ambara in the hope of reaching the Takkaze fords and extricating himself from the meshes of General Badoglio's dragnet. Band after band of his men managed to slip through, but they were instantly spotted from the air and mercilessly bombed. From Alessandro Pavolini, who was in one of the bombers, comes this description of the massacre: "The Ethiopians straggled along in disorder. There was only one road open to them, and the fords were so narrow, the rocky walls of the ravines so precipitous that they were soon jammed together in a solid mass. Even though we were flying at 1,000 meters, we could see them quite plainly. Our plane swooped down, zigzagged along the defile, sowed its seeds of death and zoomed upward." [7]

[5] Cesco Tomaselli, *Con le colonne celeri*, p. 171.
[6] Pietro Badoglio, *The War in Abyssinia*, p. 106.
[7] *Corriere della Sera* (Milan), March 3, 1936.

While Ras Seyoum was retreating beneath a hailstorm of bombs, Ras Kassa, who had established himself on Debra Amba and had not yet been engaged in action, decided to obey the emperor's orders and withdraw from Tembien. Now it was his turn to be heavily bombed as he fell back toward the Geba and the caravan trail leading to Sokota. Nevertheless, when at midday on February 29, the Eritrean columns that had been fiercely attacked by the Ethiopian rearguard at Manwe, Debra Amba, and Amba Tzellere, linked up with the Third Army Corps at a point three kilometers west of Addi Abbi, some 200,000 men of the armies of Ras Kassa and Ras Seyoum had escaped encirclement. But they were so demoralized—the last straw had been a mustard-gas attack at the Takkaze fords—that as a fighting force they were finished. As Colonel Konovaloff who was with Ras Kassa wrote: "Our retreat southward filled them with the hope that they would reach Shoa where so many of them had been born and where they would at last be able to forget the agony of the long forced march, the horrors of the air bombardment, the deadly rattle of machine guns. . . ." [8] Home—this was now their one thought, but as the two armies moved on toward the south and safety, their ranks thinned out dangerously. So much so, indeed, that when Ras Kassa and Ras Seyoum reached the emperor's headquarters at Quoram after two-weeks' march, they were virtually alone.

The Ethiopian army, which had held its positions for five long months and had vainly tried to counter two massive offensives, was now beginning to disintegrate. Haile Selassie made no attempt to hide the gravity of the situation. In a letter to Ras Imru, he wrote: "Our army, famous throughout Europe for its valor, has lost its name; brought to ruin by a few traitors, to this pass it is reduced . . . those who were the first to betray us, and those who followed their example, namely the chiefs of the Wollo forces, such as Ras Gabriel, *Dejatch*

[8] Konovaloff, *Con le armate del negus*, pp. 143–44.

Amedieh Ali and others, also of the Shoan army, namely *Dejatch* Auraris and *Dejatch* Belaineh, have all been arrested . . . Ras Kassa and Ras Seyoum are with us, but have not a single armed man with them. . . ." In conclusion, he asked Ras Imru to "come and die with us" in the battle he was determined to fight against the Italians, the battle that was to lead to the final defeat of the Ethiopians on the northern front.[9] His is the tragic letter of a man on the verge of desperation, a man who had held out for five months against an enemy infinitely more powerful than himself in the hope that the League of Nations and the democratic countries would come to his aid, who now found himself alone, betrayed even by his own chiefs who went over to the enemy for money, or who left him to his fate because they had formerly been his rivals, or simply because they were utterly base. The emperor's letter to Ras Imru is the key to the battle of Mai Chew, the battle he should never have fought, the battle he insisted on commanding in person in the vain hope of winning back the former fame and glory of his army.

By the evening of February 29 when the two corps had completed their encircling movement, the second battle of Tembien was virtually over. But the few thousand trapped Ethiopians put up fierce resistance at Mount Andino, at Enda Maryam Quarar, and Dibbuk that lasted till March 6 and roused even General Badoglio's admiration: "Occasionally, small parties of the enemy established in the caves still offered some resistance; others attempted to wrest a passage toward the south by force of arms, preferring death in battle to surrender, thus showing once again the high, warlike virtues of their race." [10] When the losses could be assessed, those of

[9] Pietro Badoglio, *The War in Abyssinia*, p. 143.

[10] *Ibid.*, p. 108. Marshal Badoglio's tribute to the courage of the Ethiopians contrasts sharply with General Bastico's gratuitous insults. On page 135 of the general's book, he calls the Ethiopian soldiers "black devils," and on page 141, "ape-headed monsters." At his most moderate, he refers to them as "brutal herds" or "savage hordes" (pp. 226–27).

the Ethiopians were, as usual, ten times as numerous as those of the Italians. Their casualties were 8,000 killed or wounded; the Italian figures were 34 officers, 359 nationals and 188 Eritreans killed or wounded.

The news of this new victory, together with the announcement that the First Army Corps had occupied Amba Alagi on February 28, threw the Italian people into a delirium of delight that recalled the early days of the war when Adowa, Axum, and Makalle had been taken. Huge headlines ran right across the front page of the newspapers, and whole pages were devoted to Toselli's heroic but ill-fated stand. Furthermore, March 1 was the fortieth anniversary of the defeat at Adowa, and the coincidence of brilliant Italian victories on this day of all days (it was hardly a coincidence, however, since Mussolini had intimated to Badoglio that unless he brought off some glittering coup he would be replaced by Graziani) provided the propaganda machine with first-class material. Thanks to the might of the Fascist regime, the dead of Adowa were at long last avenged. It was the occasion for the aged poet of Vittoriale, Gabriele D'Annunzio, to reappear on the scene. In the long flowery message he sent to Mussolini, he wrote: "All praise to you, oh Leader, who so unexpectedly made yourself the Head of a headless Italy, you who are restoring Rome to Italy as was preordained. . . . On this day, the entire nation draws a profound breath. All things are quickened, all things are animated. What I hear is the panting of destiny. It is the destiny with its own lungs, its own pleura, of our mighty nation." [11] Even the fabled, detached, and remote Vincenzo Cardarelli was intoxicated by the sweet incense of victory and sent this poem to a Turin daily:

> *Terra negata ai padri,*
> *promessa ai figli, faticata Etiopia,*

[11] *Gazzetta del Popolo*, March 1, 1936.

tu non potrai piú oltre
fuggire il tuo destino,
troppo e sí lungamente
legato al nostro.[12]

[Land denied to our fathers,
promised to our sons, battle-worn Ethiopia,
you can no longer
escape your destiny
bound so closely for so many years
to our own.]

As for General Badoglio, on March 1 he was radiant. The war correspondents saw him sitting outside his tent at Addi Quala "serene, his eyes half closed." He might have been a farmer on a Sunday afternoon surveying his land to see how many of his crops were ripe for harvesting," wrote Tomaselli. He "smiled benevolently" at the correspondents, beckoned them forward, and said euphorically, "The curtain has fallen on the second act, gentlemen. Now we must think of the third. The enemy has suffered such a shattering defeat that for the first time in his history he has lost all desire to go on fighting." [13] But despite this "shattering defeat," the Ethiopians celebrated the fortieth anniversary of Menelik's victory at Adowa in Addis Ababa. Two of the *shumbashis* who had organized the flight of the 904 Askaris from the southern front, harangued the crowd and whipped it up to a patriotic fever. The ceremony, however, was mainly of a religious nature, and ended with an exhortation by the Abuna who ordered: "All of you, great and small, men as well as women, must fast for a week, from Wednesday to the following Wednesday. During that week you must eat nothing but bread,

[12] *Ibid.*, February 29, 1936.
[13] Cesco Tomaselli, *Con le colonne celeri*, pp. 165–66.

drink nothing but water. No *talla*,* no *arak*, no meat, no eggs —nothing but bread and water must pass your lips." [14] While Rome and Addis Ababa were celebrating the victories of the present and past, Hitler decided to reoccupy the Rhineland, the first of his territorial grabs in the series that was to lead to World War II. Seven days later, when the troops of the *Wehrmacht* crossed the frontier to the alarm and consternation of all the chancelleries of Europe, the Italo-Ethiopian War became a secondary consideration, and, immersed in European problems, the League of Nations, which had done so little for Haile Selassie, more or less abandoned him to his fate.

March 1, 1936—in a little over two months, the Italo-Ethiopian War would be over. One by one, the emperor's armies were being wiped out, and another was soon to be added to the list, for on February 29, Badoglio had begun the third of his great battles of annihilation, and launched his attack on Ras Imru's forces in Shire. The Italian people thirsted for the blood of Ras Imru, for naturally the press had made a big splash of the terrible story that on February 13, he had incited his men to massacre 68 Italian laborers and overseers of the Gondrand building firm that had a yard at Utok Emme, a few kilometers from the Eritrean frontier. During the course of my interview with Ras Imru, I asked him if this allegation was true. "Yes, I gave *Fitaurari* Tesfai the order to fall on their camp at Mai Lahla," he told me. "I felt, and still feel, that this was a legitimate act of war because all these men were armed with rifles. Indeed, they defended themselves fiercely and inflicted heavy casualties on us. At least they had the means of defense whereas our people were unable to strike back when they were bombed and decimated by the Fascist air force." [15]

The emperor, who was determined to respect the international conventions of the League of Nations because he whole-

* Native beer (TRANS.).

[14] See article by Pierre Itchac in *l'Illustration*, p. 175.

[15] Information given me by Ras Imru when I interviewed him.

heartedly supported them and because it was in his own interests to adhere to them, thoroughly disapproved of this incident. In a declaration he made in July 1936, when he was an exile in London, he sought to explain what had motivated it: "Any prisoners we took we treated as guests, and the enemy might have cited to his troops the case of two of their soldiers picked up by our men in the Ogaden desert while the war was in full swing, and sent at the expense of our government to French Somaliland. Instead, he chose to quote an exceptional case when a few of our troops whose wives and children had been atrociously burned by mustard gas, revenged themselves on the brutal enemy by attacking and killing a gang of Italian laborers whose camp was situated between the Mareb and Daro Takle." [16] In reality the only crimes of violence that could be laid at the door of the race that had been depicted as the most barbarous on earth, a race that would stop at nothing in its blind fury, a race that was incapable of respecting international conventions, were the massacre at Mai Lahla, the murder and mutilation of the two air force pilots, Minniti and Zannoni [17] (the work, not of Ethiopian regulars but of nomad Somalis), and the occasional use of dum-dum bullets (most of the bullets alleged to be dum-dums were, in fact, the soft-nosed lead bullets of the

---

[16] *Une victoire de la civilisation*, p. 31.

[17] On p. 243 of *Caesar in Abyssinia*, George Steer wrote that Flight Lt. Minniti was "killed, decapitated and mutilated; his head was taken by the Somalis to Daggahbur as the proof of their loyalty to Ethiopia." In three notes to the secretary-general of the League of Nations, the Italians stated that in addition to Minniti, the Ethiopians had tortured and mutilated some fifty Italian, Somali, and Eritrean prisoners of war. When the emperor was questioned on the subject of these alleged atrocities, he said, "I will not stoop to discuss such acts of barbarity; they seldom occur, but when they do, the guilty men are punished with the utmost severity. Equally, I will not lower myself by dwelling on the atrocities carried out on the orders of Italian officers: the execution of wounded soldiers, the head men of villages crucified on trees with carpenters' nails driven through their wrists and feet, the blinding of women and children with mustard gas. Rather than go into detail about all these horrors, let me describe what has been defined as our

obsolete Gras rifles).[18] Moreover, for each outrage perpetrated
or said to have been perpetrated by the Ethiopians, the Italians carried out indiscriminate reprisals. For the heads of
Minniti and Zannoni, Graziani tells us that "we immediately
carried out a gas attack to terrorize the population."[19] In view
of these methods, it is hard to believe that ours was a civilizing
mission. It is even harder to credit it when we read this gem of
crassness and brutality penned by D'Annunzio: "Today, every
Italian cartridge means the death of an Ethiopian. The whole
jagged summit of Ethiopia must inexorably become a plateau
of Latin culture."[20]

'barbarity.' We were so 'barbarous' that when Italian planes crashed in our
lines, we buried the dead airmen in the cemeteries of our churches. Toward
the middle of February 1936, we shot down an Italian plane near Lake Haik.
I sent an official to represent me at their funeral and they were buried with
full military honors in the cemetery of the tiny church of Kidane Mehrat."
(See *Une victoire de la civilisation*, p. 28.)

[18] In a series of telegrams, dated December 17, 20, and 22, 1935, the
Italians informed the League of Nations that the Ethiopians made constant
use of dum-dum bullets. Photographs of these bullets were sent to Geneva,
together with the information that they had been supplied by Eley Bros. and
Kynoch Ltd. In reply to this smear, the British government stated categori-
cally that these two firms had never supplied Ethiopia with any such
criminal ammunition. Subsequently, the Italian government discovered that
it had based its accusation on a telegram that had been cunningly altered by
the scurrilous Colonel Pedro Lopez, alias Henry Lawrence Bernstein. Lopez
had managed to get hold of a telegram from Addis Ababa addressed to an
Ethiopian agent in London. It was an order for ten million cartridges for
light and heavy machine guns and for the appropriate ammunition, half of
which was to be delivered in *clips of five*. Lopez-Bernstein had altered this
to "half of which to be clipped." While this accusation intended to blacken
both Great Britain and Ethiopia proved to be false, the fact remains the
Ethiopians used a certain number of dum-dum bullets on both fronts.

[19] Rodolfo Graziani, *Fronte Sud*, p. 220.

[20] *Gazzetta del Popolo*, March 1, 1936.

Chapter twelve

The Battle
of Shire

February 26, 1936, was a black day for Ras Imru, the only
commander on the northern front who had not suffered defeat.
From messengers who had ridden with hot haste from the
Takkaze valley, he learned that Ras Kassa had been routed
and was retreating southward in utter disorder. Shortly before
the arrival of these messengers, he had received a long and
heartbreaking letter from the emperor, ordering him to withdraw from Shire before the enemy sprung his trap. The terrible tidings of Ras Kassa's defeat overwhelmed Ras Imru who,
with immense difficulty, had reached the Eritrean frontier,
kept the Italians bottled up for two months in the fortified
camps of Adowa and Axum, and established his advance-
guards as far as Mai Lahla, only 40 kilometers from Adowa.
To draw up a plan that would enable him to avoid the threatened encirclement, Ras Imru immediately summoned his
chiefs to a council of war; among them was Ayelu Birru who,

he was aware, was in communication with the enemy,[1] and he suspected had a hand in the revolt that had flared up in Ras Imru's province of Gojjam.[2] At the council of war, it was decided that strong contingents of regulars should remain on the heights of Semama, Addi Haimanal, and Selaclaca to cover the orderly retreat of the main body of the army, some 20,000 strong, the cattle and baggage trains, to the Takkaze.

Badoglio knew nothing of these plans, but expected to take Ras Imru by surprise and annihilate his army in the last of the great battles in Tigre. To carry out this action he brought in the Second Army Corps, commanded by General Maravigna, and the Fourth Army Corps, commanded by General Babbini. He thus could disposition 47,000 men, a force more than double that of Ras Imru. In addition his striking power was colossal compared with that of the Ethiopians who had neither artillery nor planes. Badoglio's plan was as follows: the Second Army Corps was to advance from its entrenched positions at Axum and launch the attack on the enemy, while the Fourth Army Corps, which was in the Mareb sector and would therefore have to cover far more ground in its advance through an almost unexplored, extremely difficult region, was to exert its pressure on the left flank and rear of the Ethiopian army, a pressure that would grow increasingly greater as the distance between the two forces lessened. This maneuver, whose preliminary phase was carried out as the battle of Enderta raged and the First Army Corps pushed on beyond the Alagi

---

[1] In *La guerra dei sette mesi* (Milan: Longanesi, 1965), Luigi Pignatelli writes, "The *dejatch* was, indeed, in correspondence with Colonel Talamonti, an officer who had a profound knowledge of Ethiopia, and despite the fact that Ayelu Birru's messages were ambiguous, it was obvious that the Ethiopians could place no reliance in him." (See p. 198).

[2] In January 1936, a revolt had broken out in Gojjam; the Italians helped to spread it by dropping arms to the rebels. On March 2 and 3, a few planes dropped cartridges and messages to the insurgents in the zone between Zarabruk and Benenned. (See *Cronache illustrate dell'azione italiana in A.O.*, pp. 262–63.)

passes, was a triumph for General Fidenzio Dall'Ora, who demonstrated his truly superb ability by wringing out of the port of Massawa the staggering amount of supplies needed for five army corps on the move.[3]

At dawn on February 29, General Maravigna and his force of 20,000 men left Axum and began to advance toward Selaclaca. The sky was cloudless, the terrain not too difficult and, according to intelligence, there were no enemy concentrations in the Selaclaca zone. Maravigna decided to make full use of the one existing motor road and, after taking the usual security measures to cover his movement, proceeded in formation with the divisions echeloned in depth—an imprudent course for which he was severely censured by Badoglio.[4] The long column was headed by the "21st April," followed by the Gavinana, the Gran Sasso, the Second Eritrean Brigade, and a few detachments of Spahis. All went well until midday. When the column reached the crossroads at Akab Saat, the "21st April" veered left and established itself on the surrounding heights; the Gavinana, however, continued its advance toward Selaclaca. But it had barely begun its descent into the valley than it was suddenly caught in a deadly cross-fire. It was now 1200 hours. The furious battle that ensued continued without a break till midnight. "If General Maravigna had taken the precaution of sending out patrols on the flanks of the column, we should probably not have been taken by surprise," General Dante Bonaiuti told me, "but he did not do so and we advanced as if we were on an exercise. Consequently, the Ethiopians who were hidden in the bushes fell upon us without warning and, covered by the fire of their machine guns on the

---

[3] General Dall'Ora had an entire army at his disposal: 2,500 officers, 50,000 men, 40,000 pack animals and 10,000 motor vehicles. By December 1, 1935, he had assembled on the plateau 2,003,670 shells, 291,980,270 cartridges for small arms, and 785,440 grenades, in all 29,771 tons of ammunition. Toward the middle of the war, he succeeded in provisioning 350,000 troops and 90,000 laborers, as well as 70,000 pack animals.

[4] Pietro Badoglio, *The War in Abyssinia*, p. 115.

151

slopes of Addi Haimanal, hurled themselves upon us. All we could do was form a square and, under a hailstorm of lead, our artillerymen began to set up and load the guns with feverish haste. The Ethiopians were mainly armed with 77-87 rifles that

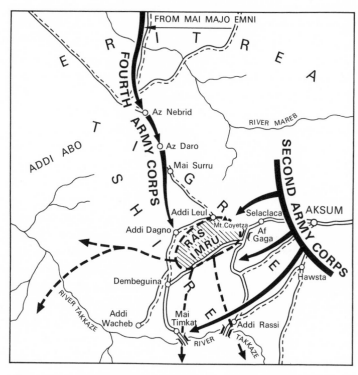

Map 8. The battle of Shire.

even predated our old Mannlichers, but they were crack shots and they soon inflicted heavy casualties on us. We were fighting at such close quarters that when the guns opened up, they had to be fired point-blank, killing our men as well the enemy." [5] This engagement in which the combatants were

[5] Information given to me during an interview.

almost equal in number and separated by only a few meters of ground (the sort of engagement Badoglio dreaded) lasted ten hours. Thousands of Ras Imru's men broke through to the road intending to capture the trucks loaded with ammunition and provisions. "We found Ethiopians who had been sawed in two by machine-gun bullets," a wounded officer told Luigi Barzini, Jr. "They threw themselves on the guns as though they could silence them. Their courage was unbelievable, they were utterly oblivious of danger. I saw a shell explode in the midst of a group of fifteen; ten men fell, but the remaining five never even noticed and rushed on frenziedly." [6]

Shaken by this ambush and possibly overestimating the strength of the enemy, General Maravigna made a second mistake: he ordered the First Corps to halt and assume a defensive position, hence it failed to reach the prearranged objectives for that day. And on the next morning, still judging his position to be critical, Maravigna was compelled to request Badoglio (who was furious) for his "authority to postpone action till the following day." [7] The immobilization of the First Corps for forty-eight hours crowned Ras Imru's maneuver with a wholly unexpected success that enabled the main body of his army to continue its orderly retreat toward the Takkaze. On March 2, the Italo-Eritreans resumed the advance toward their objective, the massif of Mount Coietza, but again they made little progress for they were violently attacked by the second force of Ethiopian regulars who were covering Ras Imru's retreat. Badoglio raged at this further holdup. "Between 1300 and 1700 hours," he wrote in his book, "the enemy set up a very determined resistance and attempted a counterattack in force, made by regulars and supported by numerous automatic weapons." [8] As usual the Italians, in order to beat them back, were obliged to pound them with all the

---

[6] *Con l'esercito italiano in A.O.*, vol. 2, pp. 406–7.
[7] Pietro Badoglio, *The War in Abyssinia*, p. 116.
[8] *Ibid.*, p. 117.

weight of their artillery and hammer them from the air.[9] "Bands of Ethiopians were surrounded but refused to surrender," wrote Paul Gentizon, "A number of them who had taken refuge in a cave were told through an interpreter that their lives would be spared if they laid down their arms, but they scorned the offer and fought on till the last." [10]

When dawn broke March 3, the area was clear of the enemy and Maravigna was left in a complete void, for despite the fact that the Second Corps had been forced to a standstill for two days, the Fourth Army Corps, which should have threatened "the left flank and rear" of Ras Imru's army, was still fifty kilometers away at Az Daro. When Luigi Abbove, an Allessandrian, reached the scene of battle on the morning of March 3, with a supply column, the only Ethiopians he saw were those killed during the engagement; their corpses were being cremated by chemical-warfare squads with flamethrowers.[11] The two corps had failed to close the trap, and the few hundred Ethiopians of the covering force who had hidden themselves in the caves, had to be driven out one by one. "The battle had been brought to a completely successful termination," Badoglio wrote in his book, ". . . even though the Second Army Corps had not succeeded in acting as rapidly, decisively, and thoroughly as would have been desirable." [12] The truth was the men of the Second Corps had fought with the greatest courage and their commanding officers were entirely to blame for the fact that, from the opening shots fired on February 29 till the evening of March 2, the covering forces of Ras Imru had it all their own way. "I recall the battle of Shire as the toughest the Italians ever fought, owing to the

[9] On page 95 of *La conquête de l'Ethiopie*, Paul Gentizon wrote, "To give an idea of the massive artillery barrage, when evening fell on March 2, the Second Army Corps, during the two days of the battle, had fired 40,000 shells and used 8 million cartridges for their machine guns and rifles."

[10] Paul Gentizon, *La conquête de l'Ethiopie*, p. 93.

[11] This evidence was given to me April 5, 1965, when I was in Dekamere.

[12] Pietro Badoglio, *The War in Abyssinia*, p. 119.

strategic qualities of Ras Imru and the tenacity of his men," wrote Paul Gentizon, "they suffered far heavier casualties in this battle than in any other. Their losses, killed or wounded, were 63 officers, 894 Italians, and 12 Eritreans." [13] The Ethiopians left 4,000 killed or wounded on the battlefield; for the first time, their losses instead of being ten to one were reduced to a mere four to one.

But the battle was not yet over, and the Ethiopian casualties were soon to rise to the usual disproportionate figure. Because the main body of Ras Imru's army had escaped, Badoglio doubted the sorely tried Second Corps would be in a fit state to pursue the enemy and, unable to make use of the Fourth Corps, which did not reach Selaclaca till the evening of March 5, he ordered the air force to carry on the battle, using all the means at its disposal. On March 3 and 4, pursuit planes and bombers zoomed over Ras Imru's army, which had reached the Takkaze fords and was within a short distance of the wild, mountainous, labyrinthine region of Tsellemti. The Fascist Air Force began by dropping eighty tons of high explosive on the Ethiopians, then, to make their work of destruction even more complete, they resorted for the first time to "small incendiary bombs." The densely wooded slopes of the Takkaze valley were enveloped in a sheet of flame and, as Badoglio says, "the plight of the fleeing enemy became utterly tragic." [14] But while he mentions the incendiary bombs, he remains, as usual, silent on the use of gas; he does not refer to the massive attacks the Italians made with mustard gas and asphyxiating gases on the fords of Mai Timkat, Addi Rassi, and Chelachekanew. Speaking of the terrible end of Ras Imru's defeated army, the emperor said, "We flung ourselves on the machine-gun nests to clear them out, we hurled ourselves against the enemy We held firm against their bombs and their containers of

---

[13] Paolo Cesarini provided me with much useful evidence.
[14] Pietro Badoglio, *The War in Abyssinia*, p. 118.

artillery. We put their tanks out of action with our bare hands. mustard gas. We cannot reproach ourselves with any taint of cowardice. But against the invisible rain of deadly gas that splashed down on our hands, our faces, we could do nothing. Yet I say again that we have no cause to be ashamed: we could not 'kill' this rain." [15] The Italian pilots who swooped down almost to ground level to carry out their last mission, that of machine-gunning the survivors (25,000 rounds were fired) "observed vast numbers of Ethiopian dead on the north bank of the Takkaze and countless bodies of men and beasts floating on the river." [16] When the Italo-Eritreans crossed the Takkaze after this massacre, they found the caravan routes "littered with thousands of corpses in an advanced state of putrefaction." [17]

Many years have elapsed since the Battle of Shire, but when Ras Imru related the facts to me with sober precision, there were moments when he could not conceal his emotion. "I succeeded in leading some 10,000 of my men across the river to safety," he told me, "But they were so demoralized that I could no longer hold them together. It had been my intention to carry on a guerrilla war in the mountainous regions of Tsellemti and Semien, ideally suited to such tactics, but when I told *Dejatch* Ayelu Birru, one of my few surviving chiefs, of my plan, he would have nothing to do with it and, with his brother Admasu, made his way to Begemder. Day by day my ranks thinned out; many were killed in the course of air attacks, many deserted. When at last I reached Dashan, all that remained of my army was my personal bodyguard of 300 men." [18] But even though Ras Imru had put a hundred kilometers between himself and the Takkaze, his tragic Odyssey was not yet over. An Italian pilot flying very low "spotted him, still

[15] *Une victoire de la civilisation*, pp. 37–39.
[16] *Cronache illustrate dell'azione italiana in A.O.*, p. 163.
[17] *Ibid.*, p. 263.
[18] Part of the story Ras Imru told me during my interview with him.

wearing his smart uniform" [19] and the gunner opened fire on him; fortunately, he escaped to the cover of some bushes. From then on, however, he was forced to leave the beaten track, and it was only under cover of darkness that he was able to resume his retreat along devious routes among a people who were growing sick of the war, who had had almost as much as they could stand in the way of air raids, and the depredations of bands of demoralized soldiers. "It was a matter of extreme urgency to contact the emperor," Ras Imru continued, "I therefore made for Dabat where there was a telephone, but as I approached the town, I realized the Italians were already at its gates. I decided to march to Gondar, but found that this town, too, had fallen to the enemy—it was only by a hair's-breadth that I escaped capture. I had no choice left but to march on to Debra Markos. Continually attacked by rebels from Gojjam, paid and armed by the Italians, it took me a month to get there, and when I did arrive, it was only to learn that the emperor had left Addis Ababa for Jibouti and that the capital was on the point of falling. I rounded up a thousand men, and prepared to fight a guerrilla war." [20]

Now that he had defeated Ras Imru's army, the gates of Ethiopia were open to Badoglio, all, that is, save one, the gate of the capital still held by the emperor with what remained of his hapless army. During the month of March, when the First Army Corps pushed on beyond the Alagi passes as far as Mai Chew, Badoglio occupied the whole of the northern regions now open and virtually undefended, and dispatched a number

[19] Episode referred to by Renzo Martinelli in *Con l'esercito italiano in A.O.*, p. 412.

[20] As Luigi Pignatelli states on p. 211 of his book, "This vast operation would have been impossible but for various favorable factors: the collaboration of certain chiefs and dignitaries, detailed knowledge of the ground that was to be covered, etc." Jacopo Gasparini, a former governor of Eritrea, played the leading political part in the preparations for the maneuver, as he had been in contact for years with many Ethiopian chiefs, particularly those who nursed grudges against the central government.

of flying columns on an arc of 600 kilometers to occupy Gondar, Debarak, Sokota, and Sardo. This operation, a vast, systematic, and successful maneuver, was carried out smoothly, and met with little opposition. (The only casualties sustained by Starace's column during the famous "March on Gondar" and the two months following, were nine men killed and nine men wounded.) The operation added a further 100,000 square kilometers to the territory already under Italian control. At the same time, Marshal Badoglio reorganized his front. A complete network of roads was constructed; supply bases were established as far forward as possible; a prudent defensive system of two lines of entrenched camps was created to protect the main lines of communication; bands of Azebu Galla and Raya Galla were paid and armed; and the main forces were reconstituted and distributed to meet the requirements of the new situation.

We have now come to the final act of the drama. Except for the emperor's army, still intact and completely loyal, the four armies that had originally faced the Italians on the northern front had all been routed and a number of chiefs, among them *Dejatch* Amare Gabre Selassie, Hailu Tesfai, and Beite Hagos went over to the enemy with their men. The Ethiopian treasury was empty and there was a desperate shortage of arms. The League of Nations had so little interest left in Ethiopia that it did not even take the trouble to study in depth the proposals for a negotiated peace put forward by the Committee of Thirteen, but allowed them to founder. Sickened, Léon Blum commented, "So it's finished. No one can read the resolution of the League of Nations without an aching heart, without blushing with shame. The League of Nations no longer condemns the Fascist act of aggression; the League 'notes,' the League 'does thus and thus,' the League 'deplores' —the League makes a hypocritical show of balancing the scales justly between the criminal and his victim, whether it is dealing with the breakdown of conciliatory measures or with

the contravention of the rules of war. Even more intolerable
are the lies concealed in these formulae, and what can be read
between the lines: the League's confession of impotence, its
abject surrender, its acceptance of the fait accompli. In short,
Ethiopia has been warned that she can no longer depend on
the League of Nations." [21]

On March 23, Mussolini, confident that he had triumphed
even in Geneva, addressed the nation from the balcony of the
Palazzo Venezia: "The sky is not yet absolutely clear, but no
matter; I tell you here and now that the few remaining clouds
must be and will be rapidly dispersed." [22] The Italians, who
had been preoccupied with anxiety for their expeditionary
force and the dread that their country might find itself at war
with Great Britain, breathed more freely, began to smile
again. In Turin, on the very eve of the decisive battle of Mai
Chew, Mario Casalegno's company opened at the Rossini The-
atre with a comedy entitled *Da Mongardino ad Addis Ababa.*
And when the song "Little Black Face" had been banned
because it was out of line with the new racist principles of the
regime, the people sang:

> Selassie, hear the trumpets
> That herald two that you know,
> Two brothers fearless, full of fire,
> Sons worthy of a mighty sire,
> Vittorio and Bruno!

As March drew to a close, Badoglio was left with one
agonizing question—would the emperor attack or would he
fall back toward Dessie or even farther south, forcing him to
engage in a decisive battle hundreds of kilometers from his
bases? "My doubt had increased every day as I remembered

---

[21] See the article "L'Histoire jugera," April 22, 1936.
[22] Benito Mussolini, *Scritti e discorsi dell'Impero*, p. 67.

his repeated recommendations to the rases not to give battle but to restrict themselves to guerrilla action on the lines of communications," wrote the marshal in his memoirs.[23] Badoglio had every cause for concern. If the emperor retreated, he would be compelled to lengthen his supply lines to a perilous extent and precious weeks would be lost, the last few weeks before the start of the rainy season. In this event the war that he counted on bringing to a triumphant conclusion in a couple of months might well continue for another year, the time foreseen, incidentally, by most foreign military experts. We can imagine Badoglio's relief, therefore, when he learned on March 21 that the negus had reached the Agumberta Pass to take command of the last Ethiopian army on the northern front. He was so overjoyed that he immediately wired to Mussolini, "Whether the emperor attacks or whether he awaits my attack, his fate is now decided—he will be completely defeated." [24]

[23] Pietro Badoglio, *The War in Abyssinia*, p. 140.
[24] *Ibid.*

Chapter thirteen

The Battle
of Mai Chew

The drama of the Italo-Ethiopian War had unfolded itself in the wild and rugged regions of Tigre and the apocalyptic wastes of Sidamo Borana and the Ogaden, but the last act was played out in a very different setting. The battle of Mai Chew was fought in pleasant, almost smiling country, with lush green plains watered by thermal springs and the Mekan torrent, gently sloping hills wooded with euphorbias and cedars, and valleys fragrant with eucalyptus and juniper. There is only one rocky mass amid all this greenery, Amba Bohora; on the morning when I surveyed the site of the battle, its summit was enveloped in heavy, rain-swollen clouds. It was market day in Mai Chew, the village so hotly contested in 1936. Not much business was being done, but there was a continuous babble of chatter and gossip. As it was a festive occasion, the women had donned dazzlingly white *shammas* richly embroidered in scarlet or black. Soldiers on leave from the nearby camp mingled with the throng beneath the shade of the eucalyptus groves that surround the village and screen it from sight. A Coptic priest cleared a way for himself, stopping every now and then to allow the faithful to kiss his massive silver hand-cross. Blind beggars and lepers stood on the verges of the mud roads, holding out their hands for alms or beating their backs as they chanted *"Abiet, abiet!"* (pity, justice) or *"Miskin, miskin!"* (Have compassion on us poor wretches.) The atmosphere of Mai Chew had not altered in the least since 1936. The only innovations were the gasoline pumps and the football field swarming with schoolboys, the only sign of the times, and a few youths who were hoping to become marathon runners like Abeba Bikila and were trotting along conscientiously through the crowd and startling the domestic animals in the courtyards—in Ethiopian villages, even villages as large as Mai Chew, domestic animals are part of the family and have the right to full citizenship!

On March 23, 1936, from his observation post on Mount Aia, the Emperor Haile Selassie gazed through his field glasses at Mai Chew, which was in the center of the positions held by the Italians. He had just arrived with the finest of his troops. At his side was Colonel Konovaloff who quotes in his book the words the negus had addressed to him two days earlier, " 'I have decided to attack the Italians at their camp near Mai Chew before they have gathered in force. This is where they are . . . I am no engineer like you and you'll probably think my draft plan a wretched one.' I saw on a leaf of his notebook the profile of the mountains drawn in perspective. 'I want you,' he went on, 'to visit these mountains with three of our officers who were at St. Cyr and make a complete plan of the region occupied by the enemy, as well as a note of possible positions for us.' " [1] The emperor, then, despite the fact that he had repeatedly reproved his commanders for fighting the

---

[1] Konovaloff, *Con le armate del negus*, p. 146.

Italians face to face, was about to commit the same error, or rather one that was still worse, since instead of waiting for them to attack his positions, he intended to launch an offensive. What had driven him to this decision? When I put this question to him thirty years later, he gave me no answer.[2] Probably Badoglio was right when he wrote, "The negus was drawn to it, not so much by the will to attack as by the advice of his chiefs, the dignitaries of the empire, and even by the empress herself, all of whom, in accordance with Ethiopian tradition, now saw a possible solution of the conflict only in a great battle directed by the emperor in person." [3] But it was a desperate venture and Haile Selassie, as we know from a telegram he sent to *Itege* Menen on March 27, put himself wholly in the hands of the Almighty: "Since our trust is in our Creator and in the hope of His help, and as we have decided to advance and enter the fortifications, confide this decision of ours in secret to the Abun, the ministers and dignitaries, and offer unto God your fervent prayers." [4]

To launch his offensive against the enemy, the emperor had at his disposition an army 31,000 strong, made up as follows: the yet untried force of Ras Getachew Abate, the Imperial Guard, consisting of six infantry battalions and a brigade of artillery (about twenty Schneider 75s and Oerlikon 37s and six Brandt mortars), the survivors of the armies of Ras Kassa and Ras Seyoum, and a few contingents of troops and bands of irregulars raised in the locality of Addis Ababa. It was undoubtedly the best army that Ethiopia had put into the field,

---

[2] For the past two years the emperor has been writing his memoirs, and he told me I would find the answer to this question and to others of a somewhat delicate nature in his book. He declined to give me his opinion of the men who had defeated his armies or governed his country: General De Bono, Marshal Badoglio, General Graziani and the Duke of Aosta. "You will have to wait till my memoirs appear," he said.

[3] Pietro Badoglio, *The War in Abyssinia*, pp. 140–41.

[4] *Ibid.*, p. 142.

but it must be borne in mind that it had virtually no radio communications and that it was utterly defenseless against aerial bombing and gas attacks.[5]

Scarcely three kilometers from the Ethiopian outposts, beyond the green plain where the Mekan swirled, the Italians had dug themselves in on the heights overlooking the valley and the village of Mai Chew. On the right, round Amba Bohora, were the Alpini of the Pusteria; in the center, the 2nd Eritrean Division, defending Mai Chew; on the left, the Askaris of the 1st Division. In all there were some 40,000 men, to which must be added the strength of another three divisions, the Sabauda, the Assietta, and the "3rd January," distributed in depth between Belago and the Alagi passes. This formation, however, was only assumed on the eve of the battle, and the Italians were in a particularly difficult position as they had not succeeded in extending the motor road for their lines of supply and communication, being hampered by the weather and the ground on which blasting had little effect. General Badoglio, who had planned to attack on April 6 was, in fact, completely taken by surprise, as the German, Colonel Rudolf Xylander noted,[6] by the threatening aspect of the Ethiopian army, and was therefore compelled to assume a defensive rather than an offensive position. For several days, parties of Alpini and Askaris were engaged in constructing a line of defense, but as Cesco Tomaselli recorded, "we had no *chevaux de frise*, no barbed wire, no mortar; we had to be satisfied with trenches dug with pick and shovel, redoubts with dry-built walls and barricades of tree trunks."[7]

On March 21, Colonel Konovaloff, disguised as a deacon,

---

[5] A few Ethiopian companies had been issued with gas masks but these were no protection against mustard gas. A hundred-page manual, translated from the German, on the use of gas masks and the precautions to be taken in the event of a mustard-gas attack, was issued to all Ethiopian officers.

[6] Rudolf Xylander, *La conquista dell'Abissinia* (Milan: Treves, 1937), p. 115.

[7] Cesco Tomaselli, *Con le colonne celeri*, p. 189.

passed through the enemy lines. He noted that the Italian defenses were flimsy, that there was only a thin veil of Askaris on the left flank, and on his return to the emperor's headquarters advised him to attack at once while the Italians were still unprepared. The negus decided to launch his offensive on March 24, believing that by this date the local population would be in full revolt against the Italians and that the Azebu Galla, to whom he was pouring out thalers, would obey his orders and ferociously assail the left flank of the Italian army. But the offensive was postponed and we know from the telegram the emperor sent to the empress that he had decided to strike "either on Saturday or Monday," March 28 and March 30. On Sunday evening, in fact, the emperor inspected the forward positions, gave orders for the disposition of the artillery and mortars, and said to his chiefs: "You will find me with the reserves on that mountain covered with cactus. I will send reinforcements whenever there is any difficulty." [8] Despite the advice of Colonel Konovaloff and several Ethiopian officers, he had given the command of the three attacking columns to Ras Kassa, Ras Seyoum, and Ras Getachew. No one knew better than the emperor that Ras Kassa and Ras Seyoum were mediocre generals who had suffered crushing defeats, but because they were high dignitaries of the empire he was compelled by tradition to favor them. He could count, however, on many leaders of outstanding quality, among them *Dejatch* Mangasha Yilma, Ligaba Tassew, Ras Kebbede Mangasha, *Dejatch* Latibelu, and *Dejatch* Wonderat. But the attack was deferred for a further twenty-four hours, and it was decided to launch the offensive on March 31, possibly because this was St. George's Day and so seemed more propitious. All this loss of time was to prove fatal for the emperor's army.

The week frittered away by the Ethiopians in war councils, banquets, and prayers gave the Italians time to strengthen

[8] Konovaloff, *Con le armate del negus*, p. 158.

their defenses, bring up their reserves, and convince the Azebu Galla with still more thalers and several thousand rifles, to support them not the emperor. Then on the evening of March 30, an officer of the Imperial Guard who had formerly served in various Eritrean battalions crossed over to the Italian lines and warned General Negri to be on the alert as the attack was imminent.[9] This was confirmed by the Azebu Galla who were well acquainted with the emperor's plans. Accordingly, at 0300 hours the men in the line were ordered to action stations and a few Askari patrols were sent out to reconnoiter in "no man's land." For almost three hours the Italians waited tensely, then at 0545 hours, as outlines were beginning to emerge in the first faint light of dawn, a Mauser barked twice and two red rockets soared up into the sky. It was the signal for the first contingents of Ethiopians to hurl themselves against the Alpini entrenched on the slopes of Amba Bohora and the Eritreans who held the Mekan Pass. The decisive battle for the empire had begun. It was to continue with scarcely a break for thirteen hours.

"At about 0400 hours we formed up into three columns, each consisting of some 3,000 men," Colonel Kosrof Boghossian told me, "Before we moved off, the emperor reminded us that on the previous evening several planes had sprayed mustard gas in front of our positions, and said 'If you smell it, change direction immediately. If you are contaminated by the gas, wash yourselves at once.' Indeed, there was a cordon of yperite, but as most of it had evaporated during the night, we were able to break through.[10] Under cover of the darkness, we got to within a few hundred meters of the enemy trenches, set up our machine guns, and waited for the signal to attack. When we heard the Mauser bark twice and saw the rockets

[9] This incident will be found on p. 200 of Tomaselli's book and also in *Eyewitness in Ethiopia* by H. L. Matthews. The former, however, gives the date as March 29, the latter as March 30.

[10] *New Times and Ethiopia News*, July 18, 1936.

shoot up, we rushed forward, shouting "Makalle! Alagi!" [11]

The Alpini of the Feltra, Intra, and Piave di Teco battalions, most of whom came from the provinces of Piedmont, Liguria and the Veneto, bore the first shock of the Ethiopian assault. Gallantly though they fought, they were forced back by the withering fire of the many heavy Hotchkiss and Colt machine guns and the shells of a 75 mm. Schneider, commanded by *Kanyazmatch* Kifle who had trained at St. Cyr, which exploded among them with deadly precision. Protected by this fire, the Ethiopians fell on the enemy trenches with that fanatical courage described in the manuals distributed to the Italian troops. "Colonel Rosa, the commanding officer of the 24th, was sending up signal rockets for artillery support when he was hit by a bullet and killed outright," reported Cesco Tomaselli, "A few minutes later, the commanding officer of the 7th fell seriously wounded. A burst of fire killed a corporal who collapsed over his machine gun; the Alpini private who was beside him immediately took his place, but within seconds, he too was killed. A third Alpini private at once stepped into the breach, but scarcely had he opened fire than he was wounded in the head and shoulder." [12] The Ethiopian commanders of a mortar battery, ex-cadets of the Harar military school, proved that they were equal to the finest European experts; with three deadly salvos, they killed all the officers of the 8th mortar battery and wounded every man in the detachment. But despite the accuracy of their fire, the fury of their onslaught, the Ethiopians were unable to break through. One reason for this failure was given by the emperor. "We were somewhat taken by surprise. Instead of trenches and low walls, the first of our infantry battalions to rush forward found

[11] Evidence given to the author in Addis Ababa on April 15, 1965. Colonel Boghossian, an Armenian by birth, was a captain in the imperial cavalry at the time of the battle of Mai Chew. He is now in charge of the imperial stables.
[12] Cesco Tomaselli, *Con le colonne celeri*, p. 202.

themselves up against solid defense works with brilliantly sited gun emplacements. The Italian engineer proved his worth to the full in this war, as was only to be expected from a nation whose genius lies in constructing rather than fighting." [13]

Too late the Ethiopians regretted that they had not launched their offensive a week earlier. Unable to break through the line held by the Alpini, they switched their attack to the Mekan Pass and the left flank of the Italian army, their main objectives. They hoped, indeed, to encounter a less stubborn resistance in the sector held by the Eritreans, and from 0700–0800 hours, they kept up a furious onslaught, brilliantly supported by the fire of a few machine guns and batteries. At the price of heavy casualties, they achieved a few gains that, as the emperor testified, instantly inebriated them: "As was traditional in war, the soldiers rushed to my headquarters to present me with the booty slung across their shoulders. While I was issuing orders and firing my machine gun,[14] they leaped about boasting of their prowess and improvising *foggaras*,* as was their custom in the days of the imperial banquets . . . But at 0800 hours, the ominous roar of engines came from the north. The planes! Pursuit planes, bombers." [15] The battle on equal terms was already over. It had only lasted for two hours. But the emperor did not lose heart. He ordered

---

[13] *Une victoire de la civilisation*, pp. 40–43.

[14] There are many testimonials to the emperor's personal courage. On December 6, 1935, when the Italians bombed Dessie, Emeny noted in his diary (see *Abyssinian Stop Press*, p. 189), "The emperor, despite the pleadings of his staff that he should take cover, ran out into the garden of the consulate and opened fire with an antiaircraft gun." Colonel Boghossian told me, "I was standing close by the emperor when the Italian planes flew over Dessie. As soon as his majesty heard the roar of their engines, he put on his steel helmet, and asked Dr. Zervos to take his son, ten-year-old Prince Makonnen, to an air-raid shelter. The emperor then went out into the garden where we had set up an Oerlikon and fired twenty bursts of flak at the enemy bombers."

* War songs (TRANS.).

[15] *Une victoire de la civilisation*, pp. 40–43.

the Oerlikons, which up to that time had supported the attacking columns, to fire at the aircraft and, donning his steel helmet, he himself set the example by opening up with one of the guns. (Of the 70 planes that took part in this action, 36 were shot down, among them the plane piloted by Vittorio Mussolini.) Toward 0900 hours, the emperor ordered the *Kabur-Zabagna*, the Imperial Guard, to attack the left flank of the enemy. The six infantry battalions, armed with modern automatics, trained by European experts, were now to receive their baptism of fire.

"This time the whole of the Imperial Guard, supported by a lively fire, moved against our positions," wrote Badoglio, "advancing in rushes and making good use of the ground, giving proof of a solidity and a remarkable degree of training combined with a superb contempt for danger." [16] For three hours, these picked troops fought with such fire and determination that almost all the officers of the 10th Eritrean Battalion were either killed or wounded. *"Zarraf, zarraf!"* * the Ethiopians yelled as they rushed forward, or "Makalle! Alagi!" the names of cities they were burning to reconquer. Defiantly, the Askaris roared out the "Song of the *Ashanfareh"* [17] and held on stubbornly to their entrenched positions. By 1100 hours, however, the 10th battalion, while it had succeeded in beating back four successive waves of Ethiopians, was almost decimated, and Lt. Colonel Zuretti signaled to headquarters: "Heavy enemy pressure between 'Reversed Finger' hill and adjoining *tukuls*. Request artillery concentration this position." [18] A few minutes later, he and the commanding officer of the 10th, Colonel Ruggero, were killed by

[16] Pietro Badoglio, *The War in Abyssinia*, p. 145.

* Raid, sack! (TRANS.).

[17] The song of the "Ashanfareh" runs: "Cudgels and rifles of the Eritrean battalions,/Ashanfareh! Ah! . . . O . . . O!/Askaris, swoop like falcons,/Like vultures on your prey!/Askianferé . . ./Askianferé . . . Ah! O. . . ."

[18] Cesco Tomaselli, *Con le colonne celeri*, p. 208.

the same burst of fire. The Neapolitan Raffaello Tarantini, one of the few surviving officers, took over. "Even the wounded are fighting here," he signaled to General Dalmazzo, who was in command of the 2nd Division, "Soon we shall all be dead men, but we shall continue to fire." [19] The situation was rendered still worse by the fact, the truly inexplicable fact, that at midday, the batteries of the 2nd Division had run out of ammunition. Consequently, when General Dalmazzo ordered his troops to counterattack and he and his officers led the way with fixed bayonets, the gunners took part in the charge toward "Reversed Finger" hill and the Mekan Pass which, despite the intensive Ethiopian machine-gun fire, they succeeded in retaking. Almost immediately afterward, however, the Ethiopians made a violent attack on the positions still farther left held by the 1st Division, and the Italians were forced to make a second bayonet charge.

On the whole, however, the Ethiopians had made little impression on the Italian line. The emperor, noting with bitter disappointment, that the enemy still held firm, ordered his forces to attack right along the front although his hope of success was not high. It was now 1600 hours. The sky was heavily overcast and rain fell intermittently. The three columns to which the negus had sent reinforcements surged forward and again reached the trenches held by the Alpini and Eritreans, but wherever they attacked, they were relentlessly driven back. Their final desperate onslaught lasted an hour, and they fought with particular fury at the point of juncture between the 1st and 2nd Eritrean battalions; and here they succeeded in taking a few trenches and did their utmost to infiltrate the positions and widen the breach. But this was their last ephemeral success. At 1800 hours, when evening began to close in, the emperor ordered his army to fall back. "We realized that unless our forces were given a respite, they would

[19] See *Chié dell'Eritrea?* p. 279.

not be able to attempt to take the enemy fortifications the following morning," Haile Selassie said later, "Moreover, these fortifications were, as we have already said, far more formidable than we had supposed. We decided, therefore, that our army should fall back to a hill not far from Mai Chew, from whose summit we could see the entire plain and the enemy positions." [20] But the Ethiopians hardly carried out what the negus described as "an orderly retreat," for in addition to being shelled by the artillery and bombed by the air force, several thousand mounted Azebu Gallas swooped down like vultures on the exhausted warriors who had battled for an entire day and had not touched food since dawn. [21]

On his return to his headquarters on Mount Aya, the emperor wired his wife, "From five in the morning till seven in the evening, our troops attacked the enemy's strong positions, fighting without pause. We also took part in the action, and by the grace of God remain unharmed. Our chief and trusted soldiers are dead or wounded. Although our losses are heavy, the enemy too has been injured. The Guard fought magnificently and deserve every praise. The Amhara troops also did their best. Our troops, even though they are not adapted for fighting of the European type, were able to bear comparison throughout the day with the Italian troops." [22] Haile Selassie had every reason to be proud of his soldiers. Sem Benelli witnessed the battle and later wrote, "We questioned one Ethiopian warrior through an interpreter. Gray matter was

[20] *Une victoire de la civilisation*, pp. 40–43. Here is Marinetti's "vision" of the end of the battle of Mai Chew (*Il poema africana*, p. 263): "At sunset, the negus who had spent the day/scratching his black beard four miles away/from his glorious, defeated battalions,/ordered the retreat of the disorderly array."

[21] Among the distinguished men killed at Mai Chew were *Dejatch* Mangasha Yilma, *Dejatch* Wonderat, who had fought and been wounded at Adowa, *Fitaurari* Assefa, and old *Dejatch* Aberra Tella, who in prewar days had been a thorn in the emperor's side for twenty years.

[22] Pietro Badoglio, *The War in Abyssinia*, p. 147.

oozing from a hole in his temple, it was obvious that he had not long to live, yet he bore himself as proudly as if he had been decorated. 'Who are you?' 'The commander of a thousand men.' 'Why don't you lie down on that stretcher? The Italians don't kill their prisoners.' 'I prefer to die on my feet.' 'What's the sense of this heroic gesture?' 'We swore to the emperor two days ago that we'd conquer or die in the attempt. We have not conquered, but we have died. Look—' and he pointed to the valley littered with corpses. Propping himself up against a boulder, he awaited his own end." [23]

According to Colonel Konovaloff, 1,000 Ethiopians were killed at Mai Chew; [24] according to Tomaselli, 5,000.[25] General Badoglio, evidently including all those who fell during the retreat, put the figure as high as 8,000.[26] The Italian losses were: killed and wounded, 68 officers, 332 nationals, 873 Eritreans. While no words can do justice to the heroic stand made by the Alpini and the gallantry of the Italian officers who set a shining example to their men, the "battle for the empire" was in fact won by the colored troops who shed their lifeblood so generously for the common cause. This afforded little comfort to Mussolini who hoped to certify that, through the State, his people had acquired a strength as solid and durable as cement. Indeed, for the next few months, he was filled with bitter disappointment. Denis Mack Smith interpreted his feelings correctly: "The Duce grieved over the fact that the fallen Italians had not even numbered 2,000 and that the war had been won at too low a price to reinvigorate the national character to the extent Fascism required." [27]

Tense and anxious though both sides were, neither of them slept that night. The Ethiopians to whom the services of the

[23] Sem Benelli, *Io in Africa*, p. 106.

[24] Konovaloff, *Con le armate del negus*, p. 163.

[25] Cesco Tomaselli, *Con le colonne celeri*, p. 211.

[26] Pietro Badoglio, *The War in Abyssinia*, p. 148.

[27] Denis Mack Smith, *Italy, a Modern History*, p. 451.

Red Cross were no longer available (the field hospitals had either been bombed to bits or their personnel had been taken prisoner), spent the hours in bearing away the thousands of wounded and in burying the dead while the Coptic priests chanted prayers and the women wailed in chorus.[28] The Italians, who expected a mass attack at sunrise, feverishly repaired their fortifications and emptied the cartridge belts of the dead. But even after they had collected these cartridges they were in desperate straits; the 1st Eritrean Division, for instance, had no more than fifteen rounds per man and two clips for its machine guns.[29] Owing to criminal dilatoriness at the base, the supply train, which had to take the slow and difficult caravan roads, did not arrive until 0800 hours on the following morning. But the attack failed to materialize. At dawn April 1, 1936, on the order of the negus, the army had set out on what was to prove an endless retreat. The battle of Mai Chew had indeed decided the fate of the empire.[30]

[28] There were always a few hundred women attached to the Ethiopian armies who cooked meals for the warriors. During the retreats these women shared the lot of the men, and large numbers of them were killed by bombs or mustard gas.

[29] Luigi Pignatelli, *La guerra dei sette mesi*, p. 226.

[30] During the battle of Mai Chew, the Italians fired 61,200 rounds of machine-gun fire against the Ethiopians, while the air force dropped 34 tons of H.E. on their positions.

Chapter fourteen

The Massacre of Lake Ashangi

It was dawn on April 1, 1936—23 *Megabit,* according to the Ethiopian calendar—and the Ethiopian warriors had not tasted food for thirty-six hours. The supply train had been spotted by reconnaissance planes between Quoram and the Agumberta Pass and bombed to bits. The men were starving as well as exhausted and to add to their misery no sooner was it light than the bombers reappeared, dropped tons of high explosives, and sprayed mustard gas on their positions. With a last anguished look at the plain littered with corpses, Haile Selassie ordered his few surviving officers to position a thin veil of troops who would cover the retreat of the main body of his defeated army, some 20,000 men in all, to the mountain ranges between Addi Assel Gerti and Enda Aya Giorgis. Although the negus realized that a second attack on the enemy positions would lead to the wholesale slaughter of his men, he was loath to leave his headquarters in a cave on Mount Aya, but during the night of April 2, he was informed that the Italians were pursuing his army and threatening it with encirclement. From this moment he gave up all hope of victory, quitted Mount Aya, and ordered his forces to fall back toward Lake Ashangi and Quoram. But this did not mean that he had given up all thought of resistance, far from it. He made up his mind from then on he would follow the course that several military advisers had urged him to take at the beginning of the war and resort to guerrilla tactics. Accordingly, he ordered Ras Seyoum to return with his warriors to his province of Tigre and rouse the population to a full-scale revolt against the Italians. Colonel Konovaloff who was present at the time noted Ras Seyoum's manifest lack of enthusiasm: "Poor Ras Seyoum! Fate had endowed him with wealth that would enable him to live without work or care and now, at the age of sixty, he was forced to become a *shifta*. . . ." [1]

Before the sun had risen on April 3, the emperor's army began its retreat toward Lake Ashangi, dragging along a few cannon and bearing the wounded on crude litters of interlaced boughs. The men were so shaken and exhausted that they no longer responded to orders but stumbled along the difficult mountain tracks like automatons. Already the chiefs had begun to give vent to accusations and recriminations. "These *Kabur-Zabagna!*" burst out one of Ras Kassa's sons convulsed with rage, "They're no better than our simple soldiers—and how much money they've cost us!" [2] The negus got out of his car, donned a khaki cloak, allowed his anxious chiefs to press a steel helmet on his head, and rode to the front of the interminable column. "As he waited impassively for the steel helmet to be placed on his head, I thought of the moment when he was crowned, the moment when he was at the zenith of his power and seemed invincible," wrote Colonel Konovaloff. [3] For most of the day the sky was overcast and the visibility poor, hence aerial activity was limited, but another enemy,

---

[1] Konovaloff, *Con le armate del negus*, p. 168.
[2] *Ibid.*, p. 164.
[3] *Ibid.*, p. 180.

equally insidious, was waiting to pounce: the Azebu Galla. From the rocky heights of ravines, they fired on the wounded, the stragglers, and swarmed down to despoil and mutilate the dead and dying. The praise lavished on these scavengers, these castrators, by Pietro Badoglio, Marshal of Italy, was little short of blasphemous, but then he was always ready to use any means to take full advantage of tribal hatred to throw the defeated Ethiopians into utter confusion. The Azebu Galla served admirably to "hasten the enemy's retreat that changed gradually to a precipitous and disorderly flight." [4]

On the morning of April 4, the sky was cloudless. Worse still, the approaches to Lake Ashangi were bare of cover; there was not a tree, not a rock in sight. Nevertheless, instead of waiting till night fell, the Ethiopians resumed their march as soon as it was light, and a column several kilometers long began to issue from the comparative safety of the Agumberta Pass in the direction of Endodo. The emperor told Marcel Griaule that he had been unable to hold back his men because their fears had been dispelled by the message on the leaflets that had been dropped by plane on the previous day. "You can safely proceed south," this message ran, "Our quarrel is with the emperor, not with you. Rest at night and march during the day. There is no need for you to conceal yourselves—we shall not attack you." [5] I have not been able to trace any of these leaflets, in fact I feel very dubious about this incident. In my opinion, the Ethiopians decided to press on because they feared the enemy would cut their line of retreat. Indeed, shortly after dawn on April 3, the First Army Corps and the Eritrean Corps had been dispatched in pursuit of the fugitives and were moving toward Lake Ashangi, in the vicinity of which they would converge.

When the column came within sight of the lake, it split in two in order to accelerate the descent. The advance-guard

[4] Pietro Badoglio, *The War in Abyssinia*, p. 148.
[5] *Une victoire de la civilisation*, pp. 45–48.

began to file through the pass leading to Mekare on the east shore of the lake, while the main body of the force took the pass that would bring it to the western shore. It was a glorious morning. The graduated terraces that sloped down to the basin were festive with waving green corn. As the survivors of Mai Chew who believed they had a day's advantage over the enemy were dreaming of the quiet, the peace that awaited them in the eucalyptus groves of Quoram, they suddenly heard the roar of engines directly overhead. Then the bombs began to fall. "From that moment a tornado of fire was unleashed," wrote Tomaselli, "Wave after wave of bombers with full loads hammered their main objective, the Ethiopian column making for the east shore toward which the Eritrean Corps was advancing . . . the bombs exploded among the dense mass of fugitives who bent double and clapped their hands over their ears as if they had been caught in a heavy hailstorm. . . ." [6] What Tomaselli does not tell us is, that in addition to dropping 73 tons of high explosives on the hapless Ethiopians, the Fascist Air Force sprayed them with mustard gas. "Of all the massacres of the terrible and pitiless war, this was the worst," the emperor told Marcel Griaule, "Men, women, pack animals were blown to bits or were fatally burned by the mustard gas. The dying, the wounded screamed with agony. Those who escaped the bombs fell victim to the deadly rain. The gas finished off the carnage that the bombs had begun. We could do nothing to protect ourselves against it. Our thin cotton *shammas* were soaked with yperite. . . ." [7]

Despite this tornado of fire, this lethal mist, the Ethiopians, particularly those who were making for the west shore and were less exposed, did their utmost to strike back at the enemy. "The planes came down to ten meters to machine-gun us, but they offered us an excellent target," said Colonel

[6] Cesco Tomaselli, *Con le colonne celeri*, pp. 218–19.
[7] *Une victoire de la civilisation*, p. 45–48.

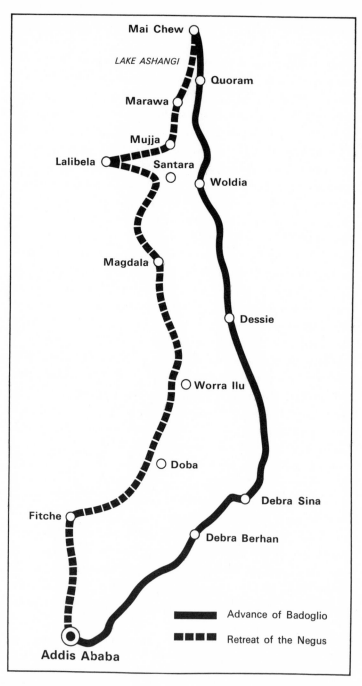

Map 9. The retreat of the negus and advance of Badoglio after the battle of Lake Ashangi.

Boghossian.[8] The Ethiopians shot down the plane piloted by
Fabbri and scored direct hits on twenty-eight others, but the
whole of the air force on the northern front darkened the sky
above the plain of Golgolo. As Badoglio tells us, "Our entire
air arm . . . had sent up its aircraft, regardless of type, even
to the last machine." [9] Throughout the day, 150 planes continued to bomb a routed, demoralized force that asked only to
be allowed to escape to the south. Of this utterly unwarranted
ferocity, Haile Selassie said, "It was no longer a war for the
Italian airmen—it was a game." [10] Even Allessandro Pavolini,
who was in one of the bombers, was sickened by what he saw,
"During other wars there have been scores of massacres on a
far larger scale, but this particular massacre was enacted in
such a small area, in so short a space of time . . . on the
slopes of the plateau, a generation fell dying or dead." [11]
Indeed, when the evening closed in and the last of the planes
was on its way back to Makalle, the plain of Gongolo was
strewn with thousands of corpses; they lay thickest on the
slopes of Benassa, around the village of Mekare and the Pass
of Chollemadur Maryam. The survivors of the Imperial Guard
who had fought so heroically at Mai Chew died in the corn-
fields, targets easily gunned down by an enemy that had lost
all sense of chivalry.

The emperor had taken shelter in a cave and was torn by
conflicting emotions: horror, anguish, despair, a passion of
black anger. Colonel Konovaloff, aware that he was almost at
the breaking point, did all he could to comfort and encourage
him, but the negus, throwing his pride to the winds, said
wildly, "I don't know what to do . . . my brain no longer
works." [12] The most terrible moment of his ordeal came at

[8] Evidence given to me by Colonel Boghossian.
[9] Pietro Badoglio, *The War in Abyssinia*, p. 148.
[10] *Une victoire de la civilisation*, pp. 45–48.
[11] Alessandro Pavolini, *Disperata* (Florence: Vallecchi, 1937), p. 266.
[12] Konovaloff, *Con la armate del negus*, p. 179.

dawn when he looked out from the entrance of the cave and saw that "the shores of the lake were ringed round with bodies. . . ." [13] During the night the wounded, panting with thirst, had crawled or dragged themselves to the edge of the lake and gulped down the gas-contaminated water. Among the heaped-up corpses were those of pack animals and wild creatures who had drunk from the poisoned source. When Colonel Boghossian described the terrible scene to me thirty years later, he kept passing his hand across his eyes as if to shut it out, and his voice was so choked with sobs that he could hardly speak. It was above all the massacre of Lake Ashangi that made me ask myself and others why Marshal Badoglio with his crushing superiority, with victory within his grasp, continued to use gas to the end. None knew its effects better than he did; had he not seen on the Isonzo the livid faces of Italian soldiers poisoned by yperite, diphenyl chloroarsine, dichloroethyl sulphide? But Marshal Badoglio is dead and the few men who hold the key to the riddle remain silent.

On the evening of April 5, the survivors of the massacre began to march toward Quoram, but when they were within a few kilometers of the city, they learned that the Eritrean Corps had got there before them. They then turned right, deciding to make for Dessie via the caravan routes of Lasta and not by the far easier Imperial Road. As they avoided the main road and only marched at night, several days passed before the reconnaissance planes spotted them. But the Azebu Galla soon picked up their trail and ferociously harried the rear guard, commanded by Ras Getachew as far south as Marawa and even beyond. The emperor, who was almost himself again, believed that it might be possible to make a stand at Dessie where large amounts of supplies and ammunition had been assembled and where the heir to the throne, Prince Asfa Wossen, could rally several thousand men. On April 8, during a halt, he issued an "Imperial Order for General Mobilization"

[13] *Une victoire de la civilisation,* pp. 45–48.

that contained these words: "Thanks to the help of Almighty God, we are still able to defend ourselves. We call upon all who are fit to take up arms and come to the aid of their heroic countrymen. Peasants, merchants! Make ready to join us and reinforce our troops who are fighting to preserve Ethiopia's independence. . . ." The *kitet* met with little response, but I have quoted it because it brings out to the full the courage, the strength of the Emperor who, even now when all was lost, thought not in terms of surrender but of resistance.

The column had passed Mujja when Haile Selassie suddenly decided to leave the main body and make a pilgrimage to the holy city of Lalibela. This expedition was both useless and dangerous and even his most loyal chiefs were taken aback and angered, for several precious days would be lost. Yet this sudden impulse that seized the emperor sheds a clear light on his strange and complex character. Accompanied by a few of the men closest to him, Haile Selassie rode off at dawn toward Mount Abuna Yosef towering majestically to the sky. At dusk, April 12, he reached the city of famed rock churches and entered the largest, Medhane Alem. As the Coptic priests hastened to pay him homage, he fell on his knees and began to pray. "We stayed for two days in Lalibela. The head of an empire about to topple had come to this characteristic center of piety to renew his spiritual strength," wrote Colonel Konovaloff with a touch of irony.[14] For forty-eight hours the emperor remained in the church hewn out of the mountain; not a crumb of *injera*,* not a drop of water passed his lips. He was alone with his God to whom he had offered up so many prayers, to whom he had brought so many of his people to pray—his God who had denied him victory.

On April 15, the negus left Lalibela and two days later rejoined his army, or rather what was left of it. Burdened with their wounded, the survivors plodded on and had almost

[14] Konovaloff, *Con le armate del negus*, p. 190.
* Native bread (TRANS.).

reached Dessie when they learned that Prince Asfa Wossen had abandoned the city on April 14 without firing a shot and that it had been occupied by the Eritreans on the following day. The emperor decided to make for Worra Ilu, but as they drew near, runners brought the news that the Italians had taken the town. Yet despite these setbacks, the Ethiopians did not give way to despair. "We had no thought of defeat," the emperor said, "Not one of us, not an officer, not a soldier, not even the most gravely wounded borne on the litters from Mai Chew showed any signs of losing heart." [15] Indeed, Haile Selassie still hoped to defend his capital, hence he ordered his forces to march to Fiche. They proceeded by devious ways unknown to their pursuers who, as a result lost all track of the remnants of the last army on the northern front. Advancing by forced marches, the Ethiopians reached Fiche on April 28 and on the following day the emperor, with a retinue of some fifty dignitaries, drove to Addis Ababa. So after an absence of four months, after the terrible retreat that had lasted for a good three weeks, Haile Selassie returned to his capital. "When he arrived on April 29, the 'New Flower' was like a sinking ship whose passengers were scrambling for the lifeboats," wrote Marcel Junod. "The station was besieged by important Ethiopian officials madly anxious to get to Jibouti and by a number of foreigners who thought it advisable to leave before the Italians arrived." [16] The agony of the capital had begun, but the negus was determined to resist the enemy to the last and was striving vainly, as we shall see, to organize the defense of the city.

In the meantime on April 20, General Badoglio had transferred his headquarters to Dessie, the forest city that for so many months had been the emperor's headquarters. Badoglio and his entire staff had been flown to Dessie in twelve large bombers. Evidently the Marshal was far less perceptive, or far

[15] *Une victoire de la civilisation,* pp. 45–48.
[16] Marcel Junod, *Les troisième combattant,* p. 56.

more vainglorious, than General De Bono, for he recorded that the population greeted him "in a manner that was truly solemn and festive." [17] Badoglio was now only 400 kilometers distant from Addis Ababa and there was no army left to oppose him; except for the pitiful procession of refugees continually bombed and machine-gunned by the air force, his road was clear. He therefore decided to "risk" the advance on the capital with a mechanized column which, thanks to General Dall'Ora's genius for organization, was assembled in Dessie between April 21–25. With 1,785 cars and trucks, Fiats, Lancias, Alfa Romeos, Fords, Chevrolets, Bedfords, and Studebakers, a squadron of light tanks and eleven batteries, this was the most powerful mechanized column ever to appear on an African road.[18] On the morning of April 26, three days before the emperor's return to his capital, 12,495 Italian troops clambered into the trucks and left Dessie on what Badoglio termed the "March of the Iron Will." In addition to the trucks filled with men, there were trucks carrying 193 horses; at the gates of Addis Ababa, the Marshal and his staff would leave their cars and ride in triumph into the capital on horseback.

To protect the column which was so constituted that it could not sustain an attack, General Badoglio had sent forward on April 24 two columns of Eritreans, each 4,000 men strong. But this precautionary measure proved to be superfluous—there was no sign of the enemy, there was nothing but rain and mud. Even at the Termaber Pass, where Badoglio had expected at least a show of resistance, all was quiet, although the mechanized column was immobilized for two days thanks to the fact that Captain Tamm had blown up a section of the road. On the

[17] Pietro Badoglio, *The War in Abyssinia*, p. 155.

[18] In some of the Italian reports, different figures are given, all below 1,725, the number that appears in Badoglio's account (*The War in Abyssinia*, p. 159). In his book, *Intendenza in A.O.*, General Dall'Ora gives the number as 1,785 (see p. 80), and since one can rely on his accuracy, I have quoted from this source.

whole, the "March of the Iron Will" was hardly more than a logistics exercise on a grand scale. As an anonymous writer put it, "It was far more of a sports event than a page in military history."

When they had passed through Debra Sina, the Italians found themselves in one of the loveliest and richest regions of Ethiopia. "Our troops were dumbfounded at what they saw," Tomaselli reported, "Marvel succeeded marvel. The men in the open trucks, their rifles between their knees, and their faces so plastered with dust that they looked like Japanese actors in a "no" play, gazed spellbound at this unimaginably fertile earth, stared at it as if it were some unguarded treasure. 'It's ours, it's ours!' their eyes wide with amazement seemed to be saying. Soon they were chattering excitedly in the language of millionaires of the crops they would sow, the harvests they would reap. 'At last we've got a real colony of our own!' they told themselves exultantly." [19] Now that the war seemed to be over, the soldiers, three-quarters of whom were peasants, were filled with an upsurge of that hope which had made their break with the homeland so easy, indeed almost joyful, and diluted the gall of seven months of bitter fighting. It was the cherished hope of throwing down their rifles and picking up their spades, of reaping their reward from the rich black earth that until now had only been furrowed by archaic wooden plows. Far more sophisticated, however, were the hopes of the poets, inevitably expressed in the high-flown rhetoric of the regime. Here is a typical effusion by Adriano Grande:

> *Il nostro sangue ha fame*
> *d'avventura e di pane, Italia: e questa*
> *favol gigantesca sino in fondo*
> *tu la vivrai: Cancellerai dai*
> *negri visi di questi popoli selvaggi*

[19] Cesco Tomaselli, *Con le colonne celeri*, p. 234.

la supina ferocia e la mestizia
antica della schiavitu; di nuovo
madre sarai, pe'l mondo
trasgociato e interte, di bellezza
e di giustizia: di favole saggie
ed eroiche, le sole
certezze che rallegrano la vita.[20]

[Our blood cries out
for adventure and bread, Italy: this gigantic
epic you will live out to the last page
you will erase from the black faces of this savage race
the dull ferocity and the ancient shame
of slavery; once more you will be
the mother of a wretched and helpless world,
you will bring to it beauty and justice,
your fabled and heroic wisdom, the only
certainties that will rekindle the spark of life.]

As they reached the gates of Addis Ababa, the Italians were delirious with joy; not a single man among them, peasant or poet, foresaw that, far from coming to an end, the war would continue for five years. The day of the spade, of seedtime and harvest, was destined never to dawn.

[20] *Gazzetta del Popolo*, April 16, 1936.

Chapter fifteen

The Battle of the Ogaden

The victorious progress achieved by Badoglio since February understandably filled the energetic and ambitious Graziani with unbounded jealousy and resentment. He was convinced, and quite rightly, that the marshal had no intention of dividing the laurels with him; consequently, he was desperately anxious to launch an offensive on Ras Nasibu's army, which was solidly entrenched in defense of Daggahbur, Jijiga, and Harar. Graziani was determined not to be cheated out of what he considered to be a certain victory and as far back as January 25, had appealed once more directly to Mussolini: "Duce, send me the motor vehicles I have already asked for and which I urgently need, also 100 more 50 h.p. caterpillars, and 200 chains. Please dispatch in one shipment so they can be speedily disembarked and Harar will speedily be yours." [1] But the motor vehicles Graziani needed for the difficult offensive were slow in arriving, and the Libyan division he had asked

---

[1] Rodolfo Graziani, *Fronte Sud*, p. 285, telegram 1073/76.

186

for to replace the Eritrean division (depleted by continued desertions), did not arrive until the end of February. On top of these delays, Graziani was faced with the vast problem of setting up an operational base thousands of kilometers from the coast. New roads, hundreds of kilometers long, had to be constructed; thousands more motor vehicles had to be acquired, and all the essentials, from water to ammunition, for an army of 40,000 men that would have to advance 500 kilometers through country bare of resources, had to be assembled.

It was while Graziani was wrestling with these vast logistical difficulties that the two men, who up till now had made only a miserly response to his repeated demands for further supplies and ordered him to play a purely defensive role, began to grow impatient and assail him with telegrams. Mussolini wished to be informed how soon he might expect him to launch his offensive. Badoglio sent him the news of his victories in Tigre, asked him when he would be ready to attack Ras Nasibu, and reminded him maliciously that "audacity pays handsome dividends." [2] Graziani, seething afresh with resentment against the marshal, wired him "his humble and heartiest congratulations," but did not fail to add with extreme asperity, "I am bitterly aware that had I been believed a year ago when I pointed out the advantage of an offensive on the southern front, I could have annihilated both the Ethiopian armies in the Ogaden, and so have brought the Italo-Ethiopian War to an end. History will attribute this failure to its proper source. My own conscience is completely clear." [3] Badoglio did not reply immediately, but a few days later he telegraphed, "Please inform me when you propose to attack Ras Nasibu. If

[2] *Ibid.*, p. 292, telegram 1624/M. It must be recalled that Badoglio, who disapproved of Graziani's offensive on Negelli, had telegraphed Mussolini in order to disclaim all responsibility for it.

[3] *Commando delle Forze Armate della Somalia*, p. 69, telegram 10381, dated March 4, 1936.

Your Excellency has already launched the offensive, kindly let me know where you have established your headquarters so that I can keep in telegraphic contact with you." [4] Beside himself with fury, Graziani wired back, "I have no intention of leaving anything to chance for an operation that calls for the most meticulous preparations and in which my entire army will be involved." [5] Then in order to conciliate Mussolini who, as usual, expected plans that had barely been drafted to materialize immediately, Graziani informed him the offensive on Harar would be preceded by a series of aerial bombardments. Indeed, from March 22–31, the air force on the southern front dropped tons of high explosives that reduced Jijiga to ruins, destroyed much of the "open city" of Harar, and caused great damage to the smaller towns of Bullaleh, Birkut, Daggahbur, and Sassabaneh.

This was not nearly enough, however, to satisfy Mussolini. On April 1, he assailed Graziani once more and wired in true *squadristi* terms, "Instinct tells me the time is ripe to give Nasibu the flogging he so richly deserves." [6] On the following day, Badoglio, overjoyed by his victory at Mai Chew, also returned to the attack: "Imperial army retreating south. First Army Corps and Eritrean Corps, as well as the air force, sent in pursuit. Time has now come to stake all on a final throw. Am sure your Excellency will profit to the full from this situation." [7] This fusillade of telegrams compelled Graziani to announce that he would launch his attack on April 18, but Mussolini, seething with impatience, urged him to attack several days earlier, while Badoglio exhorted him sarcastically: "Graziani, my old comrade-in-arms, make a vigorous beginning that will bring us yet another victory." [8] But Graziani's

[4] Rodolfo Graziani, *Fronte Sud*, p. 297, telegram 1757/M.
[5] *Ibid.*
[6] *Ibid.*, p. 302, telegram 3714.
[7] *Ibid.*, p. 302, telegram 1897.
[8] *Ibid.*, p. 303, telegram 1947, dated April 5, 1936.

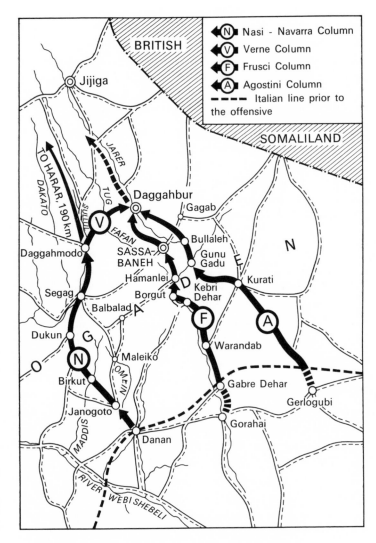

Map 10. Graziani's plan for the offensive in the Ogaden.

189

trials were not yet over. In the first week of April, a deluge fell from the skies—the rainy season had begun. Streams became dangerous swirling torrents and the tracks were transformed into morasses of squelching mud. General Nasi, who had seen so much service in Africa, advised Graziani not to launch his offensive under such adverse conditions, but the latter could no longer afford to delay since the Ethiopians, aware of his plans, had dispatched from their armed camps a number of contingents that were now marching toward him. On April 8, indeed, *Dejatch* Abebe Damtu, Ras Desta's brother, and Makonnen Endalkatchew reached Janogoto thirty kilometers from the Italian lines, and began to dig themselves in with their combined forces of 10,000 men, on the left bank of the Gorrah Wadi.

On April 13, although the formation of his three attacking columns had not yet been completed and the swollen torrents were almost impassable, Graziani flew to Danane and ordered the advance to be made on the following day. Facing him was Haile Selassie's last army, far better equipped than those that had been defeated (the Italians estimated 500 machine guns, 50 small-caliber cannon), and far better provisioned, thanks to the Jijiga-Berbera motor road. Ras Nasibu's force was 28,000 strong, as has been said; a number of contingents had established themselves in positions close to the Italian lines, while the main body garrisoned the fortified cities and manned the Hindenburg Wall. Wehib Pasha had constructed the Wall in a year and, as Ciasca reported, "It was a formidable obstacle. Wehib Pasha had made brilliant use of the ground and exploited modern military techniques to the full: he had taken every advantage of the caves to screen the troops, the machine guns and the cannon were positioned to produce a deadly cross-fire, the cave openings were protected by insuperable *chevaux-de-frise*, five thicknesses of barbed-wire entanglement and a connecting series of trenches." [9] To

[9] Raffaele Ciasca, *Storia coloniale dell'Italia contemporanea*, p. 684.

smash this armed camp in the Daggahbur-Sassabaneh-Bullaleh triangle, Graziani employed an army of 38,000 men, of which 15,600 were Italians. In comparison with the massive force Badoglio had deployed at the battles of Tembien and Enderta, Graziani's army was on the small side, but it had the advantage of being almost completely mechanized and had the support of an air force empowered—as one may read in the "Secret and Confidential Operational Memorandum for the Offensive on Harar" to make "liberal use of bombs and special liquids [mustard gas]—to inflict the maximum losses on the enemy, and above all, shatter his morale." [10] On April 14, Graziani launched a three-pronged attack on Ras Nasibu. The first column, commanded by General Nasi, was to break through the Ethiopian defenses at Janogoto, and move rapidly via Birkut-Dukun-Segag to Daggahmodo and threaten the left flank of the enemy army; the central column, commanded by General Frusci, was to move forward via Hamanlei and Sassabaneh to Daggahbur, the pivotal point of the Hindenburg Wall; while the third column, commanded by General Agostini, was to proceed via Kurati-Gunu Gadu-Bullaleh and engage the Ethiopians on the right flank.

On the very day the three attacking columns had begun to advance on a 250 kilometer front, Graziani received a telegram from Mussolini that caused his cup of bitterness to overflow. "Today, April 14, our advance-guards will reach Dessie," it ran, "Even on the international scene the rhythm of events is accelerating. There is not a moment to lose, my dear Graziani. I await the news that you have begun your offensive on Harar." [11] In his reply, 150 words long, Graziani made no attempt to hide his resentment and rancor. He reproached the Duce for not taking account of the enormous difficulties he faced, and concluded his telegram by giving full vent to his

---

[10] *Commando delle Forze Armate della Somalia*, vol. 4, p. 50, no. 609 *di protocollo op. Mogadishu*, March 3, 1936.

[11] Rodolfo Graziani, *Fronte Sud*, p. 310, telegram 4252.

feelings: "You, the one man who has penetrated my inmost mind, you who know that I would gladly die a hundred deaths for my country and for my Leader, will assuredly understand how deeply you have wounded me by insinuating that I am deaf to your explicit demand for action and the tacit demand of the entire country which, fully aware of my character, is undoubtedly asking itself why I have not swept forward with my customary energy and vigor. . . ." [12]

The first day of the advance passed uneventfully. At dawn on April 15, however, as the Nasi column came within sight of Janogoto, it was brought to a halt by intensive fire from the right bank of the Gorrah Wadi. The rain was pelting down and the swirling torrent reinforced the already solid Ethiopian line of defense. "The battalions from Cyrenaiaca were in the van," wrote Guelfo Civinini, "These Libyan troops were splendid fighters and also wary and thoroughly versed in the insidious ways of desert warfare. As soon as their men began to fall, they took stock of the situation and resorted to their patient Bedouin tactics of firing only a few shots, assessing the terrain held by the enemy and making full use of their own." [13] Not a meter of ground was gained during the entire day; from the caves that honeycombed the rocky peaks of the Wadi, the Ethiopians continued to blaze away, protected as they were from air attacks. It was only when dusk fell and the flood water began to ebb that a few platoons of Libyans managed to ford the torrent and establish a bridgehead. But at dawn, April 17, only part of the Libyan division had succeeded in crossing the Gorrah owing to the "stubborn resistance"—Graziani's words—put up by the Ethiopians. To break it down, General Nasi was compelled to bring up tanks, flamethrowers, and artillery to within a few meters of the entrances to the caves.

[12] *Ibid.*, pp. 310–11, telegram 4824/28.
[13] *Con l'esercito italiano in A.O.*, vol. 2, p. 608.

After three days of desperate fighting, the Ethiopians were forced to fall back. Civinini then did his utmost to annihilate *Dejatch* Makonnen, whom he had known in prewar days, by heaping ridicule on him: "I'm told that when he bolted off on his mule only about fifty of his men followed him. Poor chap —war isn't his métier. He is one of those civilized Ethiopians who go about in immaculately polished shoes and adore night clubs. I remember seeing him a few years ago in the New Flower night club in Addis. Beaming all over and half-drunk, he was cuddling a platinum-blonde hostess who sat on his knees. *'Oh, comme j'aime ta bombe!'* he kept repeating." [14] This was an amusing but fatuous sketch that Graziani did his utmost to cancel out by defining Makonnen Endalkatchew as a leader of "unquestionable merit." [15] Makonnen indeed had inspired his men to hold out for three days; rather than surrender to the enemy, they had allowed the machine gunners to mow them down in swathes. "The Ethiopians left a couple of thousand dead and as many rifles behind them," wrote Graziani, "as well as dozens of machine guns and one cannon. Few prisoners were taken." [16] The Libyans, it must be remembered, were Moslems, and "few prisoners were taken" because they vented their hatred of the Christians on the Shoan and Amhara warriors who fell into their hands.

On the evening of April 18, the Nasi column reached the wells of Birkut, but at 0445 hours, while it was still dark, the Ethiopian forces that had been defeated at Janagobo suddenly launched a surprise attack. Bitter fighting continued till midday, occupied Birkut. Generals Frusci and Agostini, however, Thanks to his artillery and the support of the air force, he broke down the Ethiopian resistance, and on the following day, occupied Birkut. Generals Frusci and Agostini, however, who were advancing in the center and on the right respec-

[14] *Ibid.*, p. 611.
[15] Rodolfo Graziani, *Fronte Sud*, p. 309.
[16] *Ibid.*, p. 312.

193

tively, met with no opposition, and despite the torrential rain and the appalling state of the ground, succeeded in reaching their objectives. On the evening of April 23, all three columns had taken up their positions behind the Hindenburg Wall. The Verné column, thanks to the fact that it was mechanized, had outdistanced the Nasi column and reached Daggahmodo; the Frusci column was within sight of the fortifications of Hamanlei; and the Agostini column had made contact with the enemy at Gunu Gadu. At the first light of dawn on April 24, as Marshal Badoglio began the "March of the Iron Will" on Addis Ababa, fierce fighting broke out on the entire length of the Ogaden front. From his headquarters in Bullaleh, Wehib Pasha directed the course of the battle. As Mario Bassi wrote, Nasibu's Turkish adviser had taken into account the "traditional tactics of war" of the Ethiopians, and instead of limiting them to "a static defense within the system of fortifications" had trained and "provided them with the means that enabled them to put up a subtle and spirited resistance"; a defensive, in fact, that could be transformed when the moment presented itself, into a counteroffensive.[17] Indeed, at dawn on the 24th, it was the Ethiopians who, protected by fire from their gun emplacements, attacked right along the front in the hope of relieving the pressure on their fortified line of defense.

The fighting rose to a crescendo of fury particularly in the center at Hamanlei and Borgut. For two days *Fitaurari* Malion and his men held up the advance of the Frusci column, and by making a series of sorties from their garrison, threatened it with envelopment. General Frusci, indeed, was so alarmed that he requested Graziani to send the Agostini column to ease the pressure on him, a request Graziani refused to grant. The volunteers of the Parini Legion fought with such little conviction that Frusci was obliged to throw into this hell a platoon of flame throwers as well as the Libyan Askaris, who lost 600

---

[17] *Con l'esercito italiano in A.O.*, p. 589.

men, killed or wounded, in the course of their bayonet charges.[18] The Agostini column, too, had struck a bad patch; its advance on Gunu Gadu was held up for an entire day by the Ethiopians on the right bank of the Jarer torrent, and it was not until April 25 that the Italians, at the price of heavy casualties, put paid to the Ethiopians, who had lodged themselves in caves or in hollows among the roots of trees. Graziani praised the enemy for his "skill and tenacity" and his exploitation of the terrain. He concludes his description of the battle of Gunu Gadu by telling us, "The Ethiopians resisted to the death, till they were finished off by hand grenades and bayonets."[19] During the ten-day battle, the Ethiopians lost some 5,000 men, but Graziani's army had also suffered heavily —2,000 of his men had been killed or wounded, a high figure, bearing in mind that on the northern front the ratio between Ethiopian and Italian casualties was almost invariably well over ten to one.

After the fall of Hamanlei and Gunu Gadu, and as the Nasi column increased its pressure on Daggahbur, the Hindenburg

[18] For this battle I consulted Mario Bassi's notebooks and maps (see Acknowledgments), the typed accounts sent to Graziani by the Consul-General, F. Navarra Viggiani (n. prot. 0I/576), and the detailed description of the fighting at Borgut by Major Paolo Petroni, a staff officer. On p. 11 of Petroni's narrative, we read, "Among the soldiers were a number of women, some in uniform, some not. These amazons boasted ferociously that they had never ceased firing their rifles." On page 42 we learn that "few prisoners were taken; hundreds of Ethiopians were killed. This is a war with no quarter." On p. 43 he tells us that "1,000 Ethiopians were killed (we counted the number of dead); a few dozen were wounded, and we took 36 prisoners, among whom were a few chiefs and one woman. Anyone who has been through a war will appreciate that these figures are appalling as the number of men wounded in a battle is usually twice or three times larger than that of the killed. The Italian casualties were as follows: 10 officers, killed, 11 wounded; 1 Italian soldier killed, 11 wounded; 132 Eritreans and Somalis killed, 493 wounded. The number of Italo-Eritrean-Somalis wounded was three times greater than the number killed. Yet the Italians maintained that it was the habit of the Ethiopians to finish off the wounded and kill the prisoners they had taken!

[19] Rodolfo Graziani, *Fronte Sud*, p. 326.

Wall unexpectedly crumbled and when, after a four-day halt, Graziani resumed the advance, the three columns met no further resistance. On April 29, the Italians entered Sassaba-neh and Bullaleh. On April 30, they occupied Daggahbur. From then on the only opposition Graziani had to contend with on his march to Jijiga and Harar was the everlasting rain and thick, viscous mud. On May 3, Ras Nasibu [20] and Wehib Pasha joined the emperor in Jibouti, and the army of the Ogaden, abandoned by its commander and chief of staff, broke into a hundred fragments. Some bands crossed the border into British Somaliland, others made for the mountains of Garamulata and Chercher where they were to initiate the first phase of the Ethiopian resistance.

Graziani now had only one aim: to enter Harar before Marshal Badoglio entered Addis Ababa. On May 3, he flew to Daggahbur, but the rain that had plagued him throughout his campaign had created such a sea of mud it threatened to block the road to Wehib Pasha's fortress city. In his diary under May 5, Adriano Grande, the poet, entered, "They tell me Graziani's in a nervous state. I'm not surprised. The rain that kept him inactive at Hamanlei for four days and another four at Daggahbur has held up his advance on Harar, which should have been in our hands by now. If it hadn't been for the rain, we'd have entered the city on the day Badoglio entered Addis Ababa, or even earlier. All this delay threatens to cast a shadow over Graziani's glorious campaign that has been so

---

[20] *Dejatch* Nasibu died shortly afterward of tuberculosis in a sanatorium in Davos. A poem by Baroness Maria Atzel on Nasibu's death was printed in the *New Times and Ethiopia News*, December 11, 1937:

> He fought so well, he had so brief a day,
> Leave him his dreams as his life ebbs away.
> The setting sun sheds one last ray of light
> To bid the dying warrior goodnight.
> Flowers of the Ogaden bow low with grief,
> And far away the Abyssinians chant
> A threnody for their heroic chief.

prodigiously successful. What a damned shame! We'll vindi-
cate ourselves by occupying Jijiga, Harar and Dire Dawa with
all possible speed." [21] But when the army reached the gates of
Harar, there was no *Condottiero* riding at its head, no triumphal entry. Graziani had stumbled and injured himself during
a visit to a Coptic church in Jijiga—he had caught his foot in
what he asserted was a "pitfall." Possibly Graziani's hatred of
the Coptic clergy stemmed from this incident—the violent,
unreasoning hatred that reached its peak when he sentenced
Abuna Petros and Abuna Mikael to death and ordered the
mass execution of 425 deacons and monks of the monastery
of Debra Libanos.

At noon on May 9, Marshal Badoglio with a party of officers
and men arrived by train from Addis Ababa at Dire Dawa,
where General Graziani and his entourage were drawn up on
the platform. The men of the two victorious armies presented
arms to one another in turn; illustrations of this historic
ceremony appeared on the covers of all the popular magazines
in Italy. The war was over, even in Harar, littered with debris,
sacked by *shiftas*, peace reigned once more. "The planes, at
which the Ethiopians had fired until nightfall on the day we
entered the city, circled just above the rooftops," wrote Max
David, "A few rifle shots cracked from the mountains, but
they sounded less and less frequently and finally ceased. Sometimes the bush telegraph is slow, and not all the Ethiopians
realized the war was over, that the king of kings had vanished
from the face of the earth. Tap-tap-tap—the swift beat on the
goatskin drums sent out the order: 'Cease fire.' " [22]

The war was over. On the southern front, the losses had
been comparatively low. Eighty percent of the casualties,
killed or wounded, were Libyan mercenaries, Somalis, and
Askaris. Only 390 out of a total figure of 3,139 were Italians.
A glance at the number of Italian casualties is enough to prove

[21] Adriano Grande, *La Legione Parini*, p. 217.
[22] *Con l'esercito italiano in A.O.*, p. 715.

that Pierre Bonardi, the French journalist, was a true prophet: "Before they [the Ethiopians] meet the Europeans, they will endure five levels of hells. The bombs from the air. The shelling from the long-range howitzers. The deadly splutter of machine guns. The tanks. The Askaris." [23] He forgot to mention a sixth and even more frightful hell—the hell of mustard gas.

[23] Pierre Bonardi, in *Servizio Stampa A.O.*, p. 233.

Chapter sixteen

The Train to Jibouti

"The emperor did not leave the capital voluntarily, the decision was forced on him," Colonel Kosrof Boghossian told me, "Once again, on the morning of May 1, the war drums were beaten, and we men of the Imperial Guard were ordered to encamp at Chola at the gates of Addis and await the command to attack." [1] During the long retreat from Mai Chew, Haile Selassie had developed a number of plans, none of which foresaw the abandonment of the struggle. His main preoccupation was to delay the fall of Addis Ababa as long as possible with the one striking force that remained to him, Ras Getachew's 5,000 men. He was also considering the transfer of the seat of government to Harar or, if Harar proved too vulnerable to Graziani's threat, to Gore. If worse came to worse, he had made up his mind to join Ras Imru and wage a guerrilla

---

[1] Colonel Boghossian furnished me with many valuable details.

war amid the gorges of the Blue Nile and the rugged mountains of Gojjam.

On May 1, determined to put one of these plans into action, the emperor convoked the 23 surviving members of the Imperial Council at the "Great *Gebbi.*" * Among them were Ras Kassa, Ras Getachew, Sirak Heruy, minister for foreign affairs, Lorenzo Taezaz, the negus's aide, and *Fitaurari* Birru. When these dignitaries had heard what the emperor had to say and retired to discuss his plans, Haile Selassie sent for the British minister Sir Sidney Barton, and a little later, for Bodard, the French ambassador, and told them he intended to defend his capital. But it was not to be. The members of the Imperial Council had come to the unanimous decision that the negus must leave Ethiopia immediately for Geneva to make a last appeal to the free world from the tribune of the League of Nations. The emperor began by flatly turning down this solution, but when Ras Kassa and the empress urged him to adopt it, when—and this weighed most heavily with him—Ras Getachew told him his men were too demoralized to continue fighting, he changed his mind. "We had resisted to the uttermost limits of our strength," the negus said later, "and we believed that our dead, our wounded, our people burned with mustard gas in this farce of a war, our villages reduced to ashes, our lakes poisoned with gas, our animals who died when they drank from them—we believed that the horrors we had endured would furnish the clear proof of our determination to preserve our independence. For this reason it was essential for the head of the empire to leave Ethiopia for Geneva without delay." [2]

The emperor's changed appearance showed only too plainly the agonized state of his mind. George Steer who saw him at this time was shocked: "He was dressed in khaki as a general. His aspect froze my blood. Vigor had left his face, his body

* The huge palace built for Menelik (TRANS.).

[2] *Une victoire de la civilisation,* pp. 50–59.

was crumpled up, his shoulders drooped. The orders on his tunic concealed a hollow, not a chest." [3] That afternoon, the emperor issued his final orders. The government was to transfer to Gore with Wolde Tzaddik, President of the Senate, at its head. The *Kantiba* * was to remain at his post, take what steps he could do prevent rioting from breaking out, and ensure that no resistance was offered to the Italians. Lastly, Haile Selassie begged the Abuna Kyril, the Metropolitan, to stay in Addis Ababa and do all that lay in his power to maintain calm. These provisions, of which there is ample evidence, contrast strangely with Konovaloff's description of the negus's behavior: "On Thursday night, in a fury of rage, he tore down the silk curtains from the baldachin of his throne, and shouted: 'Take what you please, sack, loot, but do not burn down the *gebbi* lest a curse fall on you. But loot, sack, pillage—leave nothing for the Italians.' " [4] The emperor may or may not have lost momentary control of himself, but it seems unlikely, to say the least of it, that he ordered his capital to be sacked since, on the morning of May 2, the police did their utmost to hold back the mob intent on pillaging and wrecking the city. [5]

[3] George Steer, *Caesar in Abyssinia*, p. 367.

* Mayor (TRANS.).

[4] Konovaloff, *Con le armate del negus*, p. 210. There are several versions of what the emperor is supposed to have said. According to Pierre Itchac, his words were, "Sack this ill-fated city, but do not burn the *gebbi*—it will bring you bad luck. I leave you all my possessions." (See *l'Illustration*, p. 200.) That most unreliable and wildly romantic writer, Henri de Monfreid, tells us that "during the night, the emperor left the *gebbi*, abandoned it to the soldiery, and gave orders to *Ato* Makonnen Habte Wold for the sacking of the capital and the massacre of all the whites." See *L'Avion Noir* (Grasset, 1936), p. 195.

[5] On p. 260 of his book, *Con le colonne celeri*, Cesco Tomaselli wrote, "The imperial guard still obeyed the orders of their officers. The chief of police had ridden along Makonnen Street, and had visited the legations to announce that the situation was under complete control and that there was no need for any anxiety. But shortly afterward, the sound of firing, the yells of the mob made themselves heard. A band of rioters surged toward the shop owned by one Gunatakis, who, although he had been born in the Dodec-

Indeed it was only when thousands of *shiftas*, Galla, Gurage, and disbanded soldiers invaded the capital that they abandoned their attempts to maintain law and order. The xenophobia that had smoldered for so long flared up with overwhelming violence, and the rioters looted and set ablaze all the shops owned by Europeans. Even some of the imperial residences and government buildings were consigned to the flames.

The emperor was on his way to Jibouti when the first column of smoke rose from the forest city. At 4:20 A.M. on May 2, he had boarded the special train with his wife, his five children, and some hundred high-ranking officers and dignitaries.[6] An unwilling passenger on the train was the august prisoner Ras Hailu Tekla Haimanot, the deposed governor of Gojjam. The negus, suspecting, and quite rightly as it turned out, that the ras would afford the Italians valuable assistance, had decided to remove him from Ethiopia. When the train stopped at Dire Dawa, however, Haile Selassie, realizing that it would not be practicable to drag the ras across Europe, set him free.[7] The train did not pull out of Dire Dawa for several hours as the emperor had telegraphed his old friend Chapman-Andrews [later Sir Edwin Chapman-Andrews], the British consul at Harar, to meet him there. In the course of their

---

anese, had retained Italian nationality. In a few seconds, his premises were looted and set alight. The police continued to try and force a way through the crowd which grew denser at every moment."

[6] Graziani had wired Rome for permission to bomb the train that was taking the emperor to Jibouti, but this was refused. "Once we had decided to leave Addis Ababa for Jibouti, we had no choice—there was no other way of getting there except by train. We were well aware that it might be bombed by the Italians, but we had to take the risk," the emperor told me.

[7] According to certain Fascist sources and to Leonard Mosley, Ras Hailu escaped from the train during the halt at Dire Dawa. When I asked Colonel Boghossian, who had accompanied the negus, if this was true, he replied, "It's utterly untrue. The emperor pardoned him, and allowed him to leave the train. He also pardoned five other traitors and let them go—one of them was the ex-ambassador to Rome, Afewerk."

conversation, the negus admitted that he already regretted leaving Addis Ababa and that he hoped to return to Ethiopia and join Ras Desta, his son-in-law, and what remained of Ras Desta's forces, in Bale. "It took me some time to dissuade him, but it had to be done," Sir Edwin told Leonard Mosley.[8] The emperor boarded the train once more and it chugged away across the Danakil desert. Within a few hours it reached Jibouti. Haile Selassie's exile had begun; it was to last until the end of 1941.[9]

The negus's departure from the capital was the signal for rioting and violence. *Shiftas* fought one another for booty and the Shoans took advantage of the wild confusion to shoot down their enemies, the Galla. *Shiftas* and disbanded warriors made vain attempts to storm the British and French legations where most of the foreign contingent had taken refuge. "Dawn, May 5—Addis is utterly silent, strangely silent. Here and there smoke curls up from burning houses. The streets are deserted . . . Every hundred meters or so, a corpse lies amid the debris. Most of the dead are Ethiopians, but among them are a few Europeans, Armenians, or Greeks murdered by the rioters who looted their shops," recorded Marcel Junod.[10] The sack of Addis Ababa, this final tragedy, the incontrovertible proof of the fragile foundations of the empire and of its profound cleavages, played right into the hand of the victors,

[8] Leonard Mosley, *Haile Selassie*, p. 232.

[9] In *L'Avion Noir*, Henri de Monfreid wrote that the negus took out of the country 117 chests of gold ingots which he deposited at Barclay's Bank in Jerusalem. Needless to say, this was grist for the mill of the Italian propagandists. While no one in their senses would have expected the emperor to leave the ingots in Ethiopia for the Italians, I must make it absolutely clear that the decision to remove the gold from the country was made, not by the negus, but by the Crown Council. The gold, a far less fabulous sum than was stated, was used to maintain the tiny court in exile and finance the resistance movement in Ethiopia.

[10] Marcel Junod, *Les troisième combattant*, p. 61. During the rioting, 500 people were killed, fourteen of whom were whites—one Englishman, one American, one Turk, four Greeks, and seven Armenians.

allowing them to appear as the saviors, of a barbarous race, the apostles of light and civilization. What a thousand pities it was that this image was not sustained, that only a year later, after the attempt on Graziani's life, the neo-squadristi of Addis Ababa carried out a massacre ten times greater and ten times less justified in the capital that so obscured the true merit of countless Italian soldiers and officials who sincerely believed they were there to rescue the Ethiopian people from utter ignorance and misery.

The agony of Addis Ababa was drawing to an end. On the afternoon of May 5, Marshal Badoglio's mechanized column came within sight of the capital. It was raining heavily and the sky was sulphurous with thunderclouds. At 1600 hours the Italians reached the gates, and the marshal, accompanied by his entourage, made a triumphal entry into the city of the king of kings. Among the riders in the cavalcade were Bottai, Lessona, and other members of the Fascist hierarchy, and Badoglio's most trusted generals, Gabba, Cona, Santini, and Pirzio Biroli. "When they reached the Kebana blockhouse, a detachment of Ethiopian customs guards presented arms impeccably to the victorious Marshal, although their rifles were of different makes and lengths; farther on, a platoon of Italian grenadiers paid him the same homage. Every *tukul* displayed a white flag." [11] The column advanced for a couple of miles, reached the suburb of Kebana, turned right, and made its way along an avenue of eucalyptus trees to the Italian legation. At 1745 hours, while a few R.O.-37 pursuit planes were giving an aerobatic display, the Italian tricolor was hoisted above the legation. "Four shouts of 'Attention!' " wrote Giovanni Artieri in jerky telegraphic prose, "Voice of Badoglio. Hushed silence only broken by patter of rain. Rain falls on faces, hands, rifle butts, bayonets, trees, flowers. Three cheers for the king, three cheers for Mussolini. Air Marshal Magliocco's face wet with

[11] Cesco Tomaselli, *Con le colonne celeri*, p. 248.

rain or tears. Badoglio's too. Suddenly they embrace one another. Marshal says as if he'd just come off best in game of bowls, 'We've done it! We've won!' Goodbye, glorious war. This is your reporter sitting on ground on cushion of mud typing out his last dispatch on his portable." [12]

For the last few days, the Italian people had known that Addis Ababa was about to fall, but when the news came late in the evening of May 5 that Marshal Badoglio had entered the capital, they went wild with excitement and heartfelt joy. They surged into the streets and packed the Piazza Venezia. In his speech from the balcony, the Duce said, "During the thirty centuries of our history, Italy has known many solemn and memorable moments—this is unquestionably one of the most solemn, the most memorable. People of Italy, people of the world, peace has been restored." [13] The crowd would not let him go—ten times they recalled him to the balcony and cheered and waved while the boys of the various Fascist youth organizations sang the newly composed "Hymn of the Empire." Four days later, the same scenes were repeated when the Duce in his speech of the "shining sword" and the "fatal hills of Rome," announced: "At last Italy has her empire." Two days earlier, King Victor Emmanuel III had conferred the Grand Order of Savoy on him, thus definitely linking the destiny of the reigning House to that of fascism: "As the Minister of the Armed Forces, he planned, directed and won the greatest war in colonial history, a war which he, as head of the king's government, had foreseen and willed for the prestige, the life, the might of the Fascist Motherland." The enthusiasm of the monarchy for the African achievement can be

---

[12] *Con l'esercito italiano in A.O.*, p. 687.

[13] Benito Mussolini, *Scritti e discorsi dell'Impero*, p. 99. The speeches he made on May 5 and May 9 were immediately translated into Latin by Nicola Festa (*La Fondazione dell'Impero*, Naples: Rispoli, 1937). Here is the old translation of the opening sentence, "*Nigra subucula induti vos novi rerum ordinis auctores!*" (The Blackshirts of the Revolution!).

gauged by the fatuous words that Princess Marie-José entered in her diary on May 5, when she crossed the Red Sea on the *Cesarea:* "The Duce ended his speech with 'Long live Italy!' —'Long live Italy!' shouted our people, 'Long live the future empress of Ethiopia!'—'Ethiopia is Italian!' . . . and the Italians on board the *Cesarea,* like all the Italians, are thrilled to think that their sovereigns are now emperor and empress! Their princess, who is tending the sick and wounded soldiers, will one day be an empress! To have lived through these hours on the *Cesarea* is to have lived a lifetime!" [14]

While the Italian people did not pay much attention to the grotesque parallels drawn by Mussolini between the Fascist empire and the Roman empire, they had good cause for rejoicing. The war had been won in far less time than they had expected at the loss of only 2,000 of their men,[15] and they had acquired a vast territory whose riches, needless to say, were magnified by the regime. As for the Fascist hierarchy, it had even more reason to rejoice, for it knew through the prefects that never had fascism been more popular. As Dr. David Thomson rightly observed: "At one stroke it [the war] quelled discontent at home, or at least drowned it in Fascist propaganda and shouts of military glory; it eased the burden of economic stagnation and created a timely diversion; and it opened a new phase in Mussolini's policy of seeking imperial

[14] Princess Marie-José of Piedmont, *Infermiera in Africa Orientale,* (Milan: Mondadori, 1937), p. 124. On p. 129, the princess wrote, "When we reached the Mediterranean, *mare nostro,* we had a kind of feeling all the other seas were ours!"

[15] According to an official statement published in the *Gazzetta del Popolo* June 3, 1936, the Italian casualties for the period January 1, 1935–May 31, 1936, were 1,304 killed in action, plus 1,009 who either died of wounds or from illnesses they had contracted. Total: 2,313. The casualty figure of the laborers was 453 dead. The number of Eritrean dead was 1,086 on the northern front and 507 on the southern front. The Italians estimated that 50,000 Ethiopians had been killed. The Ethiopians, however, put the number at 275,000; this figure included all the civilians who lost their lives during the war.

power in the Mediterranean and Africa." [16] Mussolini interpreted the national sentiment to H. R. Knickerbocker of the Hearst press: "Ethiopia has satisfied Italy's inexorable need for expansion, and has placed her among those nations who have all the living room they require." [17] A few years later, on the eve of the collapse of fascism, the Duce said bitterly to Ciano that he wished his stomach ulcer had killed him in that hour of glory.

"That was the proudest moment of his life, the grand climax of Italian Fascism," wrote H. L. Matthews, "It was the nearest this modern Icarus got to the sun. From that moment on, the course was downward to destruction. Even as he cried from the balcony that it was 'an empire of peace because Italy wants peace for all,' he was making preparations for the wanton intervention in Spain which began a few months later." [18] Inevitably, isolated as he was by his defiance of the League of Nations, Mussolini drew ever closer to an alliance with Hitler, an alliance that was to prove catastrophic for Italy. The Ethiopian war, it must be borne in mind, had cost the country the fabulous sum of 12 milliard, 111 million lire, a new and fearful deficit that left the economy hopelessly unbalanced.[19] It must also be recalled that the easy victory in Ethiopia convinced our historians and generals that Italy had become a great military power overnight. Ciasca, for instance, wrote, "Our troops had triumphed in Ethiopia where even the Romans failed, where the Arab invasion could make no headway, where the fortunes of modern military Egypt foundered, where the British army had been forced to retreat in hot haste." [20] As for Marshal Badoglio, he wrote vaingloriously, "It was a war

[16] David Thomson, *Europe Since Napoleon* (London: Longmans, 1963), p. 685.

[17] Benito Mussolini, *Seritti e discorsi dell'Impero*, p. 153.

[18] H. L. Matthews, *The Fruits of Fascism*, p. 266.

[19] Statement made to the Chamber by Thaon de Revel, the Financial Minister, on May 20, 1936.

[20] Raffaele Ciasca, *Storia coloniale dell'Italia contemporanea*, p. 689.

207

from which it will be possible to draw valuable lessons for the conduct of future wars, colonial or otherwise." [21] But four years later, those same generals who had covered themselves with glory during the Italo-Ethiopian war, suffered the crushing humiliation of defeat or of abject surrender. Ciano industriously recorded the Duce's scathing verdicts on these men in the pages of his diary.

While the Italian people were rejoicing, Haile Selassie was crossing the Red Sea on the British cruiser *Enterprise*, which had sailed from Jibouti at 1615 hours on May 4. Shaken though he was by the last, dramatic moments in his capital, the emperor had retained his customary energy, his fighting spirit. Two days after his arrival in Jerusalem, he sent a

[21] Pietro Badoglio, *The War in Abyssinia*, p. 169. I asked General Quirino Armellini what, in his opinion, had been the principal causes that had led to the Italian victory. "There were diverse reasons," he told me, "Above all, however, even though the Ethiopians greatly outnumbered us and were fighting in their own country, we won the war because of the high morale of our troops, our modern arms, the brilliance of our commanders and the overwhelming superiority of the material and means at our disposal, particularly the artillery and the air force. Furthermore, the negus himself contributed to our victory since he had been persuaded by his European military advisers into believing that he could plan and conduct a strategic battle. Possibly he had the ability to do so, but unquestionably the generals he had appointed and the men of his armies had not been sufficiently trained in the tactics of modern war. At the outset we feared the emperor might hurl the full weight of his forces against us, regardless of the heavy losses they would sustain and, had he done so, we might have been thrown into confusion. However, after the battle of Amba Aradam, we felt completely confident, for it had become clear he would not launch an offensive of this kind against us and that he intended to realize his ambitious dream of putting his forces into the field and conducting the operations he himself had planned." Now let us see what an Ethiopian general, Ras Nasibu, had to say: "If the Italians had not used poison gases against us and if the consignments of arms and ammunition intended for my army had not been confiscated by the French authorities in Jibouti, the enemy would never have broken through our lines." (See *Temps*, May 17, 1936.) General Pascek (see *Mitteilungen*, July 1936), agreed with the views expressed by General Armellini and maintained the Ethiopians threw away all chances of success by meeting the Italians face to face instead of resorting to guerrilla tactics.

telegram to the League of Nations in which he said, inter alia, "We have decided to bring to an end the most unequal, most unjust, most barbarous war of our age, and have chosen to take the road to exile in order that our people shall not be exterminated and in order to consecrate ourselves wholly and in peace to the preservation of our empire's independence . . . we now demand that the League of Nations should continue its efforts to secure respect for the covenant, and that it should decide not to recognize territorial extensions, or the exercise of an assumed sovreignty, resulting from an illegal recourse to armed force and from numerous other violations of international agreements. . . ."[22] This forceful telegram dispatched at the right moment decided several governments, among them that of Great Britain, to defer recognition of the Italian conquest.[23] But this was the emperor's last success in the diplomatic sphere. Now that the Italians had occupied Addis Ababa, the democracies hoped Haile Selassie would resign himself to his fate and, since the final act had been played out, allow the curtain to fall. Great Britain, in fact, was so anxious to avoid giving offense to Mussolini that, when the negus reached Gibraltar, he was transferred from the cruiser *Capetown* to an ordinary liner, a ruse by which the government was spared the risk and annoyance of according him a state reception.

Only one hope remained to the emperor, the hope of gaining the sympathy and support of the world by appearing in person before the tribunal of the League of Nations at the special assembly convened at the request of Sr. Cantilo of Argentina. On June 30, 1936, two months after his defeat at Mai Chew, Haile Selassie, wearing an ample black cloak that

---

[22] *Official Journal* of the League of Nations, *Minutes of the 92nd Session of the Council*, No. 6, document 1597 (June 1936), p. 660.

[23] Ethiopia will always be grateful to the four countries who refused to recognize the Italian conquest. They were, the United States of America, the U.S.S.R., Mexico, and New Zealand.

accentuated his pale face, so alive with intelligence, stood before the microphone. There was a breathless hush, and the eyes of all present were fixed on the slight, diminutive figure whose dignity Italian caricaturists had failed to destroy, whose spirit the Italian war machine had failed to break. But hardly had the President, Van Zeeland, given him the signal to speak than pandemonium broke out in the auditorium. The uproar was caused by twenty or so Italian journalists staging a demonstration, who were booing, jeering, and yelling insults at the emperor.[24] Haile Selassie stood there impassively, waiting for order to be restored. Titulescu, the Rumanian chairman, jumped to his feet and shouted: *"A la porte les sauvages!"* As soon as the Italians had been ejected and silence reigned once more, the emperor began to plead his cause with infinite courage and pathos: "I, Haile Selassie I, Emperor of Ethiopia, am here today to claim that justice which is due to my people and the assistance promised to it eight months ago when fifty nations asserted that an aggression had been committed. None other than the emperor can address the appeal of the Ethiopian people to fifty nations. . . . Given that I am setting a precedent, that I am the first head of a state to address the Assembly, it is surely without precedent that a people, the victim of an iniquitous war, now stands in danger of being abandoned to the aggressor. . . ." He then went on to speak of the events that had led up to the war and to denounce the gas attacks made by the Fascist Air Force, attacks of which he furnished proof with new and damning evidence. Ethiopia, he said, did not expect other nations to shed their blood for her, but: "I assert that the problem submitted to the Assembly today is a much wider one than the removal of sanctions. It is not merely a settlement of Italian aggression. It is collective. It

---

[24] Because of this disgraceful behavior, Giulio Caprin, Paolo Monelli, Lino Cajani, Eugenio Morreale, Carlo Giucci, Alfredo Signoretti, Engely, and Cassuto were arrested by the Swiss police and subsequently expelled from the Canton of Geneva.

is the very existence of the League of Nations . . . in a word, it is international morality that is at stake." He then turned to the delegates of the fifty nations, and asked them earnestly not to recognize the Italian conquest but to grant Ethiopia a loan to finance a resistance movement: "Representatives of the world, I have come to Geneva to discharge in your midst the most painful of the duties of a head of state. What reply shall I take back to my people?" [25]

But the emperor's deeply moving speech, his prophetic condemnation of those who were digging the grave of the ideal of collective security, met with no success. The resolution of the Ethiopian delegation was heavily defeated. Eight days later, Great Britain recalled the home fleet from the Mediterranean. On July 15, the sanctions on Italy were lifted. Mussolini's victory over the negus, over Great Britain, over the League of Nations seemed to be complete. But the Duce had underestimated the emperor and his people. Here was an emperor who would never renounce his rights, a people who would never submit. On January 1, 1939, almost three years after Badoglio's triumphant entry into Addis Ababa, Ciano recorded with dismay in his diary, "In fact, Asmara is still in a state of complete revolt, and the sixty-five battalions that are stationed there are compelled to live in temporary fortifications." [26]

[25] *Official Journal* of the League of Nations, Special Supplement no. 151 (1936) pp. 22–25. During my interview with Haile Selassie, he pronounced his final and bitter judgment on the League of Nations: "When we first turned to the League of Nations, it was to put before them all the facts that had led up to the war and to ask for aid for our country. But because this was an age of uncertainty and mistrust when men feared to take any definite line of action, our requests were unheeded. Consequently, the world which had done nothing to help us, was itself plunged into chaos. Subsequently, those in power realized that our tragedy has led to the tragedy of the Second World War. Whenever the spirit of the thirties manifests itself in this continent or that, we must remember the lessons of the past and be on our guard."

[26] Galeazzo Ciano, *Ciano's Diary, 1939–43* (London: Heinemann, 1946), p. 316.

211

Chapter seventeen

Italy's Colonial Policy

Three days after Marshal Badoglio's entry into Addis Ababa, the city began to return to life. In small groups, the 50,000 Ethiopians who had fled to the mountains of Entoto, trickled back to their *tukuls*. The debris, the putrefying corpses were cleared away. Sakerillaris, the Greek barber who had managed to save one mirror from the looters, reopened his shop. Bottai, who had been appointed governor of the capital, installed himself in the "Little *Gebbi*," and for some reason ordered the six remaining lions to be shot. Trade started to pick up and the lira had already entered into circulation; the current rate of exchange was 6 lire to the thaler. On the surface all appeared calm, but despite Mussolini's optimistic forecasts, the war was anything but over. The standing force of 426 officers and 9,934 men that garrisoned the forest city and its extensive outskirts was, in fact, almost ringed round by 50,000 leaderless Ethiopian soldiers, the majority of whom had been disbanded, but all of whom were armed. Most of the empire, indeed, was only nominally under Italian domination. About two-thirds of the country was still under the control of negusite dignitaries, while massive forces commanded by Ras Desta and Ras Imru, Generals Beyene Merid, Gabre Maryam, Makonnen Wossen, Fikri Maryam and Balcha, and *Fitauraris* Bahade Gabre, Shimellis, Shalek Asfau, and dozens of others were concentrated in Gojjam, Shoa, Jimma, Galla-Sidamo and Hararge. Many other chiefs, however, among them Ras Hailu Tekla Haimanot, Ras Kebbede Mangasha, and *Dejatch* Ayelu Birru put themselves and their men at the disposal of the Italian authority.[1]

On May 22, when the situation was at its most critical point, Marshal Badoglio returned to Italy at his own request, and was succeeded as Viceroy by General Rodolfo Graziani, the very last man to carry out the extremely difficult task of pacification. Mussolini, knowing Graziani as he did, should have advised him to act with moderation; instead, he wired to him on June 6: "All rebels captured are to be shot,"[2] thus

[1] On May 9, 1936, Ras Seyoum, who had been ordered by the emperor to stir up a revolt in Tigre, surrendered to General Bastico: "I swear to be loyal to you, your mighty king, your just Leader and your victorious general, Marshal Badoglio. Henceforth, your king is my king, your commanders are the commanders of my people." (See p. 251 of General Bastico's book.) On June 10, Ras Hailu, the Abuna Kyril, Ras Gabre Hiwot, *Dejatch* Mangasha Wubie, *Dejatch* Habte Mikael and the ex-ambassador in Rome, Afewerk, swore the oath of allegiance to Italy. On June 23, even Ras Kebbede Mangasha submitted to the Italians. "We pardon you, Ras Kebbede, as we have pardoned all those who submitted with you," Graziani told him, "but the law that lays down that a pardon is extended to the Ethiopians who submit to us is equally a law under which rebellion is a capital offense. It is a just and generous law to those who keep it; to those who break it, no mercy will be shown: they will be tried by a tribunal and sentenced to death. Keep to the road which the government of Rome has traced for you; follow it faithfully, you and your sons. By doing so, you will transform the land of your birth into a mighty and civilized country—the country that now belongs to Rome. It will be hers for ever." (See *Gazzetta del Popolo*, June 25, 1936.)

[2] See *La civilisation de l'Italie Fasciste en Ethiopie*, Press Bureau and Department of Information of the Imperial Government (Addis Ababa: Berhanena Press), p. 10. Telegram 1763/6496 dispatched from Rome at

authorizing Graziani to order mass executions and terrorize the population of entire regions with gas attacks. These brutal measures roused the burning indignation of A. C. W. Martin, the Ethiopian ambassador in London. In a letter to the press, he wrote: "General Graziani has declared all Ethiopians still fighting for their country are "brigands" to be shot immediately, not combatants to be treated as prisoners of war. Against this illegal conduct, I make the strongest possible protest." [3] But even the "strongest possible" protests were useless; from now on, every Ethiopian patriot was a "brigand." The 300 very young cadets of the Holeta Academy, who killed Air Marshal Magliocco and eleven of his officers when they boldly but rashly landed their 3 planes at Lekemti on June 27 to stir up the Galla against the Shoans and Amharas, were "brigands." [4] So were Maryam Fikre and his men who repeatedly sabotaged the Addis Ababa-Jibouti railway line. So were Ras Desta and his warriors who for another year were to harass the Italians with guerrilla warfare in Galla-Sidamo.

At dawn on July 28, when Addis Ababa was shrouded by a curtain of torrential rain, a few thousand Ethiopians led by Aberra and Asfa Wossen, the sons of Ras Kassa, swooped down from the mountains and surrounded the capital, infiltrating the outlying districts of Kirkos, Bole, and Gullale. The Italian troops beat them back almost immediately, but on the following day they attacked again, once more without success.

1435 hours on June 6 received in Addis Ababa at 0245 hours on the following day. Graziani refers to this telegram, which is of capital importance, in his telegram to General Nasi—(523/4375, dated June 22, 1936), ". . . I take this opportunity of reminding you of order of His Excellency, Head of State, all rebels captured to be immediately executed, order repeated by Duce in a second telegram No. 40." (See *Il I Anno dell'Impero*, printed in Addis Ababa, 1939. Documents in vol. 1, p. 144, and document 106.)

[3] *New Times and Ethiopia News*, June 6, 1936.

[4] The news of this tragic event was not immediately published in Italy. It did not appear in the newspapers until July 8, twelve days after it had taken place.

Graziani suspected that the instigator of this uprising was the Abuna of Dessie, Abuna Petros, and dealt with him summarily. "Abuna Petros was shot in the market place at 1630 hours July 29 in the presence of a large number of the population," he wired to Rome.[5] In a second telegram he stated, "Abuna Petros, one of the four bishops who has terrorized chiefs and population, has been executed. Repressive action continues against armed groups scattered in the bush. Inexorable repressive measures have been effected against all population guilty, if not of complicity, at least of absence of reaction."[6] These brutal and warlike acts were ambiguously described to the Italians in Ethiopia as "operations of the grand colonial policy" in order to preserve calm in the country. On October 24, Mussolini, anxious to prevent any suspicions arising at home as to the true nature of these "opera-

[5] Governo Generale dell' A.O.I., *La guerra italo-etiopica*, document no. 222, p. 284, telegram 1645/8837, dated July 29, 1936, addressed to the Colonial Minister. In 1938, in a message to all the Christian churches, Haile Selassie gave a long list of the harm done to the Coptic church by the Italians, of the destruction of Coptic churches, and the atrocities committed against the Coptic clergy: "(1) The killing of Coptic priests and Moslem sheiks after the attempt on Graziani's life when the police opened fire indiscriminately on the Ethiopians who were present; (2) The refusal of the Italian authority to allow the Christian burial of Ethiopians who had been shot and to the victims of the massacre of February 19–23. The Italian authority refused to permit the families of these victims to bear their dead away; petrol was poured on the bodies and they were consumed to ashes. (3) The destruction of the Cathedral of St. George in Addis Ababa, of the ancient and holy monastery of Debra Libanos, and many other churches. (4) The public execution in Addis Ababa of the Abuna Petros, who had refused to make an act of submission to the Italian authority and had also refused to excommunicate all Ethiopians who refused to take the oath of loyalty to the Italian authority. The Abuna Petros was shot in July 1937. (5) The removal to Rome of one of our most historic monuments, the great obelisk raised in Axum by an emperor who was on the throne in 400 A.D."

[6] *Ibid.*, document no. 225, p. 286, telegram 1667/8906 sent to the colonial minister on July 30, 1936. Part of this telegram, as well as parts of others, appear to have been omitted from the official reports of the central government in Italian East Africa; I saw the photostats of the original telegrams in the Ethiopian archives.

tions," declared in his "olive branch and bayonets" address, "It took us seven months to conquer the empire, but to occupy and pacify it will take us far less time. At this moment our troops are marching hundreds of miles into the fertile regions of the Great Lakes in the heart of Equatorial Africa, while a column of our men is on its way westward to Gore, the seat of the puppet government." [7] Mussolini ignored the fact that almost seven months had elapsed since the occupation of Addis Ababa, and did not mention that during October 173 Italian officers, soldiers, and laborers had been killed or wounded. In November the casualty list was 156, in December, 134.

If the situation was precarious for the Italian troops, it was desperate for the Ethiopian patriots. "After the emperor left for Europe, I rounded up a thousand or so men and left Debra Markos for Gore, the seat of the provisional government," Ras Imru told me, "There I met *Dejatch* Wolde Tzaddik and Mr. Erskine, the British consul, now the only representative of the diplomatic corps in Ethiopia. A few hundred cadets of the Holeta Academy who were in the city were desperately anxious to fight the Italians at all costs, but speaking from experience, I told them it would be sheer madness and advised them to cross into the Sudan and wait for better times. There was another reason for my advice. Although via Gambela we could communicate with the outside world, even with London, no money, no ammunition was sent to Gore to enable us to continue fighting.[8] Between August and September we had a series of clashes with the Italians in Wollega, and our store of ammunition became alarmingly low. So much so that I was

[7] Benito Mussolini, *Scritti e discorsi dell'Impero*, p. 183.

[8] On September 21, 1936, the Ethiopian legation in London announced far too optimistically that two-thirds of the country was still under the control of the negusite authority and that Ras Imru had assumed the supreme command, over-riding even Ras Desta, who was fighting in Sidamo, Aberra Kassa, who was operating in Salale, and *Bajirond* Fikre Selassie, who was harassing the Italians in Arussi.

216

forced to leave the city, although, owing to the unhealthy air of the marshland, a great many of my men were suffering from malaria. I decided to make my way in the direction of Jimma in order to reach Maji on the Sudan frontier. But the Italians had already cut off the road, and I was obliged to retreat and fight my way step by step to Gojjam. Of my 1200 men, some were wounded, some were sick, some had exhausted their entire supply of ammunition. They had fought for a whole year and I could not ask them to make any further sacrifices. I therefore decided to surrender and gave myself up to General Malta. In all fairness, I must state that the Italians immediately saw to the wounded and sick." [9]

For once in his life, Graziani acted generously. In the letter he sent to Lessona on December 16, informing him of Ras Imru's surrender, he even gave the reason for his leniency: "Ras Imru, surrounded by a ring of iron, defeated by Princevalle's troops, gave himself up and I therefore regarded him as a prisoner of war. Had he been captured during a skirmish, I would have given orders for his immediate execution." [10] Ras Imru's life was spared, but when he was taken to the airport at Addis Ababa at 9:00 A.M., he was followed by a crowd of Italians anxious to see this "monster," yelling insults at him, shouting "Liar! Murderer!" and for some unknown reason, "Conceited ape!" [11] Graziani did not show the same magnanimity to Ras Kassa's sons. On December 21, he wired to Lessona, "In today's action, the brothers Aberra and Asfa

[9] During my interview with him.

[10] Governo Generale dell'A.O.I., *La guerra italo-etiopica*, documents appended to vol. 2, p. 63, document no. 710, telegram 32507.

[11] In the course of my interview with him, Ras Imru told me of this ordeal. He was flown to Massawa where he was put aboard the *Colombo*. From Naples to where the *Colombo* docked, Ras Imru was taken to Ponsa (where the Duce was to be confined seven years later). He was later transferred to another prison on the Lipari Islands, and finally, he was brought back to Italy and imprisoned at Longobuco in Calabria. He was liberated by the Allies in 1943, and shortly afterward, returned to Ethiopia. He had languished for seven years in prison.

Wossen Kassa were captured. In pursuance of my orders, they were shot at dusk in the square of Fiche. Salale situation liquidated." [12] A few days earlier, Ras Kassa's third son, Wondewossen, had been captured in the highlands of the Takkaze region by the Wollo banda and summarily executed. Twenty years later, Lessona wrote in his memoirs, "I have never been able to understand why General Tracchia, one of our most experienced colonial soldiers and Graziani's closest collaborator, ordered Ras Kassa's son to be shot. It makes me angry to think of it. It was a shameful business, a terrible mistake that lowered our prestige. After this execution the population lost all faith in Graziani." [13]

The only commanders still holding out were Ras Desta and his chiefs, Bejene Merid and Gabre Maryam. These three men were as slippery as eels, and from June 26, 1936, to February 24, 1937, they eluded thousands of Italian and Eritrean soldiers, Somalis, and Ethiopian irregulars. But on October 26, 1936, their pursuers tracked them to Mount Jabassire, and a little later, to Arbagoma in the heart of the Jamjamo country. From that time on, the Geloso, Tucci, Gallina, Natale, Pascolini, and Ragazzoni columns followed their trail and engaged their forces in a series of battles in this region of vast lakes, where marshland alternated with dense forests. To avoid encirclement, Ras Desta decided to make for Gurage, his natal province, not far from Addis Ababa, but the Tucci column was hot on his heels, and on February 19, 1937, fell upon him at Gojetti. During this engagement, *Dejatch* Gabre Maryam and *Fitaurari* Shimellis were killed; Beyene Merid was wounded, taken prisoner, and shot with several other chiefs and a number of Eritreans who had gone over to the Ethiopians. Once more Ras Desta managed to escape, but five days later, the Italians tracked him down to the tiny village of Eya, and after

[12] Governo Generale dell'A.O.I., *La guerra italo-etiopica*, p. 104, document no. 763, telegram 8684/334444.

[13] Alessandro Lessona, *Memorie*, p. 305.

a brief resistance, Ras Desta was captured by the Tigrean banda commanded by the renegade *Dejatch* Toklu Mashasha.

Ras Desta was taken to Buttajera and haled before a hastily improvised tribunal. So changed was his appearance that it was hard to believe he was the man of whom Marcel Junod had written a year earlier, "he revealed in every gesture his nobility, his refinement." [14] His cheeks were hollow, his beard tangled and matted; he was only forty-three, but worn out by endless marches, the privations he had endured, and looked ten years older. Captain Tucci informed him that the tribunal had sentenced him to death, ordered Toklu Mashasha's Tigreans to form a firing squad, and a few minutes later, Ras Desta fell, riddled with bullets. After the execution Tucci wired Graziani, "Today, February 24 at 0600 hours, Ras Desta Damtu was captured. According to Your Excellency's orders, he was executed at 1730 hours." [15] The Italian newspapers printed the news in huge headlines and Guido Pallotta had the impudence to write, "The crack of the firing squad's rifles was a burst of defiant Fascist laughter at the world that so sanctimoniously condemns us, a shout of defiance to the powers who imposed sanctions on us. What a true squadristi slap in the face Captain Tucci has administered to that raddled old harlot Geneva!" [16]

The execution of Ras Desta and other veteran commanders did not bring the guerrilla war to an end.[17] The great rases, the

[14] Marcel Junod, *Les troisième combattant*, p. 34.

[15] Governo Generale dell'A.O.I., *La guerra italo-etiopica*, p. 377, document no. 1157, telegram 750/24.

[16] *Gazzetta del Popolo*, February 24, 1938.

[17] One of the rare documents on the liquidation of the emperor's routed armies is *Relazione sulle operazioni di grande polizia svolte dal 15 giugno 1937 al 31 marzo 1938*, a typewritten document written and signed by General Nasi, the governor of Harar, very few copies of which were issued by the military authority, Command Headquarters, Harar. This account of the operations in Abdullah-Kondudo, Garamulata, Chercher, Arussi, and Bale is probably the greatest testimony to the dauntless spirit of the Ethiopians, their determination to fight on against impossible odds, their

experienced generals, were replaced by men hitherto unknown, men such as Abebe Aregai who, three years later was
appointed commander of all the rebel forces in Ethiopia by the
emperor.[18]

Graziani was driven to such a pitch of fury by the activities
of the insurgents that he embarked on a reign of terror. "We
must continue with the work of total destruction," he wired
General Gallina [19] and General Pirzio Biroli, "As region not
accessible to troops, air force will clear it, bombing it daily
and using all the means at its disposal, essential attack with
asphyxiating gases." [20] In an official military document, we
read that in Bale alone "the results of the brief but bitter
actions that took place between February 22 and March 14 are

---

indomitable courage in the hopeless situation in which they found themselves. Here is General Nasi's description of the terrible retreat of the
survivors of Ras Desta's army: "Pursued by the troops of group 5, threatened with encirclement on the left by the Cubeddu column, continually
bombed by the air force, the rebels pushed on northward in the hope of
escaping from the dragnet and finding an opening in the vicinity of Lake
Zwai. The retreat became a rout, and small bands of desperate fugitives
marched, not only by day but throughout the hours of darkness by torchlight
under the torrential rain, abandoning in the forests of Gambo the wounded,
the sick, the women and children. The survivors plodded on, some on foot,
some on horseback, and when our troops caught up with them, they opened
fire on them in the hopeless attempt to halt their advance." I am indebted to
Mario Bassi (see Acknowledgments) whose notes drew my attention to this
document. The account of the retreat appears on p. 71.

[18] Abebe Aregai was the son of *Fitaurari* Aregai and the nephew of Ras
Goberna. As his son Daniel told me, Abebe Aregia, an officer in the
Ethiopian police force, left Addis Ababa on May 3, 1936, two days before
the Italians entered the capital and fled to the mountains of Entoto. From
Entoto he made his way to Debra Berhan, where he rallied the survivors of
Ras Aberra's force and initiated the resistance of the *Arbaňňoch*. *Dejatch*
Auraris and *Dejatch* Fikre Maryam carried out guerrilla operations under
his command.

[19] *La civilisation de l'Italie Fasciste en Ethiopie*, p. 39. Telegram
5506/22980, dated October 27, 1936.

[20] *Ibid.*, pp. 24–25, telegram 3386/15756, dated September 11, 1936.

eloquent: some 1,000 rebels killed, 500 taken prisoner, 3,000 gave themselves up." [21]

Driven beyond endurance by Graziani's repressive measures, a number of Ethiopians plotted to assassinate him. To celebrate the birth of the prince of Naples, Graziani had decided to distribute thalers to the neediest inhabitants of the capital. The ceremony took place on February 19, 1937, in the compound of the "Little *Gebbi*" and was attended by almost all the top-ranking Italian authorities, the Metropolitan, Abuna Kyril, and a large number of notables. At midday, the poor, of whom there were some 3,000, had just begun to file past the long white table on which the thalers were piled, when a hand grenade hurled by someone hidden in the crowd exploded just above the gate of the *Gebbi*. A second later, another *Breda* burst in the midst of the Italian group and Graziani fell, wounded in the back. In the next few minutes, seven more were thrown, injuring General Liotta, Guido Cortese, the mayor of Addis Ababa, Mario Appelius, the journalist, Ciro Poggiale, and another thirty or so people.

The *carabinieri*, convinced that many more missiles would be flung by conspirators lurking in the dense throng, lost their heads and opened fire indiscriminately. "The firing went on for three hours," an Italian eyewitness told me, "When it stopped, the compound was littered with bodies."

But the worst was yet to come. Late that afternoon a few hundred squads of Blackshirts, chauffeurs, and Libyan Askari's assembled outside party headquarters, and made for the native quarter. "They began to play 'Hunt the Moor' on an unheard of scale. They drenched the *tukuls* with petrol, set them alight, and as the inhabitants rushed out, finished them off with hand grenades. I heard one man complaining that his right arm ached from hurling so many grenades, while another

[21] Governo Generale dell'A.O.I., *La guerra italo-etiopica*, vol. 2, p. 323.

boasted that he'd 'done' ten *tukuls* with a single can of petrol. Many of these maniacs were known to me personally. They were tradesmen, chauffeurs, officials—people I'd always thought of as law-abiding and respectable, people who'd never fired a shot during the entire war—I'd never even suspected that all this hatred was bottled up in them. They knew perfectly well they were immune, that the only 'risk' they ran was of being awarded a medal. To my knowledge, the police only intervened once when the mob threatened to set fire to Muhammad Ali's emporium. The massacre went on for three days, then on the morning of February 22, notices were put up that said, 'Reprisals must cease at noon. Guido Cortese, Mayor of Addis Ababa.' I saw one stuck on the wall of *L'Alimentare,* a shop in the Corso Vittorio Emanuele. It was typed on cream laid paper. I read it and reread it. I couldn't believe my eyes. I found it incredible that the authorities had pasted up these notices that proved beyond a shadow of doubt that they had tacitly acquiesced in the massacre." [22]

While the neo-squadristi of Addis Ababa were engaged in their murderous work, Graziani, unable to trace his would-be assassins, took advantage of the occasion to liquidate the entire Ethiopian intelligentsia, every member of the Young Ethiopian Party, and all the officers and cadets of the Holeta Academy.[23] While Rome thoroughly approved, the wish was nevertheless expressed that the executions be carried out in the utmost secrecy with no witnesses present, an instruction that, needless to say, was never followed. Rankling at the thought that he had been rebuked, Graziani wired back in order to justify himself, "I cannot deny that some Ethiopians have shouted as they faced the firing squad, 'Long live Ethiopia!' I

[22] Evidence given to me by Signor D. in Addis Ababa, March 26, 1965. My informant asked me not to disclose his name.

[23] Among those executed were the three Martin brothers, sons of the Ethiopian ambassador in London, Ras Nasibu's son, Kifle, and the son of Sirak Heruy, the Ethiopian Foreign Minister.

beg to state, however, that executions ordered in consequence of attempt on my life are invariably carried out in isolated spots where no one, I repeat, no one can witness them." [24] Two days later, he telegraphed Mussolini, who was visiting Tripolitania, "From February 19 up to today, 324 summary executions have been carried out—all persons shot were tried and found guilty. This figure does not include those shot during the reprisals of February 19 and 20. In addition to executions, have sent 1,100 men, women and children to Danane concentration camp. . . ." [25]

It is difficult to say how many victims there were of these reprisals. The Ethiopians put the number as high as 30,000. The English, French, and American newspapers of the day give figures oscillating between 1,400 and 6,000 dead. According to certain Italian sources, 800 Ethiopians were executed and 2,000 arrested. [26] After I had questioned dozens of people in Addis Ababa, I came to the conclusion that the Ethiopian figure was greatly exaggerated and the total number of dead could not have exceeded 3,000. But this does not include the hundreds of soothsayers and monks executed on Graziani's orders in the succeeding months. As Lessona observed, "After the attempt on his life, Graziani regarded all Ethiopians with the blackest suspicion, and displayed an excess of cruelty that

[24] *Documents on Italian War Crimes Submitted to the United Nations War Crimes Commission*, vol. I (Italian telegrams and circulars), p. 51. Telegram 14154 from Graziani to the Colonial Minister, dated March 19, 1937.

[25] *Ibid.*, p. 51. Telegram 3974/14440 sent on March 21, 1937, by Graziani to the Duce, who was in Tripoli.

[26] Incidentally, accounts of the reprisals appeared in the Italian press; hardly any attempt was made to gloss them over. In the *Gazzetta del Popolo*, dated February 22, we read, "A number of quarters in Addis Ababa suspected of harboring seditious elements have been cleaned up by the Squadristi." And two days later, "Of the 2,000 Ethiopians taken into custody after the attempt on the life of General Graziani, several hundred were able to prove their innocence and have been set free. All those Ethiopians found to be armed or in whose *tukuls* arms were found, have been executed. The rest of the prisoners are awaiting trial."

223

led to even more widespread rebellion and finally to his removal." [27] Obsessed with hatred, Graziani saw enemies and would-be assassins wherever he looked. He saw them in the soothsayers and traditional storytellers and ordered them liquidated.[28] He saw them in the Coptic deacons and monks of the monastery of Debra Libanos, 425 of whom were shot. After this massacre he wired Rome, "In pursuance of my orders, at 1300 hours today General Maletti executed the vice-prior and 295 monks, also a further 23 guilty persons. . . ." [29] Six days later he wired, "The complicity of the deacons also being proved, I have given orders to shoot them, 129 in number, at Debra Berhan . . . thus there remains no more trace of the Debra Libanos monastery." [30]

[27] Alessandro Lessona, *Memorie*, p. 305.

[28] Graziani sent the following telegram to Lessona to justify the execution of the soothsayers: "After the attempt on my life on February 19, I learned through departmental channels and police headquarters that the greatest menace to public order came from the soothsayers, traditional storytellers and witch doctors. . . . As I was convinced it was essential to root out this unhealthy and dangerous element, I gave orders that all the soothsayers, storytellers and witch doctors in the forest city were to be rounded up and shot. Up to today, seventy have been executed. . . ." (See *La civilisation de l'Italie Fasciste en Ethiopie*, pp. 61–62. Telegram 3861/14044, dated March 19, 1937.) On March 20, Mussolini gave Graziani the authority to continue with this massacre in the telegram he dispatched from Tripoli: "Reports that our volunteers in Spain have suffered heavy reverses are appearing in English newspapers. These reports, deliberately distorted by the scurrilous British press, will undoubtedly be sent by the negus to Ethiopians in Jibouti and will ultimately filter through to Addis Ababa, awakening fresh hope in the population. Approve of your action re soothsayers, storytellers and witch doctors. Vital extirpate dangerous element and maintain absolute law and order." (*Ibid.*, p. 64. "Secret" telegram 19960/27/M, dated March 20, 1937. Following other telegrams, soothsayers, storytellers and witch doctors were hunted down in every province in Ethiopia and summarily executed.

[29] *Documents on Italian War Crimes Submitted to the United Nations War Crimes Commission*, p. 52. Telegram 25876, dated May 21, 1937, from Graziani to the Minister for African Italy.

[30] *Ibid.*, p. 53. Telegram 27136 dated May 27, 1937, sent by Graziani to the Minister for African Italy. The pursuit of Coptic priests was extended to all parts of Ethiopia, as we know from other telegrams. Here is a laconic

From then on the conviction grew in Rome that even if Graziani had never uttered the famous phrase, "The Duce shall have Ethiopia, with or without the Ethiopians just as he pleases," he was putting the second of these alternatives into practice with highly undesirable results.[31] Rome had also noted that Graziani "bolted and barred himself into the governor's residence at night, and protected himself with barbed-wire entanglements, machine guns, tanks, and a battalion of guards."[32] Obviously a man in Graziani's state could not continue as Viceroy of Ethiopia.[33] On November 20, 1937, to the great relief of all, particularly the Ethiopians, he was replaced by a man of a very different character, the humane and cultured Duke of Aosta. By way of compensation, Graziani was created Duke of Negelli; a nervous wreck, he left Addis Ababa lamenting bitterly that he had been unable to

---

message from General Geloso: "Three Amhara Coptic priests captured and executed at Borodda." (Governo Generale dell'A.O.I., p. 439, document no. 1238, telegram 160814/15, dated April 15, 1937.)

[31] The possibility that Graziani might indeed have handed over the empire to the Duce "without the Ethiopians," is clearly seen from the following telegram: ". . . extermination of all Amhara chiefs, great and small, must be speeded up for if this is not done can only expect further trouble. Once chiefs executed, the Amhara will be absorbed by us without difficulty. As well as chiefs, all Amhara officials and military commanders must be executed—none to be spared out of feeling of false pity. . . ." (See *La civilisation de l'Italie Fasciste en Ethiopie*, p. 120, telegram 8370/24709.)

[32] Alessandro Lessona, *Memorie*, p. 306. Graziani was now almost out of his mind with fear. On p. 316 of his diary, Ciano noted, ". . . they tell me that even in Italy he was so much afraid of attempts on his life that he had his village of Arcinazzo guarded by at least eighteen *carabinieri*. In Libya, he had a refuge built in a Roman tomb at Cyrene sixty or seventy feet deep."

[33] The following names appear on the list of war criminals submitted to the UN War Crimes Commission. The figures in parentheses indicate the order in which they were placed on the war criminals' list of World War II: Badoglio (18), Graziani (237), Lessona (459), Guido Cortese (128), Guglielmo Nasi (542), A. Pirzio Birolli (599), Carlo Geloso (214), Sebastiano Gallina (209), Ruggero Tracchia (821), Enrico Cerulli (122). (See *Documents on Italian War Crimes*, p. 2.)

trace the conspirators who had made the attempt on his life.
He would have been utterly confounded had he known that the
would-be assassins were only two in number, and that these
men, Abraham Deboch and Mogas Asgadom, apart from the
fact that they were unconnected with the plotters, were not
Ethiopians but Eritreans.[34]

[34] Abraham Deboch was a native of Serae; Mogas Asgadom was born in
Karakusai. The former was an interpreter at the Italian consulate in Addis
Ababa, and was suspected by the Ethiopians of being a collaborator. It
seems that the two men plotted together to assassinate Graziani to prove that
even though they were Eritreans, they were patriots. Many Ethiopians
believe, however, that their attempt to kill Graziani sprang from their
determination to avenge themselves on the Italians because of their policy of
apartheid, which separated the "blacks" from the "whites," and even
excluded Ethiopians from entrance to cinemas. While their motive remains
uncertain, it has been established that, prior to the attempt, both men sold
off all their possessions in order to raise money for their flight. After hurling
the grenades at Graziani, they succeeded in reaching Mesfin Sileshi and his
patriots, but the ras would have nothing to do with them, because they were
Eritreans, he decided that he could not trust them. Deboch and Mogas
Asgadom made for the Sudan, but were shot, possibly in error, by a few
Ethiopian peasants at Metemma.

Chapter eighteen

An Empire on the Map

In May 1936, while silver medals were raining down on Ciano, Farinacci, Bottai, Bruno and Vittorio Mussolini, and other distinguished members of the hierarchy, the great E. A. Mario sent a Turin daily a dialect poem that he said his Muse had inspired him to write. Here is an excerpt from "Imperial Tarantella":

> *Sette mise 'e vittorie; Badoglio ha*
> *scupata ll'Etiopia!/ Tutt'è "rasse" scumparze. . . .*
> *O "negusse" se mbarca pe' ll'Estero . . .* [1]

> [Seven months of victories,
> Badoglio has won the day;
> Every ras has disappeared,
> The king of kings has sailed away.]

Poets, politicians, and orators exalted Marshal Badoglio's entry into Addis Ababa, and a week later the newspapers

[1] *Gazzetta del Popolo*, May 15, 1936.

followed their example with such headlines as "Peace has returned to Ethiopia." Nor was this all. On May 24, to mark the anniversary of the day on which Italy had launched her war on the central empires, there was a military parade in Addis Ababa in which the first companies of the *Gioventù Etiopica del Littorio* * took part, and for which the aged rhapsodist Hamed had composed a special hymn of praise. One verse ran:

> Mussolini is our friend,
> And he must be, so great his powers,
> The friend of God as well as ours.

Unaware of the true situation in Ethiopia, the people of Italy rejoiced wholeheartedly when they read this unexpectedly good news. The empire they had won was already beginning to prosper, and what was more, the Ethiopians were cooperating with them, were proudly arraying themselves in the uniform of the GEL and singing the praises of their liberators. The dream of the warmhearted Italians was about to come true, the dream they had put into words that were not, to tell the truth, approved of by the regime:

> When Ethiopia's ours, we'll be
> One vast united family.

But this "vast united family" had no existence in reality. Apart from the fact that the war was far from being at an end or that any collaboration between the Ethiopians and Italians was merely a matter of mutual convenience, the empire was thoroughly ill-conceived, its institutions and criteria based on an utterly puerile racism at a time when African nationalism had already begun to evolve. In the first place, "a line was

* A Fascist youth organization in which Ethiopian boys were enrolled (TRANS.).

drawn between the Italians who were citizens *optime jure,* and
the Ethiopians who were treated as a subject people and
enjoyed no rights whatsoever, although, divided into categories according to their tribal origins, some of them were
favoured with certain 'privileges.' " [2] In the second place,
"the Italian State, automatically invested with sovereign
powers by the subjugation of the Ethiopian State" [3] took
possession of all the territory belonging to the crown, the
rebels, and the exiles, territory it intended to parcel out among
the Italian settlers. The distinction drawn between the conquering whites and the conquered Ethiopians, the taking over
of the richest land for the benefit of the colonists, propagated
all the seeds of evil apparent today in *apartheid;* Italy, in
short, made the most disastrous and irretrievable errors that a
colonizing power can commit. In 1939, when the institutions
and administrative machinery had been functioning for some
considerable time, Paul Gentizon paid a visit to the empire.
"Italian policy is dominant in every sphere," he noted, "It is
utterly without sentiment. It rejects the doctrine of assimila-
tion as both false and dangerous. Its aim is to preserve the
purity of the white race in East Africa. In this respect, racism
can be considered as the corollary, or better still, as the crown
of Fascist colonial policy." [4]

The Italians have never been racists. In Ethiopia, they
found the living room, the stimulating atmosphere they
needed, and as they were by nature affectionate and friendly,

[2] Raffaele Ciasca, *Storia coloniale dell'Italia contemporanea,* p. 713.

[3] *La costruzione dell'Impero,* vol. I, p. 189. The theory that the Italian
state had "automatically" been "invested with sovereign rights by the
subjugation of the Ethiopian state" ("sovereign rights" which enabled the
Italians to carry out repressions without infringing the international conventions of war), found its strongest supporter in Professor A. P. Sereni of the
University of Ferrara, author of *La fine del conflitto italo-etiopica e il diritto
internazionale,* which appeared in *Rivisto di Diritto Internazionale,* no. 4,
1936. See pp. 404-33.

[4] *Temps,* August 18, 1939.

they submitted with the utmost reluctance—and not all did submit—to the laws forbidding the two races to intermingle. Severe penalties were incurred by men who infringed these laws; any Italian found guilty of *"Madamismo,"* setting up house with an Ethiopian woman, a common-law wife, was liable to five years' imprisonment. All mixed marriages were declared null and void.[5] This Gobineau policy was solidly backed up by the Fascist hierarchy and by Fascist writers. "Mating with women of an inferior race is sexually abnormal . . . furthermore, it is a landslide that will end up in social promiscuity," pontificated Lessona, "and inevitably the blood of the dominant race will be diluted if we permit these unions to continue. A nation that wishes to dominate must begin by dominating itself. Every Italian in every walk of life must bear this in mind and act accordingly."[6] Angelo Piccioli, Director of Official Studies of the Italian Ministry for Africa, not only approved wholeheartedly of these laws but considered that they set an example: "Italy is the first European nation to

[5] The racial laws were decreed and enacted in April 1937 and June 1938. As early as March 1936, however, the *Gazzetta del Popolo* came out with a huge headline on the front page: "THE FASCIST EMPIRE MUST NEVER BECOME AN EMPIRE OF MULATTOS." On June 13, an article by Paolo Monelli appeared in the *Gazzetta* with a title in rhyme: "Female Black Faces in your newly won spaces." Part of this article ran, "If I were the emperor of Italian Ethiopia, do you know what I'd do? I'd send the author of 'Little Black Face' to Ethiopia, and force him to live in a *tukul* for two or three weeks—what am I saying?—two or three days, no, two or three hours would be enough—with a 'Little Black Face!' The 'Little Black Face' might be that of an Amhara, a Galla, Shangalla, or a Shoa woman—he could take his pick and good luck to him—they're all equally filthy, they stink of ancient dirt! The words of 'Little Black Face' are idiotic, and worse, they are thoroughly decadent. They spring from the kind of mentality we want nothing to do with, a puerile mentality sicklied o'er with false romanticism, a mentality that is diseased. Such a mentality, figuratively speaking, ought to be buried under ten meters of earth if we are to hold our heads high and found an empire. 'Little Black Face' is nothing less than an insult to our fine, upstanding, high-principled youth."

[6] Quoted in *Nazioni Coloniali*, compiled by the Fascist Institute in Italian Africa (Trent: Alighiera, 1939), p. 114.

uphold the universal principle of the superiority of the white race and take the appropriate steps to ensure that the purity of its blood is not polluted by miscegenation. Once again, Italy has shown the nations the way." [7] Directly after the racial laws had been passed, the attention of all Italians in Ethiopia was drawn to them by circulars. One such circular, the work of Guglielmo Nasi, Governor of Harar, ran: "His Excellency, the Head of the State, has stated that all relationships with native women are strictly forbidden, particularly that relationship known as Madamismo. . . ." [8] But the color bar went even further than this and cut the cities in two. "If we study the urban conditions, we find that there is a strong tendency toward the complete separation of the Italian and the native residential quarters," wrote Aldo Della Rocca.[9] This segregation was to lead to the exclusion of Ethiopians from cinemas, parks, etc.; as in South Africa, they were "for whites only."

The architects of the new empire who had replaced the Shoan overlords did not merely limit themselves to proclaiming a racial hierarchy, but, as Czeslaw Jesman tells us in *The Ethiopian Paradox*, they strove to create an anti-Amhara nation and build up the medieval emirates of Jimma and Harar in order to crush the Copts. But above all they did their utmost to nurture the hatred of the nomadic Somalis for the Ethiopi-

---

[7] *Gli Annali dell'Africa Italiana*, I, no. 2, August 1938 (Milan: Mondadori). See article, "La razza è l'Impero," p. 418. See also the article by Nicolo Pende in the *Gazzetta del Popolo* of June 7, 1936, in which he wrote, "It is unthinkable that Fascist Italy would ever allow . . . the finest, the best-balanced nation in the world to mix its blood with that of a negroid or semi-negroid race, a primitive race fundamentally separated from the white race because of its biopsychological characteristics. That Italians should mate with women of these Ethiopian tribes in Italian Africa is unimaginable." Nearly all the Italian people, however, rejected this concept of racial superiority; furthermore, thousands of them, prompted by the desire to make such reparations as they could, asked if they might adopt Ethiopian orphans. The Fascist Party returned a laconic "No."

[8] Circular no. 2280 dated April 22, 1937, issued by the governmental department of Harar. ("Source": Mario Bassi.)

[9] *L'Azione Coloniale*, May 9, 1938.

ans of the highlands.[10] When the war was nearing its end, Graziani wired Lessona, "Idea of 'Greater Somalia' under Italian rule now established in minds of all Somalis, even primitive woodland dwellers convinced of superiority of Somalis over Ethiopians." [11] Because of the Second World War, the plan for a "Greater Somalia" came to nothing, but we know that many of the disorders, the uprisings that are prevalent in East Africa today have their origins in the Fascist colonial policy that aimed—and let us be quite clear about it—not at finding a solution for certain knotty African problems, but at stabilizing in the Horn of Africa a new balance of population that would be favorable to the Italian program of demographic colonization.

Certain that Ethiopia was theirs for good, convinced that the Ethiopian tribes would furnish them with an inexhaustible and dirt-cheap labor force, the Italians set about providing the empire with what it lacked, in other words, practically everything; roads, railways, factories, hospitals, schools, hotels, post offices, telephone exchanges, etc. In the space of five years, the life span of the ephemeral empire, they wrought miracles; Haile Selassie was right when he said they had a genius for constructing. In five years, they endowed Ethiopia with over 5,000 kilometers of new roads, some asphalted, some flattened with steamrollers, overcoming difficulties that seemed insurmountable; the construction of the Asmara-Gondar road and the Danakil desert road presented the most formidable problems.[12] During my tour of the battlefields, I often stopped to

[10] Ceslaw Jeśman, *The Ethiopian Paradox* (London: Oxford University Press, 1936), pp. 34–35, 58.

[11] Commando Forze Armate della Somalia, pp. 88–89, telegram 10575/78, dated March 5, 1936.

[12] In his account of road-making in Ethiopia published in the *Corriere della Sera*, Cobolli Gigli, Minister of Works, stated that the Danakil road alone, constructed at a cost of 675 million lire, had involved "7,460,000 square meters of excavation and shoring-up, and 34,000 square meters of cement work and masonry for the 4 large and 1,504 small bridges. An

marvel at this monumental work that had withstood so well the ravages of time and the climate. The precipitous roads of Wolkefit and Tarma Ber were truly colossal enterprises, roads that were constructed by the "labor centurions," the most disinherited of the most disinherited provinces of Italy. These laborers broke up the lava beneath the blazing sun of the Danakil desert or spread boiling tar in the swelteringly hot regions of the Takkaze. They sweated and toiled, not to consolidate an empire, which as soon as darkness fell, reverted to the *arbañnoch*, the Ethiopian patriots, but to earn money for their wives and children. The merit for any good that came of Italy's crazy enterprise in Ethiopia is in good measure due to these humble, hard-working illiterates.

In five years, 25 hospitals, 14 hotels, dozens of post offices, telephone exchanges, aqueducts, schools and shops were built. Just as they did in America during the Gold Rush, villages not even on the map became prosperous towns almost overnight. Dekamere, for instance, which in June 1935 consisted of a few *tukuls* strung out along a small square, become a city of 14,000 inhabitants by 1938. During my brief stay in Dekamere, I met Giuseppe Gioelli who came from Alba. "Because of its situation," he told me, "Dekamere soon became the largest transport center in the empire, and consequently, the largest repair shop. There used to be as many as 3,000 heavy motor vehicles in the sheds and there was more money circulating here than in any other city. There were cinemas, dozens of restaurants and espresso bars, dance halls where there were all-night sessions; there was a football stadium, a cycling track, a dramatic society. There was everything you'd find in an Italian town, and even more." [13] And Carlo Montemanni, who came from Serravalle Scrivia, added, "Dekamere would have become a city of 100,000 inhabitants, the commercial

---

average of 32,000 laborers were employed on the construction of this road for two and one-half years, bringing the total of days worked to 17,000,000."

[13] Evidence given to me when I was in Dekamere, April 4, 1965.

and industrial artery of the empire, but the Second World War broke out and the rot set in. Now, as you can see for yourself, it's finished. Everything's crumbling away, and the grass is springing up everywhere." [14]

In the brief space of five years, the Italians could not carry out the countless projects they had in mind. There was the plan for the Trans-Ethiopian railway, which would have linked Eritrea to Somalia, there were the plans for thousands of kilometers of new railway lines.[15] There was the dream of transforming Addis Ababa into a city of a million inhabitants, a dream for which 12,000,000 lire had been earmarked. "Addis does not exist," wrote Paolo Monelli, "Addis will be built by young Italian architects; the errors that were made in Asmara will be avoided, and it will become the most beautiful city in Africa. At present, Addis is merely a Levantine street, with two or three barbaric palaces, two or three buildings copied from a handbook for architectural students, and 10,000 tukuls standing amidst the eucalyptus groves. Addis has never been a city; you couldn't call it anything more than an Imperial Palace and a market." [16] Indeed, it was an Italian architect, Arturo Mezzedimi, who thirty years later endowed the capital with its most impressive buildings, from the Municipal Building to the Africa Hall. The plan drawn up for the city by Ignazio Guidi and Cesare Valle is still of great value.

Another project that never materialized, a project which the Fascist regime probably cherished above all the rest, was that of demographic colonization, which had roused such hopes in the peasants who owned no land. At the end of the war, it was said that a million Italians would be settled on the most fertile

[14] *Idem.* Today, there are only eighty Italian residents in Dekamere. Eight hundred houses, originally the homes of Italian families, are empty.

[15] For the projects the Italians hoped to carry out in Ethiopia, see the study by Manlio Cocchieri, "Rassegna italiana politica, artistica e letteraria," published in December 1941, pp. 723–38.

[16] *Gazzetta del Popolo*, June 3, 1936.

regions of the empire.[17] A little later on, there was talk of ten million colonists. But on the eve of World War II, on 113,760 hectares of land in Shoa, Woggera, Jimma, and Chercher, only 3,550 Italian families had been settled.[18] The task of carrying out the vast agricultural program that would transform Ethiopia into the granary of Africa and Europe had been entrusted to the *Opera Nazionale Combattenti* * and three societies named after the provinces from which the settlers came: Apulia of Ethiopia, Emilia-Romagna of Ethiopia and the Veneto of Ethiopia. On the outskirts of Holeta and Bishoftu, in Jimma and Hararge, a few villages sprang up which, with their white cottages, their rustic charm, recalled those of Agro Pontino or the hamlets built in Libya for the families of the men who were improving the soil. But because of the constant dangers of the guerrilla war, because the clouds were gathering ominously over the political sky of Europe, the program of demographic colonization, claimed by the regime as its main reason for the war, was dropped.

The sector of industry that offered the greatest opportunities, the highest, almost fabulous rates of pay was that of transport. Dante Galeazzi, the ex-actor, who visited the empire at the close of 1936 when thousands of Italians were streaming to Ethiopia in the hope of getting rich quick, made a gallant attempt at writing the epic story of the transport drivers. One extract from this book runs, "We were sent to Mujja, and here at last we found happiness, the good life we'd hoped for: we

---

[17] *Riviste delle Colonie*, April 1939. On June 29, 1936, however, Marshal Badoglio had said to a *Daily Express* reporter, "I believe I am not being over-excessive when I say that we expect to settle a million emigrants." To the question, "But where will all the money come from, Your Excellency?" he replied, "The new, vigorous Italy will provide her empire with what it needs: money and youth." (See *Gazzetta del Popolo*, June 30, 1936.)

[18] Facts given by the Colonial Minister, Teruzzi, in a speech to the Chamber, April 27, 1940.

* A Fascist organization for helping ex-servicemen. The ONC settled them on the land in Italy (at Agro Pontino, for instance), in the colonies and in Ethiopia, building bungalow-type houses for them (Trans.).

got 600 lire a day, a fortune when you think that in Italy the pay for a whole month is only 350 lire! The work wasn't hard either; by loading up to capacity at the quarry, we were able to cut down the number of trips." [19] Luigi Abbove, an Alessandrian, told me: "In just 26 days I'd earned enough money by carrying loads of hay from Dekamere to Adigrat to buy myself a "634." [20] In a very short time, a transport driver became a *padroncino*, his own boss, with five, ten or even more transports; every transport on the road brought him in 15,000–20,000 lire a month. The *padroncini* were making what were in those days vast sums, and at the beginning of 1938, the authorities, outraged by the huge profits they were taking in, decided to put on the brake. As Angelo Appiotti wrote, "The wealth these men are accumulating is not legitimate. They are plundering and robbing and improverishing the State which up till now has been the sole source of their riches." [21] The *padroncini* grumbled at the taxes imposed on them, nevertheless they remained in Ethiopia. Marshals, generals, labor centurions, federal officials, and Italian residents vanished forever from Ethiopia, but not the *padroncini*. Even today, more than thirty years after their first appearance on the appalling roads of Tigre, two hundred of them drive along the imperial highways, their felt hats crammed on their heads, their revolvers, like their wine bottles, within handy reach in case they are attacked by *shiftas*. The *padroncini* are the sole survivors of Italy's African "Far West."

During the five years of occupation, only 300,000 Italians were absorbed into Ethiopia, more than a third of whom were soldiers.[22] This was a laughable figure since the regime had

[19] Dante Galeazzi, *Il violino di Addis Abeba* (Milan: Gastaldi, 1959), p. 108.

[20] Evidence given to me in Dekamere.

[21] *La Stampa*, January 7, 1938.

[22] At the beginning of 1939, there were 38,882 Italian residents in Addis Abada, 49,139 in Asmara, 4,265 in Harar, 5,283 in Jimma, 3,542 in Dire Dawa, and 2,000 in Gondar.

foreseen the influx of all Italy's unemployed, who amounted to millions. As we know from data provided by the Italian councillor, Fossa, in addition to the settlers, there were 986 professional men, 540 agricultural concessionaires, 4,007 industrialists, who had invested a total capital of 2 milliard, 700 million lire, and 4,785 businessmen and shopkeepers whose total investment was over 1 milliard, 100 million lire.[23] The huge amount of capital sunk in Ethiopia speaks eloquently of the faith the Italians placed in their empire, their conviction that it would last forever; when, suddenly and unexpectedly, it collapsed and the account was closed, the debit of the African venture was in the order of tens of milliards. Mussolini had realized from the first that for years Ethiopia would absorb capital on which it would make no return. "Ethiopia is so vast, its sources of mineral wealth have been so little explored that it is quite impossible to say how long we shall have to wait before it pays dividends. It will certainly not do so for several decades." [24] To the men who were closest to him, the Duce said that in his estimation Ethiopia would be fully developed in fifty years' time and, taking into account the enormous potentialities of the country, we can say that it would have undoubtedly become self-supporting with a flourishing export trade by 1960. But at the end of five years, this rosy prospect faded away, and the Italian government that had risen from the wreckage of Fascism was forced to expend, as was only right and just, milliards of lire on war reparations.

While the Fascist adventure in East Africa burdened Italy with a huge load of debts, Ethiopia, on the other hand, reaped many benefits from the Italian occupation, and although this did not make amends for the wrongs the regime had done to her, it certainly did much to repair them. On this point almost all the authorities on Ethiopia, as well as many members of the new Ethiopian society, agree. As F. J. Simoons, the Associate

[23] *L'Azione Coloniale*, July 1939.
[24] Benito Mussolini, *Scritti e discorsi dell'Impero*, p. 155.

Professor of Geography at the University of Wisconsin wrote, "The Italian occupation of Ethiopia from 1935–41, brief as it was, was the time of the most energetic construction, and the motor roads, airports, radio stations, telephone systems, electric plant, hospitals, schools, and public buildings built by the Italians largely for their own ends, proved an enormous contribution to the Ethiopian government that succeeded them." [25] Unquestionably the network of roads and communications, even though incomplete, helped to speed the development of Ethiopia, a development that continues to make steady progress thanks to the investment of capital from abroad. The Italian intervention in Ethiopia also led to the centralization of the ruling power and the elimination of the feudal system of the rases, the system Haile Selassie had vainly strived for years to bring to an end.

While I must repeat that nothing could compensate Ethiopia for the crimes committed against her by the Fascist regime, the benefits that resulted from the Italian occupation undoubtedly went a long way toward reconciling the two countries. As Paolo Cesarini remarked: "The highly intelligent Ethiopian elite drew the requisite line between the neo-squadristi of Addis Ababa and the thrifty, hard-working, anti-racist, apolitical, warmhearted, constructive Italian people. Even the ordinary Ethiopians who were, we discovered, good, honest, pious, unfortunate folk, folk we were sincerely anxious to help, were bright enough to see in us those qualities that caused a far more civilized race, the Greeks, to differentiate sharply between the Italians and Germans." [26]

---

[25] Frederick J. Simoons: *Northwest Ethiopia, Peoples and Economy* (Madison: The University of Wisconsin Press, 1960), p. 18.

[26] For the program of colonization and the first attempts at settling Italians in Ethiopia, see *Prospettiva di colonizzazione dell'Africa Orientale Italiana* by Vincenzo Rivera (published in the series *Scienze e Lettere*, Rome, 1939). See also *Territorio di pace e di civiltà*, by Fernando Santagata (Milan: Garzanti, 1940).

Chapter nineteen

The Guerrilla War of the Arbaňňoch[*]

On December 27, 1937, Amadeo D'Aosta, the "Saharan Prince," arrived at Massawa on the cruiser "Zara," and two days later, was installed as the new viceroy in Addis Ababa. It had been impressed on him that he was to pacify the country at all costs but that he was to achieve this end by more humane, more conciliatory methods than his predecessor. The Duke, a cultured and liberal-minded man, was by nature ideally equipped for the task of persuading the Ethiopians to cooperate with the Italians, but the errors made by Graziani were irreparable. The troops he had dispatched in pursuit of the rebels had left death and destruction in their wake, as witness this telegram chosen at random among a hundred: "Colonel Garelli reports reprisals carried out with complete success over more than ten kilometers of front. Areas 18 and

* Patriots (TRANS.).

239

19 razed, thousands of *tukuls* burned down. Some hundred villagers in league with rebels executed. . . ." [1] And here is another: "During a halt at Buje, 152 Amhara rebels captured in the vicinity executed on orders of Captain Molinero." [2]

Graziani's brutal methods had terrorized even those Ethiopians who had been prepared to accept Italian rule because they realized instinctively that it would lead to the rapid development of their country. Some of these men who had taken the oath of loyalty now thoroughly distrusted Italian authority, while others broke the oath and went over to the rebels. This was a tragic state of affairs since, after the occupation of Addis Ababa, there had been every reason to believe that a fruitful collaboration between the two peoples would be achieved. In a confidential document drawn up by the Abyssinia Association, the exiles in London had been apprised of the fact that, after the defeat of their armies, "The majority of Ethiopians seemed ready to accept Italian rule and had offered very little resistance to the Italian troops who occupied the peripheral centers. Only in the mountainous regions to which the survivors of the Ethiopian armies had fled was there any stubborn resistance. Italian propaganda had succeeded in convicing the people that a new era of freedom and prosperity was about to dawn." This had been a bitter pill for the emperor to swallow.[3]

But Graziani's savage and indiscriminate reprisals, the liquidation of the Ethiopian intelligentsia, the deportation of the notables of the Amhara bourgeoisie to the concentration camp at Danane,[4] had almost completely disillusioned the Ethiopi-

---

[1] Governo Generale dell'A.O.I., p. 447. Document no. 1251, telegram 1285, dated April 21, 1937, from General Maletti to the governor-general of Addis Ababa.

[2] *Ibid.*, p. 451, document no. 1255, telegram 174114/25/G.G.S., sent by Lt. Colonel Serraglia to the governor-general of Addis Ababa.

[3] *Memorandum on the State of Affairs in Ethiopia* (confidential), London, March 8, 1940, text in English, cyclostyled, p. 1.

[4] Ethiopians who had been interned in this concentration camp described the conditions as appalling. In an affidavit, Mikael Tessema, an official of the

ans, and by the time the Duke of Aosta was installed as viceroy, a new form of resistance had developed. This came not from the Ethiopian forces (largely wiped out by the operations of the "grand colonial policy"), but from the people themselves who were convinced that the Italians intended to exterminate them. It was particularly in Amhara, the refuge of the few notables and dignitaries who escaped the massacre in Addis Ababa, and the Coptic clergy, who observed with dread the effects of the Italian pro-Moslem policy, that the resistance movement gained ground. These new centers of resistance were coordinated by the Committee of Unity and Collaboration, which was in rapport with Haile Selassie in London.[5] The Metropolitan Abuna Kyril, who had originally agreed to do what he could to calm the country and who would undoubtedly have lightened the task of the new viceroy, was no longer in Ethiopia; outraged by the mass execution of the deacons and monks of Debra Libanos, he had gone to Alexandria to recuperate from the effects of the wound caused by the grenade that had been flung at Graziani, and had flatly refused to return. The Italian authority had appointed in his stead an old, almost blind priest, Abraham, who had immediately been excommunicated by the Synod of Alexandria.

The Duke of Aosta, who could not have inherited a more disastrous situation, did all that he possibly could to regain the confidence of the Ethiopian people. He gave orders there were to be no more summary executions and that unless they were attacked, the Italian troops who garrisoned the country were not to open fire. But these orders came too late, for the resistance movement had by this time assumed alarming proportions. "In September 1937, directly after the Feast of Maskal strong forces of armed men, as if they had been given

Ethiopian Ministry of Justice, stated that 3,175 of the 6,500 detainees died of undernourishment and dysentery. He accused a Dr. Antonio (no further particulars given) of having hastened the deaths of a number of prisoners with injections of arsenic or strychnine.

[5] George A. Lipsky, *Ethiopia* (New Haven: HRAF Press, 1962), p. 25.

a simultaneous command, attacked our residencies and garrisons in the Lasta area," wrote Luigi Lino, reporting on the operations of the Italian colonial policy in the region of Gondar. "From Lasta, the rebellion spread in a few days to Begemder and Gojjam, taking our military and civil authorities completely by surprise. Many isolated residencies fell into the hands of the insurgents. They wiped out whole detachments of troops, most of them Askaris that garrisoned vast regions thought to be completely pacified." [6] At Rab Gebya in Gojjam, Colonel Umberto Carrano was seriously wounded and several of his officers taken prisoner by *Dejatch* Mangasha Jambari. In Jimma Guenet, Lt. Gennaro Barra fired his machine gun at the rebels till all his ammunition was exhausted; as his assailants rushed at him, he battered them with his camera, defending himself to the last. At Dorba on the River Omo, Lt. Giorgio Pollera was killed. A new, insidious, and far more difficult form of war had begun: a war of ambuscades in which superiority of arms counted for little. From that time forward, the Italian press was silent on the subject of military activity in Ethiopia. There was not even a mention of the men who fell, thus they were doubly erased. [7]

As the result of an investigation, the *Manchester Guardian* gave a list of the rebel leaders: *Dejatch* Mangasha Jambari and *Dejatch* Mesfin Bezebe in Gojjam; *Dejatch* Hailu Belau in Amhara; *Gerazmatch* Geresso in Gurage. But the list was incomplete. It should have included *Fitaurari* (later Ras) Mesfin Sileshi and Ras Gerassu, who were at the gates of

[6] My conversation with Luigi Lino took place March 23, 1965, in Addis Ababa.

[7] Neither the Italian nor the Ethiopian archives provides much light on this long period. The story of the Ethiopian resistance from 1938–41 has yet to be written. The only two books on the resistance are very short and sketchy and are in Amharic. One, *The Years of Torment*, by Tadesa Zewalde appeared in 1963; the other, *Fascism's Five Year Reign of Terror in Ethiopia* by Second Lt. Meleselegn Anlei, came out in 1955. (Both books published by the Berhanenna Selam Press, Addis Ababa.)

Addis Ababa; Belai Zelleka, *Fitaurari* Zewde Abbakora, the
brothers Dagno and Tesselma Imam, *Fitaurari* Negash
Kebbede, and dozens more.[8] Above all it made no mention of
Abebe Aregai, who was appointed commander of all the patriot forces at the beginning of 1939. Abebe Aregai occupied a
stronghold near Ankober, the ancient capital of Shoa, and his
men continually fell upon the convoys on the most important
of the highways, the Asmara-Dessie-Addis Ababa road. The
Italians made attempt after attempt to capture him in their
dragnet, but although he was wounded on a dozen occasions,
he succeeded in slipping through the meshes and making his
way to the mountainous, densely forested regions of Yfat and
Argobba. Abebe Aregai was as cunning as the proverbial fox;
at intervals, he would feign submission to the Italian authorities in order to gain breathing space, but scarcely had he taken
the oath of loyalty and received the commendation of the
Italians than he was off, ready once more to resume the
struggle.

I talked about Abebe Aregai's war against the Italians, a
war of skirmishes, ambushes, and counterambushes, with his
son, Daniel Abebe, governor of Arussi: "Toward the end of
1937, my father decided that although I was only fifteen, the
time had come for me to fight. 'I expect you to set an example
to my men,' he said to me. But I didn't have much chance of
setting an example because I was wounded during my very
first battle. I wasn't anywhere near my father when I fell, and
I would have been finished off by some Somalis who flung
themselves on me if they hadn't been driven back by the
Italians. I was taken to Debra Berhan and locked up in prison.
General Maletti wouldn't allow me to have any treatment for

[8] It was traditional for Ethiopian women to fight side by side with the
soldiers, and many young women of high birth and girls of the Amhara
bourgeoisie played an active part in the resistance. Among those who
distinguished themselves by their heroism were *Waizero* Belainesh, *Dejatch*
Aberra Kassa's widow, and Abebech Charkoze.

243

the wound in my foot and it became infected; you can imagine what it was like at the end of three months—it was a mess of blood and pus. I should have died if it hadn't been for the vice-governor, Cerulli; he was very angry indeed with Colonel Maletti when he saw the condition I was in, and drove me in his own car to the hospital in Addis Ababa, now the Ras Desta Damtu hospital. When my foot healed and I was discharged, Cerulli took me into his home and treated me like a son. The Italians made me an allowance of 50 lire a day; it was such a fabulous sum that I never knew how to spend it. Suddenly, however, I was snatched away from this paradise and handed over to Major Lucchetti of the *carabinieri*. This was on the day when my father had refused for the hundredth time to give himself up. Major Lucchetti told me that I was to pay for his refusal with my life and that I was to be hanged in the morning. You can imagine what a dreadful night I spent. I never stopped crying; I lit candle after candle to the Madonna. When dawn broke, they came to fetch me, but they didn't hang me after all. They'd decided to send me back to my father and see if I couldn't persuade him to surrender. I rode to Ankober on a splendid white horse, but when I rejoined my father, he wouldn't listen to me; he said flatly that he would never give himself up. I stayed with him and fought with him till 1941 when our war with the Italians came to an end." [9]

The Ethiopian insurrection that had flared up after Maskal in 1937 was kept alight by outside support, particularly by the support of the French who had become increasingly conscious of the threat to their tiny East African colony. As early as 1936, De Jonquières, the head of the "Study Section" of Jibouti, had written in a secret report, "We may find ourselves

[9] Commander-in-chief of the resistance movement though he was, Abebe Aregai had never brought himself to hate the Italians. Toward the middle of 1941, when the British were rounding up the Italians in Ethiopia and sending them to internment camps, Abebe Aregai hid a few dozen of them in his own house. Dante Galeazzi refers to this in his book, *Il violino di Addis Abeba* (p. 172).

at war with Italy and to prevent Jibouti falling into Italian hands . . . we should lose no time in fanning the flame of revolt throughout Italian East Africa." He then proceeded to outline his plan: "We should (a) make our policy fully known to those chiefs with whom we are in contact; (b) maintain the hostile attitude of the Ethiopians toward the Italians by means of clandestine propaganda; (c) support insurrections by smuggling in money and arms to the leaders; and (d) take a census of the Ethiopian refugees in our colony and encourage the formation of bandas, again supplying money and arms." [10] The French government approved of this plan, and from the middle of 1937, kept in regular contact with Abebe Aregai and Ras Gerassu. But the Italians maintained a strict watch on the frontier, hence the French were obliged to send consignments of arms into Ethiopia through the Sudan. During this first phase, Captain Appert and Captain Jean Trocard were conspicuous for their daring, particularly the latter, who carried out a number of highly dangerous missions in Ethiopia. The British Intelligence Service, however, failed to grasp the importance of these subversive activities, and it was not until the middle of 1939 that they decided to participate in them. From this time on, Khartoum became the center of support for the insurgents.

The negusa nagast, who was living in Bath, did what he could with his small personal means and the sums donated by pro-Ethiopian societies, to furnish a means of subsistence to the Ethiopians who had fled from their country. Thousands of them were in the Sudan, many others had taken refuge in French Somaliland, British Somaliland, and Kenya. Through these men, most of whom were ex-soldiers and political exiles, contact was made with the Ethiopian patriots; when World War II broke out, they formed the cadre of the Ethiopian

[10] See the article, "La participation française a la résistance éthiopienne," by Lt. Col. Yves Jouin in *Revue Historique de l'Armée*, no. 4 (Paris, 1963), pp. 157–58.

Army of Liberation. The emperor's staunchest supporter in England was Sylvia Pankhurst, who had taken up the cudgels on his behalf when Mussolini threatened to invade his country, and had upheld his cause ever since. In her paper the *New Times and Ethiopia News,* she kept the British public informed of the rebel activities in Ethiopia.[11] To raise funds for Ethiopia, she organized dinners, meetings, film shows (the most interesting of these films was "How Mussolini makes War"), roped in anyone who might help, and seized on every occasion that might serve to further her campaign. To Stephen Wright, she wrote, "As you know, Toscanini is giving a concert in Oxford in June. As you also know, he loathes fascism and has refused to conduct in his own country. It would be excellent if we could make a prominent display of the *New Times and Ethiopia News* while he is in Oxford. . . ."[12] In another letter to Mr. Wright, she asked for the addresses of various organizations and societies that might lend their support to Ethiopia, and added an urgent S.O.S.: "As many Members of the League of Nations will urge that the Italian annexation be recognized at the Assembly on September 13 [1937], it's absolutely essential that the Westminster Conference should be a tremendous success . . . We are holding it on September 9 in the Central Hall. . . ."[13] But on May 14, 1938, the emperor suffered his final and gravest defeat at Geneva. He came to the rostrum, spoke a few words, but was too ill to continue, and Lorenzo Taezaz read his speech, part of which ran as follows: "Italy in Ethiopia controls only those cities and villages where there are garrisons, and there are many Ethiopian provinces where they have little or no control

[11] It is a pity that some of the material published in the *New Times and Ethiopia News* is drawn from unreliable sources. Many of the facts have clearly been exaggerated, and the figures given cannot be taken seriously.

[12] From the collection presented by Stephen Wright to the Addis Ababa Library on June 2, 1937.

[13] *Ibid.,* letter dated August 1937.

. . . an implacable guerrilla warfare is being waged against the Italians and will continue until either they are driven out of the country or the Ethiopian people are exterminated. . . ." [14] But these words produced no effect and the democracies, including Great Britain, decided to recognize Italy's right to remain in Ethiopia.[15]

It was a right that cost Italy dear. After the first round of defeats at the hands of the rebels, the military authorities had decided to abandon the most isolated residencies, build small stone forts at intervals along the principal roads, and raise native battalions of 500–600 men, commanded by 8 to 10 Italian officers, battalions that would resort to the guerrilla tactics of the insurgents. But it was not merely to deal with the rebels that these native contingents were mobilized. Mussolini had in mind the creation of a "black army" powerful enough to defend Ethiopia if she were attacked. On February 22, 1937, he had wired Graziani, "At the beginning of September essential you recruit and begin training first 100,000 men of the 'black army'; objective: ability to mobilize at least 300,000 men by date our own rearmament complete. [1940–1941.] If war breaks out, mother country will not ask for help, but remember will not be able send help to empire. . . ." [16] The new recruits were mainly Eritreans, Somalis, Tigreans, and Galla, but there were also a good many Amhara, whose inclusion in the "black army" created a climate of civil war in Ethiopia. Shortly after Ras Kassa's sons had made the unsuc-

[14] Quoted by Leonard Mosley, *Haile Selassie*, p. 247.

[15] Another paper that supported Ethiopia's cause was *The Voice of Ethiopia*, edited by G. Balfour Bovell, and the first issue came out in New York on January 1, 1937. Many Negroes in Harlem subscribed to this paper; with the money raised by these subscriptions, a fund was established to help Ethiopians who were living in exile. In London, in addition to the Abyssinia Association, excellent work was done by the Friends of Abyssinia founded by Hazel M. Napier under the distinguished patronage of Princess Tsahai Haile Selassie.

[16] Ministero della Difesa, Stato Maggiore Esercito, Official History: *La Guerra in Africa Orientale* (Rome: Regionale Press, 1952), p. 16.

cessful attempt to occupy Addis Ababa, Ras Hailu Tekla Haimanot and Ras Kebbede Mangasha had put their forces at the disposition of the Italian authority, but Ras Hailu regarded the guerrilla war of the patriots as his own personal war and led his men against them. "Ras Hailu is frequently absent from the capital," noted the German reporter, Luisa Diel, "He is helping the Italians to trap the rebels. Long experience has taught the ras and his warriors how to deal with bandits and political troublemakers." [17]

Despite the Duke of Aosta's leniency, the repressions continued even though they were not as savage as those of Graziani. "At least the patriots had the right to a valid trial even though they were almost invariably sentenced to be hanged," Luigi Lino told me, "This was the penalty for all those who disobeyed the order to lay down arms and give themselves up. If the accused men were chiefs, they usually justified their defiance of the law by saying 'I did what I did for my country'; if they were ordinary rank and file, they said: 'I did as my leader did.' As I was a reporter, I was present at several executions, and I was greatly impressed by the courage, the pride with which these men met their end. *Fitaurari* Tesselma, for instance, put the rope round his neck with his own hands and kicked away the rough platform on which he stood. My admiration and pity were shared by many Italians who witnessed the scene." [18] The introduction of more legal methods of dealing with the rebels was confirmed by Signor Rizzi, the lawyer who had acted as president of the military tribunal of Dessie during this period: "When Graziani was Viceroy, any Ethiopian suspected of being a rebel was summarily executed, but when the Duke of Aosta arrived, there was a very decided change for the better. Only those Ethiopians who were found to be armed when captured were sentenced to death." [19]

[17] See *AOI, Cantiera d'italia*, by Luisa Diel (Rome: Ed. Roma, 1952), p. 16.

[18] Evidence given to the author.

[19] Evidence given to the author in Addis Ababa on April 3, 1965.

At the beginning of 1939, it became apparent that the resistance movement was weakening, and the Italians took advantage of the fact to reoccupy all the centers they had been forced to abandon on 1937. "The patriots suffered incredible hardships," Luigi Lino said, "They were denounced by collaborators, tracked down, and cornered by our troops. There was hardly any contact between the countless groups of resistance fighters. They had so little ammunition left they could make little use of their machine guns during a battle. They were desperately short of all supplies, but worst of all, they had no doctors to see to their wounded and sick. Indeed, rebels who had been wounded would present themselves at our headquarters with ingenious stories to account for their injuries; our men, who knew perfectly well that these tales were quite untrue, nearly always pretended to believe them, and gave them the medical aid they needed." [20] Under March 14, 1939, Galeazzo Ciano entered in his diary, "The Duke of Aosta spoke with considerable optimism about the condition of the Ethiopian Empire—I must, however, add, that among the many people who have come from there, he is the only optimist." [21] In fact, the revolt soon regained its original momentum. The insurgents were supplied with money, arms, and advice by Colonel Paul-Robert Monnier, Lorenzo Taezaz, and a few anti-Fascists who had been recruited by the French colonel. Among these men, who had served in the International Brigade during the Spanish Civil War, were two Italians, Ilio Barontini and Velio Spano, who remained in Gojjam until April 1940. [22]

In May 1939, French and British intelligence officers met secretly in Aden to coordinate military plans in the event of a war with Italy. General Le Gentilhomme stressed to his British

[20] Evidence given to the author.

[21] Galeazzo Ciano, *Ciano's Diary, 1939–43*, p. 44.

[22] One of these Italians, Velio Spana, if I am not mistaken, went under the alias of Paul Langrois. He spent nearly two years at the headquarters of Gwila Giorgis south of Lake Tana.

colleagues the importance of extending the revolt to every region of Ethiopia: "I believe that we should proceed with extreme caution, that we should wait until sporadic uprisings break out in every part of the country. Once these fires have been lighted, we should intervene and send massive consignments of arms and ammunition to those centers where the insurrections have the best chance of succeeding. . . ." [23] By this time, Great Britain realized the importance of stirring up rebellion in Ethiopia, and accordingly dispatched Brigadier Sandford, who knew the country through and through, to elaborate a program of ways and means to support the patriots. Sandford arrived in Khartoum in October 1939, and immediately ordered a census to be taken of all the Ethiopian exiles in the Sudan. Munition dumps were set up on the Sudan–Ethiopia frontier, and a start was made at establishing contact with the leaders of the insurgents.

During the first months of 1940, the Ethiopian Intelligence Bureau, headed by Major Cheesman, began to function, while the first Frontier Battalion made up entirely of Ethiopian exiles was formed by Major Hugh Boustead.[24] The Italians got wind of these activities by the British, and under April 6, 1940, Ciano noted in his diary that even the Duke of Aosta was losing his optimism: "He said when I saw him this morning that it was not only extremely problematical whether we can maintain our present position because the French and British are already equipped and ready for action and the local population, among whom rebellion is very much alive, would revolt as soon as they got any inkling of our difficulties." [25] Three days later, at the meeting of the Chiefs of Staff that Badoglio had convened in Rome, the Marshal said, "As regards the insurrection in the empire, this comes within

[23] *Revue Historique de l'Armée*, p. 152.

[24] See *Orde Wingate* by Christopher Sykes (London: Collins, 1959), pp. 236–57.

[25] Galeazzo Ciano, *Ciano's Diary*, p. 232.

the province of the Viceroy who is taking the necessary measures to deal with it. From information I have received, I have been made aware of the existence of a Franco-British underground movement whose object is to stir up the population to revolt against us. Even if we succeed in subduing Shoa, Amhara, and the territories immediately to the north, we do not have at our disposition a military force sufficiently large to defend the empire. . . ." And Graziani, who had not yet recovered from the effects of the bitter pill he had been forced to swallow, seized the opportunity to deplore the Duke of Aosta's moderation: "The situation in East Africa is critical. Amhara [i.e. Begemder] is in full revolt. Gojjam is in full revolt. Mangasha Jambari is cock-of-the-walk . . . Eight months were wasted in useless negotiations in Shoa before action was taken against the insurgents. During those eight months, Abebe Aregai had ample time to build up his store of arms and ammunition, consignments of which were dispatched to him under our very noses from Jibouti." [26]

On May 10, 1940, a month before Italy entered the war, a number of British intelligence officers left Khartoum, crossed the frontier into Ethiopia, contacted the most important rebel leaders in Gojjam, Begemder, Wolkeit and Armachaho, and gave them this message from the G.O.C. of the British forces in the Sudan, General Sir William Platt: "Peace with you. England and Italy are now at war. We have decided to help you in every way to destroy the common enemy. If you are in need of rifles, ammunition, food or clothing, send as many men and animals as you can spare to the place where our messengers will tell you. . . ." [27] At this same moment, Brigadier Sandford and nine other British and Ethiopian officers of Mission 101 arrived in Ethiopia to organize the full-scale revolt of the population. Now that the wind was changing, a

[26] From the minutes of the meeting held April 9, given in Vanno Vailati's book, *Badoglio risponde* (Milan: Rizzoli, 1958), pp. 341–42.
[27] Quoted by Leonard Mosley, *Haile Selassie*, p. 249.

number of chiefs who had collaborated with the Italians, among them Ras Seyoum and *Dejatch* Ayelu Birru, decided that they were backing the wrong horse, and joined the arbañ-ñoch in their mountain fastnesses. This convenient change of heart was not an exclusively Ethiopian phenomenon; a good many otheer countries have witnessed the eleventh hour transformation of traitors into patriots.

Chapter twenty

The Return of the Exile

"Italy has entered the war as the ally of Germany." The Italian people had been expecting this announcement, which Mussolini made from the balcony of the Palazzo Venezia at 6:00 P.M. on June 10, 1940, just as they had expected the announcement of the war in Ethiopia. This time, however, their reaction was very different; it was cold, almost hostile. Even the Duce's customary purple passages, his rhetorical images of "British battleships blazing from stem to stern," failed to kindle their enthusiasm. The only Italian in fact to radiate satisfaction was Mussolini himself, who had finally overcome the reluctance of the chiefs of staff and achieved his cherished ambition of personally conducting the war as Commander-in-Chief of the Armed Forces of Italy. "The adventure begins—God help Italy," Ciano wrote in his diary.[1]

Three days later, in the small airport of Poole Harbour, a mysterious Mr. Strong took his seat in a Sunderland seaplane

[1] Galeazzo Ciano, *Ciano's Diary*, p. 264.

bound for Egypt. Mr. Strong, who was no other than Haile Selassie, was accompanied by his son, Prince Makonnen, his aides, Lorenzo Taezaz and Wolde Maryam, and George Steer of *The Times*. For the emperor, who had become a highly important pawn on the British chessboard, this was the start of the journey that was to take him back to his country and place him once more on his throne. Little did he dream how tortuous this journey was to be, that it was destined to last for almost a year.[2] Its very outset was in the nature of a "thriller." The Sunderland was obliged to fly over France, over-run by Hitler's army, over the Mediterranean, patrolled by Italian pursuit planes. On June 25, it touched down safely at Alexandria, and seven days later, the emperor, now transmogrified into Mr. Smith, was flown to Khartoum where the invasion of Ethiopia was being organized.

On July 4, however, two days after Haile Selassie's arrival, the Italians, taking advantage of their temporary superiority, crossed the Sudan frontier at several points and occupied Cassala, Gallabat, and Kurmuk. In the months that followed, three Italian columns commanded by General Nasi invaded British Somaliland and overcame all resistance within six days. These victories, which were no more than a show of strength—six months later, the Italians were driven out of British Somaliland—caused the British great concern for the emperor's safety, and they took such elaborate precautions to ensure his safety that Christopher Sykes (biographer of Orde Wingate, the new hero who now appeared on the scene) commented, "he was treated more like a prisoner than the

---

[2] Winston Churchill had given his blessing to the emperor's journey. A few months earlier, however, Haile Selassie had received scant sympathy from the British government, which regarded him as a burden. Leonard Mosley tells us that because of the treatment accorded him for two years, the negus became a victim of melancholia. "It was not until June 10, 1940, when Italy entered the war against Great Britain that his mental depression was dissipated." (*Haile Selassie*, p. 248.)

sovereign ally of his British hosts." [3] But Haile Selassie, inured as he was to every hardship, every humiliation, comforted himself with the thought that the news of his return to Africa, his presence on the Ethiopian frontier had been circulated to his people, producing on them "an electrifying effect, particularly on the Amhara." [4] From his villa at Jebel Awlia, he could see the majestic Nile, a sight that gladdened his heart: *"C'est l'eau de mon pays,"* * he said to Edwin Chapman-Andrews.[5]

On November 6, while the officers of Mission 101 were stirring up the insurrection in Ethiopia to its highest peak, Major Orde Wingate arrived in Khartoum with orders from General Wavell to lead the first Frontier Battalions into Ethiopia. Wingate flew to Faguta in Gojjam—an extremely dangerous flight, incidentally—made contact with Brigadier Sandford, acquainted himself with the difficulties of the terrain, and returned to Khartoum. In less than two months, the Scotsman, "the Napoleon of guerrilla warfare," whose name will be remembered for all time, organized Gideon Force, a force of 100 Britishers, 2,000 Ethiopians, and 15,000 camels loaded with arms and ammunition. On January 18, 1941, while General Platt was attacking the Italians in Eritrea, the Gideon Force reached the little frontier village of Um Iddla. Two days later the emperor joined Wingate, and at 1240 hours on the day of his arrival, he crossed the line of demarcation and set foot in his own country. After five long years the standard of the Lion of Judah was once more raised in Ethiopia, and a company of his own men presented arms to the negusa nagast. As he stood there with his two eldest sons, Asfa Wossen and

[3] Christopher Sykes, *Orde Wingate*, p. 243.

[4] For this information I am again indebted to Luigi Lino.

* The emperor had been tutored in French, which was his second language (TRANS.).

[5] Leonard Mosley, *Haile Selassie*, p. 252.

255

Makonnen, and old Ras Kassa, Haile Selassie could not hide his emotion. A few weeks later while Gideon Force was thrusting its way through the dense forests of Gumur, he issued a proclamation that proved to all, particularly the Italians, that he was humane to a degree, a true Christian: "Assemble in a convenient place all Italians who surrender to you; armed or unarmed, they are to be treated as prisoners of war. Do not make them suffer for the suffering they inflicted on us. Show them that you are worthy to be called soldiers, that you are honorable and merciful men. Do not forget that during the battle of Adowa, our heroic warriors took the Italians they had captured to the emperor and so enhanced the luster and nobility of our country's name. . . ." [6]

By this time the Italians were under no illusions. They knew only too well that they would be unable to hold out for long. With no help from the mother country, more or less abandoned to their fate, they faced a population up in arms against them and three armies advancing from the Sudan and Kenya. The Italians, who numbered 7,000 officers and 84,000 men, were reinforced by the 200,000 strong "black army," but at the first reverse, the colored troops began to desert, and in increasing numbers went over to the rebels.[7] Surrounded by the enemy, with no hope of replenishing their supplies,[8] the Italians sang with a kind of desperate irony:

> Against the English, against all Ethiopia,
> We'll fight for you, beloved Motherland,
> With only native bread to stave off hunger,
> We'll suffer, struggle, make a final stand.

[6] *La civilisation de l'Italie Fasciste en Ethiopie*, p. 9.

[7] According to the figures given in the Official History of the Ministry of Defense, the Italians in Ethiopia disposed of 3,313 machine guns, 5,313 other quick-firing guns, 672,800 rifles, 24 "M" tanks, 35 "L" tanks, 126 armored cars, 325 planes, 994 cannon and mortars, and 6,286 motor vehicles.

[8] In all, 346 tons of supplies and mail were dropped to them, and they were reinforced by 1,759 parachute troops.

Though victory is now but a chimera,
We will not yield although all hope is gone,
We'll hoist our country's flag beneath our standard,
For honor's sake alone we will fight on.[9]

Fight on they did. They fought like proverbial lions at
Keren and on the Juba, but at the end of two months, they
were forced to yield to an enemy whose arms were far superior
to their own and whose supplies were regularly brought up
without difficulty. By the end of March as Gideon Force,
whose ranks were swelled by an ever-increasing number of
patriots, was advancing toward Debra Markos, the Italian
forces had abandoned Eritrea, Somalia, British Somaliland,
and the Ogaden, and had retreated to Gondar, Amba Alagi,
Dessie, and Jimma where they dug themselves in. On March
26, Harar fell. On April 6, when Haile Selassie made his
triumphal entry into Debra Markos where his old enemy Ras
Hailu Tekla Haimanot made a formal act of submission to
him, General Sir Alan Cunningham occupied Addis Ababa.
There were still some 40,000 Italians in the city, and fearing
that the sudden return of the emperor to his capital might
result in a bloodbath, General Cunningham ordered Wingate
to suspend his military operations and detain the negus in
Debra Markos. For a short time, Haile Selassie was filled with
the uneasy feeling that the British had teamed up with the
Italians to prevent him from regaining his throne, but he soon
overcame this suspicion and resigned himself much against his
will to his enforced stay in Debra Markos.

Meanwhile, the Italians in the capital lived in dread of
reprisals by the Ethiopians, particularly the neo-squadristi,
who had played their bloody game of "Hunt the Moor" after
the attempt on Graziani's life. As they were Europeans, General
Cunningham allowed them to keep their rifles and revol-

[9] Quoted by Rinaldo Panetta in *Culqualber fine dell'Impero* (Rome: Volpe, 1965), p. 88.

vers; he also allowed their disbanded police force to resume its duties temporarily and patrol the streets. Unfortunately, a few of these men behaved irresponsibly, possibly because their nerves were ragged; one party of auxiliaries opened fire on a prison yard, killing and wounding sixty-four Ethiopian detainees, while another was involved in a street fight in the course of which seven Ethiopians were killed and fourteen wounded. The British authorities were obliged to disarm the auxiliaries, and entrust the task of maintaining law and order to the Ethiopian police and to patriots who had been hurriedly instructed in their duties by South African officers. At last, on April 27, the emperor was given authority to make his solemn entrance into Addis Ababa and, escorted by Orde Wingate and his heterogeneous force, he immediately left Debra Markos. But for Haile Selassie, this last stage of his journey was not so much a triumphal march as a sorrowful pilgrimage to the towns and villages where his people had suffered martyrdom. In the marketplace of Fiche, where the two sons of Ras Kassa had been executed, he remained awhile in prayer. Farther on, in the quiet and silent valley where General Maletti, acting on Graziani's orders, had shot the 296 deacons and monks of the monastery of Debra Libanos, he prayed for the repose of their souls.

On May 5, 1941, exactly five years after Marshal Badoglio's entry into Addis Ababa, the emperor reached the green hills of Entoto and looked down at his capital. Only a few kilometers lay between Entoto and Addis Ababa, but Haile Selassie mastered his desire to cover them at full speed and entered the little church of Maryam, screened by eucalyptus trees, to give thanks to God. Wingate had managed to get hold of a magnificent white horse so that the negus might ride into the city in triumph, but the emperor rejected this romantic proposal and decided to make his entry in the open Alfa Romeo limousine he had requisitioned from Ras Hailu.

Let us follow Haile Selassie on the gentle descent from

Entoto. He passes the tiny church of Kusquam Maryam on the right, passes Ras Desta's *gebbi;* at last he reaches the outskirts of the New Flower and the inhabitants shout and wave in a delirium of joy. And now he enters his capital where, to prevent the people from flinging themselves on the emperor's car and overwhelming him in their excitement, Ras Abebe Aregai's patriots line the road, their hair, which they had vowed never to cut till they had driven the enemy out of their country, falling on their shoulders. There should only have been 700 of them, General Cunningham's orders; instead, there are 10,000. But not a single ugly incident occurs, not a hair of an Italian's head is harmed. On a rostrum in front of the "Great *Gebbi*," General Cunningham and a guard of the King's African Rifles await the emperor. He reaches the rostrum, and the guard presents arms, he and the general shake hands. A few handshakes with other officers, a few bows, a few trumpet fanfares, and the long and tortuous journey, the journey on which the king of kings had set out almost a year ago, has reached its joyful conclusion. The crowds cheer and "loo-loo" wildly, but they listen in breathless silence while their emperor addresses them: "My people," he says, "Do not repay evil with evil . . . do not stain your souls by avenging yourselves on your enemies. . . ." [10] (Thirty years later the negus told me, "When we returned to our country, thanks to the grace of God, we never even contemplated reprisals. Our most urgent task was to organize and develop our empire. . . .") [11]

That night the emperor gave a small reception for General Cunningham, Orde Wingate, and their officers. On the hills that surrounded the capital, countless fires were blazing, but this time the flames did not spring from burning *tukuls,* they were *feux de joie.* As the negus gazed at the ring of fire, reliving the events of that momentous day, he murmured to his friends: *"Vraiment j'ai été très emotionné."*

[10] Leonard Mosley, *Haile Selassie,* p. 268.
[11] During the course of the interview granted me by the emperor.

Thirteen days after the negusa nagast had returned to his capital, the Duke of Aosta, who had been attacked on May 1 at Amba Alagi by the Anglo-Ethiopian force, was compelled to surrender after a heroic resistance that provoked the admiration of the enemy. "As our many wounded were in urgent need of medical treatment and as the situation had deteriorated to such an extent that we could not hold out much longer, I was obliged to ask the enemy for an honorable truce which they immediately accorded me," he wired Mussolini on May 19.[12] Three months later, the Italians were broken in Jimma, and Ciano wrote in his diary, "Mussolini is in extremely sour humor because there was the usual surrender in large numbers with generals at their heads, despite a large amount of arms and modern equipment."[13] On December 7, he noted, "This morning the Duce was very much irritated by the paucity of our losses in East Africa. Only 67 fell at Gondar in November; 10,000 prisoners were taken. One doesn't have to think very long to see what these figures mean."[14]

But the figures given by Ciano are incorrect, and Mussolini's "irritation" was utterly unjustified. The Italians in Kulqualber and Wolkefit fought magnificently to prevent the enemy from taking Gondar, a position that was not worth the sacrifice of so many lives; moreover, they continued to fight on although they knew that "victory was but a chimera."[15] On the

---

[12] *Un anno di guerra* (Rome, 1941), p. 61. Marshal Caviglia criticized the Duke of Aosta with extreme severity for his decision to fall back on Amba Alagi: "Today, the Duke of Aosta is exalted for the stand he made at Amba Alagi, nevertheless, his decision to establish himself in this position was puerile since he had simply allowed himself to be influenced by the fact that Toselli's heroic resistance had made the Amba historic. If there was ever a position he should not have chosen, it was Amba Alagi, a rocky massif with no water supply and where food for his troops was unobtainable. He should have made for Jimma and rejoined the main body of his army." (*Ibid.*, p. 340.)

[13] Galeazzo Ciano, *Ciano's Diary*, p. 364.

[14] *Ibid.*, p. 406.

[15] For the defense of Gondar, see R. Panetta, *Culqualber fine dell'Impero.*

rocky slopes of Kulqualber, they left not 67, but 513 dead and 404 wounded, and around Gondar itself, another 517 killed and wounded. But far from admitting his own political and strategic errors, Mussolini chose to heap odium on the Italian soldiers and express his fervent wishes that the cartridges they had left behind them would be ruined by the cold. Yet he was perfectly well aware of the conditions under which they were fighting; he was perfectly well aware that their supplies had almost given out and that their position was hopeless. As General Nasi, the commander of the last Italian force to fight in Ethiopia wrote, "The men are half-starved, their uniforms are in rags, many of them are barefoot. We cannot pay the native contingents regularly. We are short of small arms, and many of those we have are useless. Our tanks, if you can call them that . . . are of local manufacture. Our artillery is out of date, many of the guns are worn out and we are desperately short of ammunition; our small stock of shells is in such poor condition that two out of three fail to explode. We have no antitank guns, no planes, and very few motor vehicles. Our carbide has decomposed. We are reduced to black bread that has fermented and is full of maggots. The men have no tobacco, no letters from home. We are surrounded by the enemy and threatened by Ethiopian rebels. Yet in spite of all this, the Italian soldiers gathered round the last tricolor in Ethiopia continue to manifest the utmost devotion·to duty." [16]

With the surrender of Gondar on November 18, Italian resistance in Ethiopia came to an end. The empire, which had been an empire more in name than in actual fact, had ceased to exit. In the futile attempt to defend it, 5,000 Italians and 10,000 colored troops were killed, almost triple the number killed during the war of conquest.[17] Three months later, at

[16] Ministry of Defense: Official History, p. 329.

[17] The casualty figures given by the Ministry of Defense are: killed—426 officers, 4,785 enlisted men, and 10,000 native soldiers; wounded—703 officers, 6,244 enlisted men, 16,000 native soldiers.

3:45 A.M. in the military hospital in Nairobi, Amadeo D'Aosta died. "With him disappears the noble figure of a prince and an Italian, simple in his ways, humane in spirit. He did not want this war. He was convinced that the empire could only hold out for a few months," Ciano wrote in his diary.[18] Haile Selassie himself paid tribute to the Duke of Aosta. *"Il a bien administré mon peuple,"* he said to Italian Minister Preti.[19]

The emperor, who had shown so much generosity to his enemies of yesterday, displayed the same mercy toward those men who had betrayed the national cause. If ever a man deserved to be executed, it was Ras Hailu Tekla Haimanot,

---

[18] Galeazzo Ciano, *Ciano's Diary*, pp. 441–42. Nino Costo dedicated a poem to the dead Duke. Costo imagined Amadeo d'Aosta describing his stand at Amba Alagi to his father. Written in Piedmontese dialect, part of it runs:

> Senssa riserve—senssa munission—
> pochi testard antorn a na bandiera.
> Da tute part la romba d'ij canon . . .
> noi, anciodà sle ponte 'd na rochera.
>
> Sle ponte dla rochera d'Amba Alagi
> per trenta dí l'oma spetà la mort.
> Ultima arsorssa l'era 'n nostr coragi,
> Ultim confort: avei pí gnun confort.
>
> [With no reserves—no ammunition,
> With only a handful to uphold the Flag,
> While all around us the cannons thundered,
> We held on grimly to Alagi's crag.
>
> To Alagi's crag we held on grimly,
> Death was expected by almost every one.
> Our last resource was our unflinching courage,
> Our final solace—but solace there was none.]

(These two verses of Costo's poem are taken from *Amedo di Savoia, Viceré di Etiopia* by De Vecchi di Val Cismon (Rome: *Istituto per l'Enciclopedia De Carlo*, 1942), p. 119.

[19] My informant was Luigi Lino. In a letter dated July 6, 1965, prot. no. 069998, Preti wrote, inter alia "When I met the emperor, he also spoke highly of General Nasi, and he went on to voice his admiration for the vast improvements we had made in his country."

who had collaborated with the Italians and led his force of 30,000 men against the patriots, yet the negus merely sentenced him to a long term of imprisonment. He was equally lenient with other archtraitors, among them Ras Kebbede, Ras Getachew, *Dejatch* Mangasha Wubie, and Gebreyesus Worq, the former Ethiopian ambassador in Rome. He did not even pass the death sentence on Ras Haile Selassie Gugsa, who had gone over with his men to the Italians on October 15, 1935, a heavy blow to the Ethiopian forces on the Makalle front. As for Ras Seyoum, that eleventh-hour "patriot," the emperor not only spared his life but allowed him to retain his possessions, his titles, and the offices he had held.[20] But perhaps he showed his greatest generosity in the case of the telegraphist, Worku Itateku, who had passed on all the secret Ethiopian messages to Graziani. The court martial clamored for the head of this man who was guilty of high treason, but the negus commuted the death sentence into one of 20 years' imprisonment, and when Itateku had served his term, restored all his property to him. Conversely, Haile Selassie showed himself implacable toward the Azebu Galla who had no intention of surrendering the arms with which the Italians had supplied them from 1935 onward. He waged a long and difficult campaign against them, a campaign that lasted until 1943 when British officers organized Ras Abebe Aregai's forces and supported them with a squadron of Blenheims.

The rebellion of the Azebu Galla was possibly the least of the difficulties Haile Selassie was forced to contend with when,

[20] The emperor was indeed magnanimous to Ras Seyoum, who had actually headed a delegation of Ethiopian notables to Rome, and during an audience with Mussolini had said, "Ethiopia is now completely Italian, not only because the Italians conquered her materially, but because, thanks to the great wisdom and generosity of Your Excellency and all those who serve you, they succeeded in a very short time in conquering her spiritually. We are, therefore, deeply gratified, Your Excellency, to be able to renew to you in person our oath of loyalty. . . ." (*Gazzetta del Popolo*, February 6, 1937.)

after six years, he took up the reins of government. In the first place, the British were not yet prepared to recognize his full authority; they considered Ethiopia to be conquered, not liberated country, and placed it under the control of OETA, Occupied Enemy Territory Administration. In reply Haile Selassie appointed seven ministers and announced that he was forming his postwar government. Immediately, Brigadier Lush, acting on the orders of Sir Philip Mitchell who had established OETA, rushed off to the "Little *Gebbi*" and said angrily to Wolde Giorgis, the emperor's chief aide: "His majesty cannot fully reassume his status and powers as emperor until a peace treaty has been signed with Italy. Until that happens, the King of Italy remains the legal ruler of Ethiopia." [21] The negus immediately wired Winston Churchill, and on January 31, 1942, the first Anglo-Ethiopian Agreement which stated that "Ethiopia is now a free and independent State" was signed. True, the British asked for and were conceded enormous privileges in the country, a good many of which they retained after the second Anglo-Ethiopian agreement was signed on December 19, 1944. Indeed, the Ogaden remained under British control until 1950. To judge from Sylvia Pankhurst's report, British administration in this part of Ethiopia was anything but clement. *Barambaras* Abdullah Faraq, the deputy for the Ogaden, told her: "I regret to say that the British authority in the Ogaden has committed worse crimes than the Fascists." [22] Thanks to the continual interference and Machiavellianism of the British, Haile Selassie began to turn more and more toward the United States and to draw closer to a reconciliation with Italy. Italy now had a new government and, crippled though she was by the war, she showed that she was ready to meet her obligations, which included reparations to Ethiopia for the wrongs done to her by the Fascist regime.

[21] Leonard Mosley, *Haile Selassie*, p. 275.

[22] Sylvia Pankhurst, *British Policy in Eastern Ethiopia, the Ogaden and the Reserved Area* (1948), p. 27.

Chapter twenty-one

The

Reconciliation

Despite all the adversities, all the difficulties Ethiopia has encountered, the Addis Ababa of a million inhabitants, the "Imperial Addis Ababa" of which the Italians dreamed in 1935, has become a reality. Fortunately, Addis is a completely African city and has never been torn in two like the white cities of Cape Town and Johannesburg. The capital has developed with unexpected rapidity during the last few years and has acquired the appearance of a stable metropolis, so much so, indeed, that the "Legionaries" who occupied it on May 5, 1936, without firing a single shot, would be hard put to recognize it. Addis Ababa is a city of wide streets and divided highways, lit by sodium lights. A city as large as Paris where architects are not cramped for space and where they set their finest buildings on the stately pedestals of the surrounding hills. A city as tree-lined and full of green spaces as Washington, a city as ambitious as New Delhi. A forest city that is being transformed into a garden city. At one time it seemed that Addis would be built in the severe, almost funereal Piacenzan style; fortunately, it is being developed far more imaginatively and attractively, though there is a decided tendency toward the theatrical. Addis has all the amenities of a modern capital: an international airport, television studios, the largest municipal building in Africa, and the most luxurious hotels, superb golf courses, exquisite churches, a number of smart night clubs, and a casino.

But Addis Ababa is not Ethiopia. Outside its radius, the rhythm of life slows down almost completely. One rarely sees a car on the roads, the signs of progress are barely perceptible. For centuries time has stood still in Ethiopia, and on the wretchedly tilled land, one sees the true representative of present-day Ethiopia, the peasant in his dirty white *shamma* turning up the soil with a plow that dates back to biblical times. Between the peasants—and ninety percent of the population are peasants—and the inhabitants of the capital, there is a great gap that instead of decreasing grows increasingly wider. I saw this gulf for myself in the course of my long journey through all the provinces of the country, the gulf that yawns between Addis Ababa and the archaic, changeless world of the peasants. In "cities" such as Debra Markos and Dargila, for instance, slates have only just begun to replace thatch. The old evils of famine and plague are still rife. The contrast between these two worlds of Ethiopia shows up even more sharply today than it did thirty-odd years ago. Ethiopia has a fleet of jets, yet there are entire provinces where the earth has never been furrowed by the wheels of a tractor. The Imperial Guard has the most powerful American tanks, yet in Arussi and Dankali the weapon of war remains the spear. The lounges of the Ghian and Imperial are as luxurious as those of the palatial hotels on the Via Veneto in Rome, yet ninety-nine percent of the houses are *tukuls* with no electric light, no running water, no sanitation. In Addis Ababa, thirty percent of the children go to school; in the country, only four percent.[1]

[1] In 1960, we are told by George A. Lipsky (*Ethiopia*, pp. 88–99), 95 percent of the population was illiterate. Out of a total population of

Africa Hall, the magnificent prestige building where the Secretariat of the OAU (Organization of African Unity) has its permanent headquarters, cost several millions to erect, but there is only one hospital bed available for every 4,000 residents in the capital, only one doctor for every 400,000 patients.[2] In the First and Second Five-Year Plan, great stress was laid on agrarian reform, but two-thirds of the land still belongs to the great landowners, the Coptic church and the crown.[3] As regards the legal system, we are told by Czeslaw Jeśman: "Western judges are employed in the courts, but a man can still be tried and convicted for sorcery." [4]

Ethiopia, of course, is not the only country where past and present rub shoulders. Almost immediately after his return to his capital, the emperor dedicated himself with his customary energy to the task of modernizing his empire, but while he has

---

20,000,000, only 200,000 children attended school. The education figures were as follows:

Children attending primary, elementary and secondary schools:	100,000.
Children receiving rudimentary education at Coptic church schools:	100,000.
Children attending mission schools of various Christian denominations:	8,000.

[2] The Health Service, which is totally inadequate for the needs of the country, causes the government the greatest concern. In 1960 (George A. Lipsky, *Ethiopia*, pp. 148–68), there were only 54 hospitals with a total of 5,774 beds; 170 doctors (most of them in the capital), 1,300 nurses, and 180 midwives. The gravity of the situation is increased by the fact that certain diseases are rife: tuberculosis (30–40 percent of the population suffer from tuberculosis) ; syphilis and gonorrhea (over one-third of the male population has contracted V.D.) ; leprosy (in Gojjam alone, there are more than 100,000 persons suffering from leprosy) ; not to mention such endemic diseases as typhus, malaria, dysentry, and such tropical diseases as bilharzia, etc. An epidemic that swept the country in 1958 caused the deaths of 400,000 persons in Tigre alone.

[3] George A. Lipsky, *Ethiopia*, pp. 238–58. The first Five Year Plan, which came to an end in 1962, did not reach all its objectives. For the second Five Year Plan, the government voted the sum of 2,760 million Ethiopian dollars (667 milliard lire).

[4] C. Jeśman, *The Ethiopian Paradox*, p. 54.

achieved some gratifying results, experts believe that little can be done without massive loans from abroad, so great are Ethiopia's needs, so vast its territory, so deeply seated the ills and difficulties that arise from lack of communications and poverty. In order to facilitate the social and economic transformation of his country, the negusa nagast enacted new laws, and in 1955 drew up a new constitution which, while it lays down that he shall continue to reign as an absolute monarch, promised the people free elections and the vote.[5] Under the constitution, the emperor cannot declare war "without the advice and consent of Parliament." But, as G. W. Shepherd, Jr., observes: "Despite his reforms, Haile Selassie has shown little desire to establish a constitutional monarchy . . . Nor does he permit the existence of rival political factions. A pacific transfer of power to educated Westernized leaders appears unlikely in Ethiopia." [6]

While he was proceeding cautiously with his work of reform, Haile Selassie, despite the fact that he had been so shabbily treated by the League of Nations, was taking steps to re-establish his country, which for six years had merely ranked as a colony in the international sphere. These steps were successful, and on July 28, 1942, Ethiopia became a charter member of the United Nations. Six years later, to show his solidarity with the Western powers, the emperor sent a token force of a few thousand men to Korea. In the following years, he paid state visits to Great Britain, America, the U.S.S.R., India, and Yugoslavia with the aim of forming ties of friendship with these countries that represented the two world blocs, and above all, of forging economic links with them. But his outstanding success was the federation of Eritrea with Ethiopia. This federation had been proposed by the U.N. in 1952

[5] The members of the Senate (*Yehege Mewensenhā Meker Bet*) are appointed by the emperor and hold office for a period of six years.

[6] George W. Shepherd, Jr., *The Politics of African Nationalism* (New York: Praeger, 1962), p. 37.

when the future of Italy's former colonies was being dis-
cussed; the federation was achieved in 1962. Naturally, there
were vehement protests from the Eritreans, and because of the
threat that they may rebel,[7] because Somalia has her eye on
the Ogaden, because of Nasser's never-ceasing subversive
propaganda, Ethiopia is obliged to maintain a standing army
out of all proportion to her needs; this defense program accounts for almost thirty percent of the state expenditure in a
budget that is already badly overstrained.[8]

While the great landowners and the Coptic church considered that the emperor's reforms and concessions were far too
sweeping, the young Ethiopians who had taken degrees at
American and European universities, even though they acclaimed Haile Selassie as the Bismarck of Ethiopia, accused
him of allowing himself to be influenced by the reactionary
clergy and refusing to remove the old rases from office. The
rases, in fact, while they had served the country well during
the war, were thoroughly bad administrators; in addition,
many of them were rapacious to a degree and utterly corrupt.
The young army officers, who had done their military training
in more democratic or more dynamic countries, were equally
dissatisfied with the limited nature of the reforms, and although they had no wish to harm the emperor, had formed for

[7] The Four Power Commission found that only 48 percent of the
population were in favor of the federation with Ethiopia. An important
section of Eritreans had hoped that the former Italian colony would become
an independent state. In July 1960, various groups of Eritrean intellectuals
who were violently "anti-Federation," formed themselves into a party, the
Liberation Front of Eritrea, an underground movement that distributed
clandestine propaganda. In September 1962, this movement led to an open
rebellion whose epicenters were the mountainous regions of Keren and the
plateau adjoining the Sudan frontier; the Second Ethiopian Division was
dispatched to deal with the insurgents. There are still rebel elements in
Eritrea, and these are sustained by Cairo and Khartoum.

[8] The Italian government is partly responsible for the trouble with
Somalia. In 1959, it relinquished its ten-year trusteeship without reaching an
agreement on the delimitation of the frontiers.

some time a plan to overthrow the government and replace it with one that was genuinely progressive. The emperor's departure in December 1960 on a foreign tour that included West Africa and Brazil was the long-awaited opportunity for revolution. At midnight on December 13, under the leadership of General Mengistu Neway, the commanding officer of the Imperial Guard, Germame Neway, the Governor of Jijiga, and Workeneh Gebeychu, the Chief of Police, the 4,500 men of the Royal Bodyguard secretly occupied the "Little *Gebbi*" and all the key points of the capital. By means of a ruse, nineteen cabinet ministers fell into the hands of the revolutionaries who held them as hostages in the palace. On the following morning, the people learned of the coup d'ètat over the radio. Most significant of all, they learned of it from the heir to the throne, Prince Asfa Wossen. In his broadcast he outlined a wide program of reforms and denounced the corruption and nepotism whose attendant ills had bedevilled the late regime. He further promised to serve the country and the new government on a fixed stipend like any ordinary Ethiopian official. Whether he spoke of his own free will or at gunpoint is not known to this day.

But the revolution only lasted for three days. While arrangements were being made in Brazil to fly the negus back as quickly as possible to his country and while, from Abuna Basilios' personal plane, thousands of leaflets were showered over the capital announcing that the emperor was on his way back and that the Crown Prince was being held prisoner by the rebels, General Merid Mangasha, the Chief of Staff of the regular army which had remained loyal to the negus, brought up tanks and surrounded the *gebbi* with troops. The game was up, and since the hostages no longer served any purpose, General Mengistu ordered them to be shot. All nineteen were summarily executed in one of the reception rooms of the palace. It was against these corrupt and rapacious men rather than the emperor that the revolution had primarily been directed. Among them were Ras Abebe Aregai,* the old double-dealer Ras Seyoum, the scheming Abba Hanna, and the Minister of Commerce, Makonnen Hapte Wolde. Two of the leaders, Germame Neway and Workeneh Gebeyehu, committed suicide; General Mengistu, who had been wounded during the fighting, was captured and imprisoned. When the emperor arrived in Addis Ababa on December 17, the revolution was over. Three months later, General Mengistu was tried; a member of the Permanent Court of International Justice at the Hague was present at the proceedings. General Mengistu was found guilty of high treason and sentenced to death. Told that he might plead for mercy, he replied, "I prefer to die. I shall be able to tell the rest of them up there that the idea of revolution is beginning to take root." On the following day, 10,000 people crowded into the market square where the gallows had been erected. The condemned man turned to the executioner. "It shall never be said that General Mengistu died at the hands of another," he said proudly, and tightening the slipknot of the noose, strangled himself.

Once more the old emperor showed clemency to the men who had opposed him. It seemed, however, that the officers' revolt had provided him with a useful lesson. In the months following the abortive *putsch,* while he maintained the paternalistic rule of fifty years, causing the younger members of his government to chafe, he allowed Parliament a greater measure of autonomy and handed over a number of functions to the prime minister, who up till now had been little more than a yes-man. In addition he set up commissions to study constitutional, administrative, and agrarian reforms. As the Coptic clergy were plethoric, largely ignorant, and an obstacle to progress, the emperor founded a theological college with an Armenian bishop at its head where young men who wished to

* He had been appointed Minister of Defense by the emperor and, as Leonard Mosley says, "He held out his hand to arms salesmen from all over the world" (TRANS.).

enter the Church would be trained on modern lines. In 1962, the Ministry of Labor was established, trades unions were organized with the help of American and Yugoslavian experts, and the Ministry of National Commissions for the Interior Community Development was set up. In the same year, Ethiopia's first university came into being in Addis Ababa; significantly, Haile Selassie presented his own palace as its center, the palace that had been the scene of the revolution which, short-lived as it was, had in a sense brought about the fall of the theocratic Ethiopian state.

The revolt of the Royal Bodyguard indirectly affected the external, as well as the internal policy of the country. It led Ethiopia to bind herself more closely to the other African countries, to identify herself with their vicissitudes, protests, and ambitious designs. In order to restore his prestige shaken by the revolution, the emperor espoused Africa's campaign for liberty and unity; he sent the Tefik Brigade to the help of the Congo, which was in the throes of a bloody tribal war; in 1963, he convened the conference of the heads of African States in Addis Ababa, a conference that gave rise to OAU; and he acted as mediator in the dispute between Algiers and Rabat.

While they are flattered by these achievements, the most progressive Ethiopians are not blinded by all the Pan-African slogans, but continue to press for drastic reforms in their own country. "To be progressive in external affairs and conservative at home is bound to lead to discontent," a young civil servant told me. X, a cabinet minister, said, "I would be the last to deny that the emperor has done a great deal for Ethiopia, but I blame him for not delegating more of his vast power to others." Far more violent are the charges of the clandestine Marxist "Ethiopian People's Movement." [9] But while there are grounds for some of the accusations made

[9] See *Rapporto sull'Etiopia*, published in the *Bolletino* of the *Centro di Documenti*, no. 1 (Milan: Fanon, February 1965), pp. 37–47.

against the negus, while, as Smith Hempstone observes, he continues to rule as if he were an emperor of the Ming dynasty or a Tudor monarch rather than as a modern sovereign, we must never forget the kind of country, the brief space of time in which he has enacted his reforms. As Sir Harry Luke wrote, "There is a limit to what can be accomplished in a lifetime, and even the emperor's best intentioned critics sometimes forget how recently the country was a collection of centrifugal, mutually warring kingdoms and principalities, ever resentful of central control, even of common links." [10] And Leonard Mosley: "Writers abroad study this method of government and roundly condemn it as archaic, despotic and ruthless. But it works, and for the moment the only alternative is likely to be anarchy, terrorism and an eventual return to the chaotic days of the tyrannizing rases." [11]

This opinion is shared by the vast majority of the 16,000 Italians who live in Ethiopia; the former enemies of Haile Selassie are now his staunchest supporters. Yet it cannot be said that the relations between Ethiopia and Italy began auspi-

---

[10] *The Times* (London), February 26, 1962.

[11] Leonard Mosley, *Haile Selassie*, p. 293. Many Ethiopians ask themselves whether the weak and ambitious heir to the throne, Prince Asfa Wossen, will be able to hold together the complex mosaic of peoples as his father has succeeded in doing. Other Ethiopians believe that owing to the equivocal behavior of the crown prince during the three days of the palace revolution, the negus will bequeath his empire to his young grandson, Eskender Desta, the commander of the Ethiopian fleet. Still others maintain that Haile Selassie will be the last of the emperors and that after his death Ethiopia will become a republic. In this event the power will probably pass into the hands of the generals, who, ever since they put down the revolutionaries of the Imperial Guard, have carried more and more weight in the country. Many Ethiopians are of the opinion that General Merid Mangasha is the only man capable of cementing the vast country into a unified state; they base this opinion on the fact that he is the most efficient and progressive of the leaders in Ethiopia and that the officers of the regular army (of which he is commander-in-chief), trained at the military academy in Harar by Indian officers who trained at Sandhurst, represent the bourgeoisie, the class that is beginning to consolidate itself between the Coptic clergy and the old aristocracy.

ciously. Indeed the emperor's generosity to our co-nationals who had remained in Ethiopia and who were, so to speak, his hostages, was ill-repaid by Rome. To begin with, at the peace talks in 1945, De Gasperi and Bonomi urged that Eritrea should be mandated under Italian control, and when this proposal was rejected they activated a Pro-Italian Party in the "first-born" colony that added to the confusion and stirred up trouble and unrest. The peace treaty was signed on February 10, 1947, but diplomatic relations between Italy and Ethiopia were not resumed until 1952, and it was not until March 5, 1956, that agreement was reached on reparations.[12] The dilato-

---

[12] Ethiopia claimed the sum of 185 million sterling (326 billion lire) for reparations. The figure finally agreed on was 6,250,000 million sterling (10½ billion lire). In a "Memorandum" presented by the Ethiopian government to the Conference of Commonwealth Prime Ministers held in London September 1945 (see St. Clement Press, 1946), the following detailed account was given:

		Lire
(1)	Amount expended by the Imperial Exchequer on arms, ammunition, etc., to resist the aggression:	26,813,155
(2)	Loss of Imperial Income during the Italian occupation:	25,402,868
(3)	Other losses:	132,530,000
		184,746,023

Details of (1) :	(a) Equipment for 365,000 soldiers:	3,650.000
	(b) Arms and ammunition:	3,513,155
	(c) Transport, provisions, etc.:	9,125,000
	(d) Pay of soldiers for 10 months at £3 per capita:	10,450,000
	(e) Cost of 15 planes destroyed:	75,000
		26,813,155

For the churches and houses destroyed, for all the Ethiopians killed during the war and the occupation, the Ethiopian government demanded the following compensation:

	Lire
Destruction of 2,000 churches containing valuable libraries and pictures:	2,000,000

riness of this agreement allowed Italy to snatch back 10 billion
lire; these billions, instead of appearing on the "reparations
account" figured on the bill that she presented to Ethiopia
under the heading of "financial and technical aid."

Despite ten years of this policy which seemed to betray
symptoms of Italy's former arrogance and the resentment that
had resulted from the "Adowa complex," the Italian settlers
consolidated themselves and prospered. They held the monop-
oly in the fields of technology and construction, and Italian
became the lingua franca. The emperor took every opportunity of praising the Italian community. At a conference of
thirty heads of African states held in the Africa Hall on May
22, 1963, the negus said in the course of his speech, "We must
live at peace with our former colonizers. We must not indulge
in recriminations or harbor bitter feelings. We must realize
that revenge and reprisals are futile. Let us purge ourselves of

525,000 houses and *tukuls* destroyed, each valued at £20

275,000 officers and men killed in the war

75,000 patriots killed during the five years of the Italian
Occupation

17,800 women, children and old people killed by the
Fascist Air Force during the Occupation

30,000 persons killed in the massacre of February, 1937

24,000 patriots tried by the Italians and executed

35,000 persons who died in concentration camps

300,000 peasants who died of hunger and privations after
the destruction of their villages

Total of dead: 760,300 at £100 per capita

Lire

76,030,000

Animals destroyed:

5,000,000 cattle at £5 per capita	25,000,000
7,000,000 sheep and goats at £1 per capita:	7,000,000
1,000,000 horses and mules at £5 per capita	5,000,000
700,000 camels at £10 per capita	7,000,000
Total:	44,000,000

hatred which corrodes the spirit and poisons the heart." [13] During the many interviews that Haile Selassie granted me in 1960, he invariably stressed the fact that he had "always distinguished between Fascism and the Italian people." On one occasion he said to me, "There are no obstacles standing in the way of true understanding and a fruitful collaboration between our two countries. We have ample proof that the Italians in Ethiopia welcome ever-closer ties of friendship. They have shown themselves to be model citizens and the work they are doing in our country gives us every cause for satisfaction." [14] To Giuseppe Faraci, who wrote to him asking which qualities he most admired in the Italians, the emperor replied, "Above all, their character. I also admire them for their industry and for their many other virtues. The Italians who decided to remain in our country have fitted into the framework of its life. The money they earn here is spent here and so they and their families are contributing toward the economic stability of our empire." [15]

The reconciliation between the two countries was almost complete when I was in Ethiopia. By a curious transference, the Italian residents of Addis Ababa have wound up by substituting Haile Selassie for the Duce they had adored. But one wish of the emperor still remained unfulfilled: his desire to cement the new friendship by paying a state visit to Italy. During the past ten years, he had often spoken of this wish to the Italians he received in the *gebbi*. To an architect he dwelt on the beauty of the mosaics in the basilica of St. Mark; to a diplomat he talked of his memories of his long-ago visit to Rome; to a prelate he spoke of the cemetery in Turin where his daughter was buried. To me he said with a trace of bitterness, "In the course of the past ten years, I have paid

[13] See page 3 of cyclostyled pamphlet distributed to those who attended the meeting of OAU.

[14] *Gazzetta del Popolo*, July 19, 1960.

[15] *La Stampa*, March 9, 1965.

many visits to Europe, but I have never been to Italy because I have never been officially invited to do so. I know, however, that now Fascism is a thing of the past, I can count on many friends in your country." [16] But in Rome, while the government was well aware of the emperor's desire, it acted as though it knew nothing about it; subsequently, it shilly-shallied, doubtful whether it would be a wise move to invite him. The years slipped by and Italian journalists on their return from Addis Ababa spoke more and more despondently of the emperor's wish, which seemed doomed to remain unfulfilled. As Rome continued to remain silent, the Italians in Ethiopia grew increasingly indignant and protested as loudly as though they themselves were to blame.

But at long last the official invitation arrived. The date was fixed, all the arrangements were made, but at the eleventh hour, President Segni fell ill and the visit had to be postponed. Once again the government dithered, tested the diplomatic climate, hemmed and hawed. Finally, at the end of another year, the invitation was renewed. Haile Selassie expressed his gratification and arranged to visit Italy in the autumn of 1965, thirty years after that autumn when cargoes of arms and ammunition were pouring into Massawa, and the Italian people were wild with excitement as the first troopships sailed for the "Promised Land." By a strange quirk of fate, the emperor arrived in Rome on the very day that the Fascist aggressors had launched their invasion of his country.

Broadly speaking, the negusa nagast, Haile Selassie I, the Elect of God, the Conquering Lion of Judah, can claim that he has attained all his objectives, satisfied all his ambitions. Destiny was on his side; during the darkest hours his faith sustained him. But first and foremost, it was through the sheer strength of his will that the king of kings triumphed—his obdurate, his unconquerable will.

[16] *Gazzetta del Popolo*, July 19, 1960.

GLOSSARY OF ETHIOPIAN WORDS
IN THIS BOOK

Abuna	(Abun if not followed by name) Title of the head of the Coptic church, also used for other important prelates
Amba	Flat-topped mountain
Ato	Polite form of address—"Mr."
Bajirond	Court official, treasurer
Dejazmatch	(abbrev. Dejatch) "Commander of the Door," senior official, dignitary, general
Fitaurari	"Commander of the Spearhead," rank below Dejazmatch
Gerazmatch	"Commander of the Left Wing," rank below Fitaurari
Kanyazmatch	"Commander of the Right Wing," same rank as above
Itege	Queen—title of the empress of Ethiopia
Ligaba	Court official, master of ceremonies
Lij	Prince
Shum	Tribal chief or district leader

Index

Abate, Ras Getachew, 163
Abbeakora, Zwede, 243
Abbi Addi, 77
Abbove, Luigi, 154
Abebe, Daniel, 243
Abyssinia. *See* Ethiopia
Abyssinia Association, 240
Adagamos, 49
Addi, Akeiti, 130
Addis Ababa, 51, 163, 199; after
  Ethiopian War, 265–66; before
  Ethiopian War, 30–31; departure
  of Haile Selassie I from, 203–4
Adigrat, 44, 47
Admasu, *Dejatch*, 104
Adowa, 21, 43, 44, 47, 74, 144
"Adowa complex," 3–9, 12, 275
Advisory Committee on Slavery, 35
Afewerk, 117
Af Gaga, 77
Africa, Africans, 5, 31, 38, 51, 57.
  See also Ethiopia; Italy, Italians,
  significance of Africa to
Africanus, 32
Africa Society, 9
Agostini, General, 120, 191
Aia, Mount, 162
Alagi, Amba, 53, 99
Alfieri, Dino, 62
Ali, Hussein, 116
Ali, Wodaju, 49
Alpini, 58, 166
American Committee for Ethiopia,
  38

Amhara, 38, 241
Amsterdam World Congress against
  War, 37
Anderson, Dr. Robert Blackwood, 94
Anglo-Ethiopian Agreement, 264
Aponte, Salvatore, 62
Appelius, Mario, 62
Appert, Captain, 245
Appiotti, Angelo, 236
Aradam, Amba, 95, 99, 127 (map),
  132–33
Arbitration Commission, 19, 21
Aregai, Abebe, 220, 243, 251, 263,
  271
Arimondi, 47
Armellini, Quirino, General, 71, 110
Arussi, 116
Asar, Mount, 75
Asfa Wossen, 70, 180, 182, 214, 270
Asgadom, Mogas, 226
Ashangi, Lake, battle of, 174–85
Askaris, 50–51, 75, 122, 197
Asmara, 17–18
Assab-Dessie road, 14
Association of Ethiopian Patriots,
  39
Auberson, 34
Austria, 25
Austrian Nazi Party, 25
Austro-German army, 107
Axum, 72, 77
Azebu Galla, 134, 165, 166, 176, 180,
  263

281

Babbini, General, 150
Babitcheff, Mischa, 91
Badoglio, Pietro, Marshal, 14, 87, 94, 204; enters Addis Ababa, 212; and Lake Ashangi, battle of, 176, 182–84; and Enderta, battle of, 124–29, 134; and Italo-Eritrean expeditionary force, 70, 71, 76–77; and Italy's preparations for war, 27–28, 51–54; and Mai Chew, battle of, 163; and Ogaden, battle of, 187–88, 197; and Shire, battle of, 150, 159–60; and Tembien, first battle of, 98–110 passim; and Tembien, second battle of, 137, 141, 145
Baistrocchi, General, 21, 77
Balau, Dr., 93, 95
Balcha, Kiferra, 19, 33
Bale, 116
Balfour, Patrick, 86
Barbusse, Henri, 37
Barontini, Ilio, 249
Barra, Lt. Gennaro, 242
Barton, Sir Sidney, 131, 200
Barzini, Luigi, Jr., 64, 126, 153
Basch, Victor, 38
BASE (British Ambulance Service in Ethiopia), 94
Baskerville, Beatrice, 9
Bassi, Mario, 194
Bastico, General, 102
"Battalion of Death," 40
Beauplan, Robert de, 35
Begemder, 74
Begnac, Ivan de, 62
Belau, Dejatch Hailu, 242
Belgian Military Mission, 36
Belgians, 88, 89
Benelli, Sem, 27, 64, 99, 171
Beonio-Brocchieri, 65
Bergamo, Duke of, 56, 61
Bergonzoli, General, 120
Bey, Shukry Yasr, 111
Bezebe, Mesfin, 242

Birolli, Pirzio, General, 82, 141
Birru, Dejatch Ayelu, 16, 25, 60–61, 74, 150, 200, 252
Blackshirts, 21, 58–59, 128
Blum, Leon, 158
Bodard, 200
Boghossian, Kosrof, Colonel, 166, 179, 180, 199
Bohora, Amba, 166
Bonaiuti, Dante, 133, 151
Bonardi, Pierre, 198
Bonomi, 274
Borana, Sidamo, 88
Bottai, Giuseppi, 23, 60, 212
Boustead, Hugh, Major, 250
Boy Scouts, 40
Brancato, Signor, 3–4
British Foreign Office, 131
British Intelligence Service, 245
British Somaliland, 196, 245, 254–55
"Buy Italian" campaign, 68

Callafo, 117
Cambier, Captain, 88
Cantilo, Sr., 209
Cardarelli, Vincenzo, 144
Carrano, Umberto, Colonel, 242
Casalegno, Mario, 159
Casini, Gherardo, 60
Castellano, Professor, 80
Cerulli, 244
Cesarini, Paolo, 45, 57, 58, 238
Chabod, Federico, 12
Chapman-Andrews, Edwin, 202, 255
Charkoze, Waizero Ababath, 40
Chessman, Major, 250
"Christmas offensive," 100, 73 (map)
Ciano, Count Geleazzo, 59, 207, 208, 249, 262
Ciasca, Raffaele, 77, 106, 116, 207
Cimmaruta, Roberto, Captain, 19
Cismon, Cesare Maria de Vecchi di Val, 9
Civinini, Guelfo, 192

Clausewitz, 71
Coatit, 28
Colson, Everett, 34
Committee of Five, 39
Committee of Thirteen, 158
Committee of Unity and Collaboration, 241
Congo, the, 272
Conscripts, 57–61
Coppola, 9
Corradini, 9
Correspondents, war, 62–68
Cortese, Guido, 222
Criniti, Major, 75
Crispi, 9
Critica Fascista, 23
Cunningham, Sir Alan, 257
Cyrenaica, 9

Da Bormida, 47
Daggahbur, 87
Dagnerai, 117
Dall'Ora, Fidenzio, General, 22, 151
Dalmazzo, General, 170
Danakil road, 6
D'Annunzio, Gabriele, 61, 144, 148
Danquah, J. B., 38
D'Aosta, Duke Amadeo, 61, 225, 239, 241, 248, 260, 262
Daoud, Prince Ismail, 38, 94
Dassios, Dr. George, 93, 95
Davanzati, Forges, 9
David, Max, 197
Deboch, Abraham, 226
Debois, Armand, Captain, 88
De Bono, Emilio, General, 48 n; and first phase of war, 49, 50–54 passim; and Italy's preparations for war, 4, 13–22 passim, 28–29; and occupation of Negelli, 117; and suppression of slavery, 48
Debra Markos, 74
De Fraippont, Lieutenant, 88
De Gasperi, 274
Dekamere, 233

Delery, Major, 88
Della Rocca, Aldo, 231
Del Valle, Captain, 90
Dembeguina, 62
Dembeguina Pass, 75
De Meo, 16
Dessie-Makalle, 70
Desta, Ras, 88, 116, 119, 122, 213, 218
Deutsche Schule, 25
Diamanti, General, 102
Diel, Luisa, 248
Di Modica, Giovanni, 57
Dinle, Olol, 116
"Directives and Plan of Action for the Solution of the Italo-Ethiopian Question," 19
Dolfin, Nino, 60
Dolo, 119, 120
Donahue, James, 41
Dothee, Major, 36, 88
Drouillet, 91
Durand, Mortimer, 66
Dutch Red Cross, 94

Egyptian Red Crescent, 94
Emanuele, Enrico, 63
Emeny, Stuart, 131
Emmanuel, King Victor, III, 7, 15, 205
Endalkatchew, *Dejatch* Makonnen, 193
Enda Yesus, 98
Enderta, battle of, 124–36
England. See Great Britain
Enticho, 44
Eritrea, Eritreans, 166, 274; and Ethiopian resistence, 122–23; and Italian invasion, 8, 14–15, 21–22, 39, 51, 73; opposition in, to federation with Ethiopia, 269. See *also* Eritrean Corps
Eritrean Corps, 138, 141, 176–77
Erre, Sergeant, 16
Erskine (British consul), 216

Ethiopia, 7–8, 12, 89, 130, 143 n;
after Ethiopian War, 267–68; development of, by 1935, 30–32, 34–
36; effect of occupation of, 237–
41; and Italian propaganda, 14,
85; Italians in, 6, 13, 48; and
League of Nations, 20 n, 109 n;
and preparations for war, 40, 47;
and world opinion, 37–38, 77, 96–
97
Ethiopian Air Force, 92
Ethiopian Army of Liberation, 246
Ethiopian Intelligence Bureau, 250
"Ethiopianism," 38
"Ethiopian People's Movement," 272
Ethiopian Red Cross, 39, 93
Europe, Europeans, 77, 86, 146. See
also names of individual countries

Faldella, Emilio, General, 54, 77, 80,
91, 109
Faltin, Professor, 94
Faraci, Giuseppe, 276
Farago, Ladislas, 132
Faraq, Abdullah, 264
Farinacci, Roberto, 60
Fascism, Fascists, 6, 12, 16, 25, 26,
67, 68, 83, 206, 276
Fascist Air Force, 87, 155, 177, 210
Favrod, Charles-Henri, 17
Federici, Luigi, 67
Fifth Army (Italian), 134
Finnish Red Cross, 44
First Army Corps (Italian), 125,
144, 153, 176
Five-Year Plans, 267
Foa, Vittorio, 139
Fourth Army Corps (Italian), 150
France, French, 12 n, 245, 249
Franchetti, Baron, 16
Frankfurter Zeitung, 24
French Somaliland, 147, 245
Frère, Lieutenant, 88, 119
Fronte Sud, 118
Frusci, General, 119, 194

Fuller, General, 166
Futurism, 23 n

Gabre Maryam, General, 213, 218
Gabriel, Ras, 142
Gadom, Amba, 124–25
Ganale Doria, battle of, 120–23
Gandi, Adriano, 64
Garavelli, General, 130
Garvey, Marcus, 38
Gas, poison, 54, 78–79, 80–81, 83 n,
108–9, 120, 155–56, 164, 166, 177
Gashorki Pass, 47
Gassassa, Dejatch, 74
Gatre, Bahade, 213
Gavinana army division, 20, 21
Gebeychu, Workeneh, 270, 271
GEL (Gioventù Etiopica de Littorio),
288
Gentizon, Paul, 48, 66, 121, 128, 154,
229
Gerar Bay, 3
Gerassu, Ras, 242
Geresso, 242
Gerlogubi, 117
Germany, Germans, 23, 25, 41, 253
Getachew, Ras, 165, 180, 199, 200,
263
Gideon Force, 255
Gioelli, Giuseppe, 233
Giua, Michele, 139
Gojjam, 74
Gondar, 151
Gongol, Fitaurari, 118
Gorahai, 117
Gore, 201
"Grand Design," 15
Grande, Adriano, 184, 196
Grandi, Dino, 15, 80
Graziana, Rodolpho, General: and
first phase of war, 88; and occu-
pation of Negelli, 112–16, 118,
120; and Ogaden, battle of, 186–
88, 191–92, 196; and preparations
for war, 21, 77; as Viceroy, 213–

Graziana (*Continued*)
25 passim, 248; describes Wehib
Pasha, 87
Great Britain: and Anglo-Ethiopian
Agreement, 264; favors arms em-
bargo, 131–32; and guerrilla war
of the Arbaňňoch, 249–50; and
Italy, 12–13, 15, 26, 27, 67, 159,
209, 211, 247; public opinion in,
22–23, 246; volunteers from, for
Ethiopia, 41
Griaule, Marcel, 176
Griniti, Major, 75
Gugsa, *Dejatch* Haile Selassie, 13,
14, 16, 47, 49
Guiliani, Padre Reginaldo, 104
Guillén, Nicolàs, 38
Gunther, John, 17
Gunu Gadu, 87; battle of, 195

Hagos, Beite, 158
Haile Selassie I, Emperor, 7, 8, 13,
14, 21; and army doctors, 94, 95;
and Lake Ashangi, battle of, 174–
75, 179–80; described by Italians,
32–33, 34–36, 42 n; on Eritreans,
122–23; and Gugsa (son-in-law),
49; and League of Nations, 29,
81, 146–47, 208–11, 246; leaves
Addis Ababa, 199–211 passim;
and Mai Chew, battle of, 142–43,
159–71 passim; on mustard gas,
81, 108–9, 155, 166; and preparations for war, 36–37, 41; and reform in Ethiopia, 33–34, 35; re-
turns to Addis Ababa, 253–60;
withdrawal tactics of, 45–47
Haimanot, Ras Hailu Tekla, 13, 202,
248, 257
Halpert, de, 34
Hamanler, 118
Hanna, Abba, 271
Hanner, Dr., 39
Hapte Wolde, Makonnen, 271
Harar, 62, 119

Harar, Duke of, 40
Hararge, 116
Hastie, Roy MacGregor, 67
Hauzen, 138
Hempstone, Smith, 17, 273
Heruy, Sirak, 200
Hindenburg Wall, 116, 190, 194–95
Hitler, Adolf, 18, 132, 146, 207
Hockman, Dr. Robert W., 93
Hoeta, 36
Holeta, 89
Holeta Academy, 214, 222
Hooper, Dr., 93
House of Savoy, 61, 64
Hylander, Dr. F., 93, 95

Ichac, Pierre, 89
Imam, Dagno, 243
Imam, Tesselma, 243, 248
Imperial Council, 200
Imperial Guard, 36, 37, 40, 163, 166,
169, 199, 266
"Imperial Order for General Mobi-
lization," 180
Imru, Ras, 7, 68, 71, 72, 75, 76, 78,
100, 104, 137, 143, 146, 149, 156–
57, 199, 213, 216, 217
International African Friends of
Ethiopia, 38
Italian Air Force, 92, 119, 128
Italian High Command, 15
Italian Military Command, 82
Italian Nationalists, 12
Italian Somaliland, 8, 9, 22, 39, 116,
119
Italian Supreme Command, 36
Italo-Eritrean expeditionary force,
70
Italy, Italians: attitude toward war
in, 14, 23 n, 26–28, 53, 57, 68,
111 n, 159, 205–7, 253; and Ethiopians, 48; and League of Na-
tions, 20 n; *padroncini*, 236; and
peace with Ethiopia, 274–76; and
preparations for war, 13; post-

Italy, Italians (*Continued*)
war colonial policy of, 212–26, 242; significance of Africa to, 4–7, 18, 20, 26 n, 57; war casualties of, 197–98; war correspondents for, 62–67, 85; and world opinion, 25, 39, 67, 81, 247
Itateku, Worku, 263

Jambari, *Dejatch* Mangasha, 242
Janagobo, 87
Japan, 25
Jeśman, Czelaw, 231, 267
Jijiga, 87
Jones, A. H. M., 19
Jones, Elizabeth, 36
Jonquières, De, 244
Julian, Hubert Eustace ("The Black Eagle"), 92
Junod, Marcel, 95, 119, 182, 203, 219

Karavasilis, Musa Saba, 90
Kassa, Ras, 70, 71, 76, 100, 103, 107–8, 131, 137, 142, 165, 200
Kebbede, Negash, 243, 263
Kelly, Dr. Percy James, 94
Kenya, 36, 122, 245
Kenyatta, Jomo, 38
King's Own African Rifles, 36
Knickerbocker, H. R., 207
Kokuryu Ku society (Black Dragon), 25
Konovaloff, Colonel, 47, 71, 90 n, 138, 142, 162, 172, 175, 201
Kyril, Abuna, 201, 221, 241

Labriola, Arturo, 27
Latibelu, Bajirond, 104, 165
Laval, 22
Lavora, Il, 63–64
League of Human Rights, 38
League of Nations, 12, 13, 20 n, 23, 26, 29, 35, 37, 45, 47, 51, 81, 95, 109, 143, 146–47, 158–59, 200, 207–11, 246, 268

Le Gentilhomme, General, 249–50
"Legion of Amazons," 40
Lessona, Alessandro, 51–52, 81
Libya, Libyans, 9, 12, 113, 192, 197
Libyan War, 8, 9
Lino, Luigi, 242, 248
"Little *Gebbi*," 31
Lucchetti, Major, 244
Luke, Sir Harry, 273
Lush, Brigadier, 264

"Madamismo," 230–31
Magliocco, Air Marshal, 214
Mafia, 4
Mai Chew, battle of, 122, 143, 161–73
Mai Lahla, 147
Mai Timkat, 74
Makalle, 76
Makalle-Takkaze, 52
Makonnen, Ras Tafari, 12. *See also* Haile Selassie I
Maletti: Colonel, 118; General, 243–44
Malka Murri, 120
Malladra, Captain, 16
Manamba, Amba, 75
Mangasha, General Merid, 270
Mangasha, Ras Kebbede, 165, 248
Maravigna, General, 44, 150, 151, 153
"March of the Iron Will," 183–84, 194
March on Gondar, 158
Mareb, River, 43
Marinetti, F. T., 23 n, 56, 62, 105, 129
Mario, E. A., 227
Mariotti, Delio, 44, 133
Martin, A. C. W., 214
Martini, Ferdinando, 3
Maryam Fiki, 213
Mashasha, *Dejatch* Toklu, 219
Massawa, 3–4, 22, 57, 79
Matthews, Herbert L., 26, 66, 207

Mekan Pass, 166, 170
Melly, John, 31, 94, 95
Menan, Empress, 39
Menelik II, Emperor, 8, 16, 33, 43
Mengistu, General, 271
Merid, Beyene, General, 141, 213, 218
Mezzedimi, 30
Mikaele, *Dejatch* Amde, 116, 132
Mila, Massimo, 139
"Milan Plan," 117
"Minculpop," 30, 63
Ministry of Labor, 172
Ministry of National Commissions for the Interior Community Development, 272
Minniti, 81
Mitchell, Sir Philip, 264
Mogadishu, 18, 57
Molinero, Captain, 240
Monelli, Paolo, 107, 234
Monfreid, Henri de, 34, 66
Monnier, Paul-Robert, Colonel, 249
Monroe, Elizabeth, 19
Monroe, John, 34
Montagna, Giovanni, 58
Montanelli, Indro, 64
Monte, Augusto, 139
Moramarco, Colonel, 122
Mosley, Leonard, 31, 54, 70, 203, 273
Mulugeta, Ras, 70, 76, 100, 103, 107, 126
Munroe, A. H. M., 36
Mussolini, Benito: and announcement of peace, 205–7; and first phase of war, 52, 53; and Mai Chew, battle of, 172; and occupation of Negelli, 115, 120; and Ogaden, battle of, 186–88, 191; plans conquest of Ethiopia, 8–9, 12–15; post-war colonial policy of, 213–16, 247; and preparations for war, 20–24; and return of Haile Selassie I, 260; and Shire, battle of, 159; and Tembien, first battle

Mussolini, Benito (*Continued*) of, 77, 111; and war correspondents, 62; and world opinion, 25, 38, 51, 67
Mussolini, Bruno, 59
Mussolini, Vittorio, 59–60, 111 n
Mustard gas. *See* Gas, poison

Naples, 21
Napolitano, Gian Gaspare, 64
Nasi, Guglielmo, General, 190, 191, 231, 254
Nasibu, Ras, 116, 117, 186–87, 191
Negelli, occupation of, 112–23
Negri, General, 166
Nesbitt, L. M., 16
Neway, Mengistu, General, 270, 271
Norden, Herman, 33
Norwegian Red Cross, 94

OAU (Organization of African Unity), 267, 272
OETA (Occupied Enemy Territory Administration), 264
Ogaden, 116, 119; battle of, 186–98, 189 (map)
ONC (*Opera Nazionale Combattenti*), 235
Orano, Paolo, 113
Oriani, Alfredo, 9
Orlando, Vittorio Emanuele, 27

Padmore, George, 38
Padroncini, 236
Pankhurst, Sylvia, 38, 246, 264
Parini, 60
Pasha, Wehib, 86, 87, 90, 116, 190, 194
Pastori, Tullio, 16
Pavolini, Alessandro, 45, 54, 141
Pedrazzi, 9
Peloritana, the, 20, 115
Permanent Court of International Justice, 271
Peru, 96

Petros, Abuna, 197, 215
Piccioli, Angelo, 230
Piedmont, Princess Marie-José of, 61, 206
Pirzio, General, 44
Pistoria, Duke of (Filiberto of Savoy-Genoa), 56, 61
Pitassi-Manella, General, 130
Platt, Sir William, General, 251, 255
Plezzo, 107
Politica, 31
Pollera, Giorgio, Lieutenant, 242
Popolo, Morelli di, General, 120
Pro-Italian Party, 274
Project OME (Ordini Militari Eritrea), 15

"Rastafarians," 38
Red Cross, 54, 92, 173; Dutch, 94; Ethiopian, 39, 93; Finnish, 94; Norwegian, 94
Rietti, Mario, 83
Rizzi, Signor, 248
Roatta, General, 80, 111
Robinson, John, 86, 92
Roghi, Bruno, 62, 129
Rosa, Colonel, 167
Roscigno, 6
Rosen, Count Carl von, 92, 96
Rosselli, Carlo, 37
Royal Bodyguard, 273
Ruel, Leopold, Colonel, 88
Ruggero, Colonel, 169
Russo, Alfio, 52

Sacrifice of the wedding rings, 68
Salan, Raoul, 66
Salvatorelli, 59
Samantar, Omar, 19
Sanctis, Gino de, 65
Sandford, Brigadier, 250
Santini, General, 44
Sassabaneh, 87
Scalea, Prince, 14
Scarfoglio, 9

Schuppler, Dr., 86, 93
Scorza, Carlo, 60
Second Army Corps (Italian), 44, 150, 154
Second Eritrean Division, 103
"Secret and Confidential Operational Memorandum for the Offensive on Harar," 191
Segni, President, 277
Selaclaca, 75
Senussi uprising, 113
Seyoum, Ras, 29, 47, 68, 70, 71, 76, 100, 137, 165, 175, 252, 263, 271
Shepherd, G. W., Jr., 268
Shire, 68, 74; battle of, 149–60, 152 (map)
Sicily, 4
Sidamo, 116, 119
Sileshi, Mesfin, 242
SIM (Servizio Informazione Militare), 80
Simon, Sir John, 15
Simoons, F. J., 237
Smith, Denis Mack, 20, 67, 172
Somaliland, Somalis, 12, 51, 197
Spain, 207
Spanish Civil War, 249
Spano, Velio, 249
Spoleto, Duke of, 61
Stanco, Francesco, 60
Starace, Achille, 60, 61, 72
Strunk, Roland von, Captain, 66
Steer, George, 128, 200, 254
Suardo, Senator, 56
Suez canal, 21, 67
Sujimura, Yotaro, 25
Swedish mission, 89
Swiss Red Cross, 95
Sykes, Christopher, 254

Taezaz, Lorenzo, 200, 246, 249
Tafari, Ras, 32
Takkaze, River, 71, 72, 81
Tamm, Captain, 89
Tana, Lake, 74

Tarantini, Raffaello, 170
Tassew, Ligaba, 165
Taulud Bay, 3
Tembien, 68, 100; first battle of, 101 (map), 102–11; second battle of, 137–48, 139 (map)
Tenagne, Worq, 117
Termaber, 6, 89
Teruzzi, Attilio, 4–5, 60
Tesfai, Hailu, 158
Tesfazien, *Shumbashi* Wandom, 50–51, 122
Third Army Corps (Italian), 100, 104, 125, 138, 142
Thompson, Dr. David, 206
Tolmino, 107
Tomasselli, Cesco, 45, 125, 145, 164, 167, 177
Toselli, 47, 99
Treaty of Friendship and Arbitration, 8, 14
Tripolitania, 9
Trocard, Jean, Captain, 245
Tzaddik, Wolde, 201
Tzellere, Amba, 72, 77

Ulland, Dr. Gunnar, 94
United Nations, 268
United States, 38, 41, 264

Vaccarisi, General, 107
Valli, Federico, 62
Vickers and Soley Arms, 131
Villasanta, General, 43
Virgin, Erik, General, 34, 36, 89
Volunteers, 41 n, 57–61, 88, 96 n

Volta, Sandro, 112, 121

Wal Wal incident, 15, 19, 20, 39
War correspondents, 62–68
Warieu Pass, 72, 77, 103–4
Wells, Linton, 109
West Indies, "Ethiopianism" in, 38
Westminster Conference, 246
Winckel, Dr., 94
Wingate, Orde, Major, 255
Witmeur, Gustav, Lieutenant, 88
Wittlin, Major, 90
Wolde, Giorgis, 264
Woldie, Mashasha, 141
Wolie, Ras Gugsa, 33
Wolkefit, 6
Wonderat, *Dejatch*, 165
Wondewossen, 70, 104
World War II, 146, 232, 245, 251
Worq, Amba, 140
Worq, Gebreyesus, 263
Wossen, Aberra, 70, 104, 214
Wossen, Makonnen, 213
Wright, Stephen, 246
Wubie, Mangasha, 263

Xylander, Rudolph, Colonel, 164

Yasu, Emperor *Lij*, 13, 33
Yilma, *Dejatch* Mangasha, 165
Young Ethiopian Party, 222
"Young Ethiopians," 117

Zangrandi, Ruggero, 26, 68
Zelleka, Belai, 243
Zoppi, V., 35
Zuretti, Lieutenant Colonel, 169